BY LOUISE J. KAPLAN

THE DOMESDAY DICTIONARY with Donald M. Kaplan and
  Armand Schwerner
ONENESS AND SEPARATENESS: From Infant to Individual
ADOLESCENCE: The Farewell to Childhood
THE FAMILY ROMANCE OF THE IMPOSTOR-POET THOMAS
  CHATTERTON
FEMALE PERVERSIONS: The Temptations of Emma Bovary

NO VOICE
IS EVER
WHOLLY
LOST

LOUISE J. KAPLAN

A TOUCHSTONE BOOK
Published by Simon & Schuster

TOUCHSTONE
Rockefeller Center
1230 Avenue of the Americas
New York, NY 10020

First Touchstone Edition 1996

TOUCHSTONE and colophon are registered trademarks
of Simon & Schuster Inc.

Designed by Irving Perkins Associates

Manufactured in the United States of America

1   3   5   7   9   10   8   6   4   2
1   3   5   7   9   10   8   6   4   2 (Pbk)

Library of Congress Cataloging-in-Publication Data
Kaplan, Louise J.
No voice is ever wholly lost / Louise J. Kaplan
p.   cm.
Includes index.
1. Loss (Psychology) 2. Parent and child. 3. Bereavement--
Psychological aspects. 4. Psychoanalysis.
5. Freud, Sigmund, 1856-1939.
I. Title.
BF575.D35.K37   1995
155.9'24--dc20   94-47923
CIP
ISBN 0-671-79868-5
0-684-81820-5 (Pbk)

In memory of Donald M. Kaplan
May 8, 1927–September 20, 1994

His generous voice inspired the creative spirit
of his family, students, and colleagues.

Until my husband's death, this book was to have been dedicated to Harry A. Slochower (1900–1992). His intellectual originality and his 1945 *No Voice Is Wholly Lost* meant so much to Donald and me during the years we were exploring the connections between psychoanalysis and culture.

CONTENTS

INTRODUCTION

I am writing about loss as an emotional process that embodies the vitalities of the human spirit rather than about death with its connotations of decay, finality, and the termination of relationships. I do so in order to bring into focus the psychological forces that inspire and sustain the human dialogue.

This dialogue—the heartbeat of human existence—begins with an exchange of gestures between parent and infant. Through these intimacies of everyday life, the parent transmits to the child the emotional language of his species and eventually the verbal language and symbolic communications that enable the child to participate in human culture. Once having entered into the human dialogue, we cannot live without it. The dialogue continues even after the body of a loved one is lifeless.

Mourning rituals and conventional behaviors of the bereaved are designed to give a semblance of order and rationality to the unruly passions of bereavement. Convention tells us something important about the state of mind of the bereaved, but I am more interested in the latent madness that goes on behind the veils of custom—the rediscovery of the lost beloved in the restoration and resurrection of lost dialogues.

My interpretations are informed by a particular version of psychoanalysis—the version that gives an account of feelings, fantasies, and thoughts that are otherwise unconscious; the version that gives as much credence and credibility to unconscious events as to the conventional behaviors that disguise them. Long before I became a psychoanalyst, while I was still in college, I found in Freudian psychoanalysis a way of thinking about human dilemmas that was conducive to the questions I wanted to pursue. At the center of the psychoanalytic endeavor is a sustained reflection on the problem of what it means to be human.

I have made the range of examples wide, from an ordinary child coping with brief separations from his mother to the phenomenon of a child with a "dead" mother—a physically alive mother whose passions are still bound up in a frozen dialogue with a child she has lost, or a lost childhood illusion, or a lost aspect of herself, or a lost ideal of virtue. In her depression and continuing preoccupation with the someone or something she has lost, such a mother is emotionally dead to the needs and desires of her living child.

In fact, it was just such a child of a dead mother who inspired this book. She is a fictional child. Her name is Berthe Bovary. Her mother, Emma, is the protagonist of the nineteenth-century novel *Madame Bovary* by Gustave Flaubert. By the time Berthe is born, her mother has lost every illusion that had made her life a life worth living. When finally all hope of recovering these illusions is gone, Emma commits suicide, and one year later her grieving husband dies of heartbreak. Berthe, who lost her mother and father between the ages of five and six, is one of the several children you will meet. The child who has lost a parent is herself lost—unless someone notices and finds her.

Unlike Berthe, the other lost children and lost parents in this book are actual persons or are based on actual persons. Sometimes this is a young child or adolescent who loses a parent and must find a way to continue the dialogue. Sometimes, however, the child has been lost, and the parents are left behind to grieve. The death of a child is an extraordinary blow to a parent's entire being, his or her sense of self-worth and self-esteem. This reversal of the natural order of things, wherein a child is meant to outlive the parents, brings into question a parent's capacity for generational transmission. A parent who loses a child interprets the unborn or dead child as a sign of his or her own degeneration. Very often the parents are consumed by a never-ending grief.

Freud appears throughout the book both as the author of works that address these ordeals of the human spirit and in his everyday guises as father and grandfather. Shortly after the end of World War I, Freud lost his favorite daughter, Sophie. We follow the fate of Sophie's first child, Ernst, from the time he is eighteen months old until he is eighty and examine his remarkable quest to reconnect with his lost mother.

Our cultural attainments, the sentences we utter or sign, our poems, dances, monuments, paintings, symphonies, and songs are a rediscovery and restoration of lost dialogues. Several children and parents who transformed their losses into creative ventures are portrayed; the inventor of a childhood game, an adolescent poet, a sculptor, a painter, the author of a memoir, a teller of tales, a rescuer of lost infants, a weeping mother who transformed her lost child's diaper into a banner of social protest. Creative artists are not necessarily more enlightened about the meaning of loss, nor are they blessed with a unique attunement to the mourning process. They *do*, in addition to their talents and gifts, have the opportunity to express what goes on unconsciously in every person who suffers loss.

I recall the paintings and sculpture of the Belgian surrealist artist René Magritte, whose severely depressed mother, Régina, like Berthe Bovary's mother, also eventually committed suicide. Magritte's visual depictions of the uncertain borders between animate and inanimate, real and unreal, resonate with the emotional consequences of derailed dialogue. Magritte's artistic visions, which are the cultural legacies of his childhood losses, make us "see" his dead mother as he experienced her when she was still alive and as she continued to influence him after her suicide.

Régina Magritte appears to us in her son's paintings, much as Anne-Justine-Caroline Flaubert speaks to us through the letters and novels of her son, Gustave Flaubert. Madame Flaubert, a typical middle-class mother from nineteenth-century France and Hebe de Bonafini, a working-class mother from twentieth-century Argentina, responded in distinctly different ways to the losses of their children.

The lost children and lost parents we encounter lived out their lives against the background of the social calamities, wars, and holocausts of modern times. The parents were not the best of all possible parents. The children did not grow up in the best of all possible worlds. And yet, despite all the personal and social calamities that befell these children and parents, the human dialogue survived.

✺

CHAPTER ONE

THE HUMAN
DIALOGUE

Your mother is dead. She has completed her journey to the place of the dead. She will never return. So reason tells you. In your not-so-rational heart, you know that she still exists. When you speak of her you say "She is lost," "I have lost her." If your mother is merely lost, you reason unconsciously, then you might find her again. Actually, you chat with her each morning over coffee and rolls.

You find yourself doing things your father would have liked you to do when he was alive—but not until now, when it is too late. He would complain about your messy habits. He would berate you for not making your bed, for not picking up your wet towels and dirty socks. But you never listened, and his nagging became part of the background noise of your daily existence. Now, six months after his death, there you are folding and refolding the laundry into neat little piles, straightening the pictures, picking up specks of dust. You and he are reunited, together again in these little gestures of everyday life. The dialogue goes on.

You see your mother strolling down the street, her shoulders slightly hunched over, her straw hat jauntily tipped, shading her eyes from the bright sun. Your heart leaps. You wave and start to run toward her. Then you remember. Your mother died a long time ago and will never walk on any street, not ever again. You scold her for fooling you. You recall one of the silly jokes she used to tell you when you were a child, and you smile.

Perhaps you are a small child and you have lost your mother. You repeat what you've been told: "Mommy is dead. She is never coming back." At night you dream that you are falling down, down, through a bottomless chasm and there is no one to catch you. Then you jump, half-waking from this nightmare, and Mommy's there, holding out her arms to comfort you and rock you back to sleep. But when morning comes, there is no Mommy. Not in the closets, not in the cabinets, not at the kitchen table. Your mouth forms the words again. "Mommy is gone. She won't ever come back." But silently you murmur, "Where are you? Why did you leave me? I want you back."

Perhaps you have lost a child. Each month you rake the leaves away from her gravestone, pretending to brush her hair. Each night you tuck in his teddy bear and whisper word for word his favorite bedtime story, as though it were a prayer he just might hear. Grief becomes your companion, your child, your sustenance, your soul. But this romance with grief must be a secret. Mourning is something you are supposed to do and get over, you are told. You must put on the mask of the still living. No one must ever know about your dialogue with the dead.

The rituals of burial and mourning, which are socially sanctioned, are an effort to give a semblance of order to the madness of bereavement. These rituals acknowledge the magnitude of the event and offer to the bereaved a quota of time apart from ordinary life. Like the dead, who, while passing from the realm of the living into the realm of the nonliving, exist in a "liminal time," so too are the grieving ones allowed a time of abeyance. During this time, in some cultures, we are permitted to tear out our hair, to lacerate our skin, to hurl ourselves into the grave, to cry, to scream, to gather with friends and tell stories about how and why the dead one passed away. We are allowed to hire a professional mourner to personify the torment of our suffering, to shriek and wail while we stand dignified, quietly observing. We are allowed to give special foods to the dead ancestor. We may dance, either solemnly or wickedly or joyously. We may strut in a noisy parade or shuffle in a slow procession. We may chant holy hymns or shout ribald limericks. We may sacrifice animals or plant seeds to honor one's everlasting existence. Or we may pretend that nothing has happened and make a point of avoiding all mention of the dead one. Whatever we do or don't do during this liminal time, society demands an eventual return to real time, when we must get on with the business of living.

Within the same religion the ritual process of mourning may vary considerably from one society to another. Religions take root in vastly different cultural soils, and therefore religious rituals and customs are less bound by religious ideals than by social ideology. The mourning rituals of the Muslims of Egypt, for example, are very different from those of the Muslims of Java and other parts of Asia.

Egyptian Muslims are encouraged to dwell profusely on their sorrow and grief. They are enjoined to speak of the deceased and to tell and retell the tragic circumstances and events surrounding the death for many months, years—decades, if the mourner wishes it. The mourner is visited daily by sympathizers who enjoy the chance to relate the stories of *their* dead beloved and how they died. The visitors do not upstage the mourner but simply display their compassionate love for her in mournful laments and shrieking tirades about those they have lost. The mourner is encouraged to speak of the dead; to tell and retell the story of his life and his death. The greater and more dramatic the display of grief, the more likely the mourner will recover from her suffering. To hold back her feelings or to try to contain them is perilous; a threat to her physical and mental well-being.

The Muslims of Bali, on the other hand, are enjoined to be placid and composed when the beloved dies. Sadness is dangerous to the mourner; it makes her physically weak and confused, and at the slightest sign of overt sadness the mourner's friends and family begin laughing and trying to make her laugh. The Muslims of Bali believe that sadness is contagious; the mourner's sadness could not only overwhelm the entire community but also distract the deceased. If the lost one sees tears or sadness in the face of his mortal beloved, he too may be overcome with longing and be unable to find his way to heaven.

The composure and silence of the Balinese mourner is a measure of her depth of feeling. Though the Balinese have no word for grief, the bereaved is extremely vulnerable to longing and all too easily captivated by nuances and shades of grief. As one mourner explained, "We are very sensitive. We have no defense. Feelings overwhelm us. Sadness could make us crazy. So we laugh away the sadness. We need our masks."

A mourner obeys the societal or cultural rituals, doing and saying precisely what is expected of her, all the while unconsciously preparing to rebel. The ritual process is about conventionalizing the longing, subduing the tantrum of protest, tidying up and wiping away the tears so that the bereaved can resume her ordinary social life. Real mourning takes its own sweet time. After we bury the dead in the prescribed way, our unruly unconscious, in which no voice is ever wholly lost, instigates a dialogue with the dead. When the public mourning is over, the personal mourning begins. The rediscovery of the lost one commences.

Death is the inevitability we share with all living things. However, the human experience of loss is about our ongoing and everlasting dialogues with the dead. Domesticated animals and those mammals and primates whose family structures and social arrangements resemble ours also experience sorrow and grief in response to the death of mates, companions, children, and parents. But for them, the death of a beloved eventually achieves finality.

When the beloved dies, these animals are bereft. They howl. They run in circles around the body. They sniff the places where the scent of the beloved lingers. They wrinkle their brows in puzzlement over the riddle of living and nonliving. They poke and nuzzle the corpse, trying to coax the beloved back to life. She, of course, remains inert and impervious to the grief and longing of the bereaved.

A chimpanzee infant may be unable to leave the corpse of his dead mother. He cuddles against her, rests a paw on her breast, pokes at her body and tries to pry open her eyelids. He refuses comfort and food. Some die of heartbreak. A gorilla mother may carry her dead infant with her for weeks, refusing to leave him behind when the troop moves on. In the usual course of events, however, in a few hours, or days, or weeks, the bereaved animal resumes her ordinary existence of foraging for food, grooming her loved ones, paying social calls. She eventually surrenders the corpse to nature. Profound and passionate as their attachments are, these animals, so nearly human in their ways of reacting to death, are not eternally bound to the past.

We are the only animal species that possesses—and is possessed by—history, personal and cultural. We are never entirely free of the past. The physical death of the beloved is not the end of our attachment to him. His presence will always be with us—in one form or another.

Even the rigidly prescribed rituals of burial and mourning give some token recognition, implicitly or explicitly, to the idea that physical death is not the end of the emotional tie between the bereaved and the beloved. Much as the rituals aim to impress the mourner with the irrevocability of death, they also allow some leeway for rebellion by designating a legitimate way for the bereaved to continue her dialogues with the dead. Nevertheless, there is a proviso—the departed one must be transformed into another sort of presence, be it an angel, a ghost, a shadow, an ancestor, a spirit, a soul, an ideal of virtue, or an aspect of conscience.

In the Shinto and Buddhist religions, for example, it is prescribed that each household should have an altar dedicated to family ancestors. The altar is meant to facilitate continuing contact with the deceased. After death, a beloved one is gone but his ancestral presence is forever accessible. One can get up in the morning and smile at his face in the photograph and tell him about the dreams one had the night before. One can buy him presents and offer him tokens of love and affection. Amends can be made to the ancestor for past negligence or ill will. The past angers and hurts in relationships with the beloved can be rectified by the new relationship with the ancestor. The ancestor is a friendly presence, and each contact with him brings solace and comfort to the bereaved.

In other cultures, the rituals of burial and mourning stress the necessity of severing the bond with the deceased as soon as possible. It is believed that the process of death has transformed the beloved into an alien Spirit and that mortals must not have any contact with Spirits. They may not speak of the Spirit or even touch the belongings of the Spirit. The Hopi, the Peaceful People, believe that contact with death is polluting. Mortuary rites are quickly accomplished. On the day or night of a death, the hair of the deceased is washed by a paternal aunt. The body is wrapped and quickly buried by the eldest son. A "cloud" shroud is placed over the head. The body is placed in the ground in a flexed position, readied for movement. A stick is inserted into the grave to serve as an exit for the soul.

As the Hopi soul departs from the dead body, the Hopi is transformed into a depersonalized, supernatural Spirit. On the fourth day after death, the Spirit begins the journey into the land of the dead, into the Underworld, the place from which the Hopi once emerged to be born into mortal existence, the place he "visited" when he negotiated the passage from childhood into adulthood. The Spirit is propitiated with feathers by his clan members and enjoined to forget the living. The trail from the burial ground back to the village is ceremoniously closed. As he is reborn in the Underworld, his life's journey ends, but he lives on in the world of Spirits.

For the Hopi, there is a Spirit-being in every object of nature—every cloud, animal, bird, plant, rock, mountain. The severing of the ties between the earthbound and the Underworld is an expression of the Hopi belief in the continuity of life after death and a sign of the mourner's everlasting emotional connection with the departing Spirit.

The bereaved Hopi affirms the depth of her emotional connections by sharing the ritual of burial with her clan, but she also obeys the ritual prescription of keeping the pain of her bereavement to herself. As with the Balinese mourner, the Hopi display of "no feeling" masks her loving concern for others. To expose her grief to other family members or neighbors would contaminate the living with the pollution of the dead, and the Spirit must be protected from the mortal passions, for if the dead one were to witness the suffering of the bereaved, he might be distracted from his journey into the Spirit world.

Thus in the Hopi religion, while physical death signifies a total and irrevocable severance of all relations between the bereaved and the deceased, there is an implicit recognition that the lost one continues to exist in the form of a Spirit. The prescribed dialogue with the dead is a dialogue of avoidance, but a dialogue nevertheless.

In modern Western European societies, the process of bereavement has been studied "objectively." By scrutinizing the bereavement behaviors and fantasies of humans of all ages, religions, and cultures, social scientists have identified two major stages of bereavement—an initial acute stage and a later chronic stage. The grief reactions of the first stage, though normal and expectable, can be acutely painful. They are sometimes likened to an illness of the soul. It is generally agreed that true mourning, the second or chronic stage of bereavement, though less consciously painful, is a long, possibly endless, internal process called "the *work* of mourning."

The acute stage of bereavement begins with a conscious registration of the fact of death and some tentative evaluation of the consequences of the loss. Then, as the shock of reality hits, we very quickly find ways to ignore and deny this so-called reality. We protest that the calamity could not have happened, and if it did not happen, then surely the beloved will return. But this blunt denial of the facts doesn't work for too long. Within a few hours or days we become acutely aware of a dreadful, aching emptiness inside us—as though, when our beloved departed the world of the living, he also vacated our inner world, leaving it in a state of collapse and disarray. We feel guilty about having survived our loved one. We feel ashamed of the cruel and insensitive things we said and did. We feel helpless and hopeless. We have no appetite and have trouble falling asleep. We find it impossible to concentrate on work or study and have little interest in the activities that used to bring us pleasure.

The second stage of bereavement, the work of mourning, concerns the long and emotionally difficult process of recovering from this illness of the soul. Bit by bit, the bereaved acknowledges that her beloved is gone and will never come back. She consoles herself with memories of the good and not-so-good times she shared with him. Eventually, she accepts the finality of his death. At this point, when the person *seems* to have come to terms with the reality, seems to have detached herself from her dead beloved, and seems to have recovered enough of her sanity to once again be capable of work, pleasure, joy, and love, it is said that the bereaved has completed the work of mourning.

However, this logical progression of acknowledgment, detachment, and return to reality leaves no room for spirits, ghosts, shadows, angels, demons, or other presences. The process of mourning is not only about detachment and the gradual relinquishment of the lost one, it is also about a reconfirmation of our attachments. The *full* work of mourning encompasses the rebuilding of our inner world and the restoration of the beloved in the form of an inner presence—if not precisely a Spirit or a ghost, an aspect of ego or conscience, an ideal, a passion. Over the course of time, these inner presences may undergo further development and revision, but they will never leave us. We can call on our inner presences to join us in the morning over coffee and rolls, to help us fold the laundry properly, to guide us in planting a garden, to inspire a painting, to give us the courage to protest social injustice.

Long after the return of logic and reason, long after we rejoin the world of the living, we are still attached to our lost ones. The human dialogue—that which makes living a life worthwhile—goes on. In the absence of this dialogue, we are lost.

Dialogue is the heartbeat of a human existence. Were it not for this dialogue, the chaotic excitements and crude appetites of the infant could not be transformed into the desires and longings that enable him to live a fully human life. Were it not for this dialogue an infant would not learn how to express love or give love to others. Love can only be learned in an atmosphere of prolonged physical contact and emotional intimacy with another human being, a caregiver who is capable of engaging in a dialogue with a baby.

Around the middle of the twentieth century, psychologists studying infant-mother relationships became aware that a mother's embrace and warm, enfolding presence were more vital to an infant's survival than the milky substance that filled its tiny stomach. Until then, the word *nurturance* had been equated solely with the satisfaction of physical hunger and physical need. It didn't take elaborate experiments to deduce that an infant would die from want of food. But it took centuries to figure out that infants can and do perish from want of love. The essential nutriment is love, and nurturance is about giving and receiving love.

Some of the more famous experiments on the nature of love were conducted by the psychologist Harry Harlow in the late 1950s and early 1960s. Harlow questioned the long-standing assumption that an infant's love for its mother is derived from associating her presence with the ingestion of milk and the alleviation of hunger. He hypothesized that the infant's suckling and the mother's gratification of the infant's hunger were of secondary, even minor importance. According to Harlow, the essential nutriments of love are the mother's offering of bodily contact and bodily warmth.

Harlow's studies proved that contact comfort is a vital element in learning to love, but his well-intentioned experiments had some unforeseen and devastating effects on the emotional development of the infant rhesus monkeys who were his experimental subjects. It seems love is a bit more complicated than Harlow had anticipated.

In Harlow's study, eight rhesus monkeys were separated from their biological mothers immediately after birth. Each infant was placed in its own private cage with a cubicle containing two surrogate mothers, neither of them alive. One was a "terry cloth mother"—a block of wood layered with spongy rubber and covered with terry cloth. The other was a "wire mother"—a wire mesh construction of the same size and shape as the terry cloth mother. For four of the infants, only the terry cloth mother was fitted with a feeding nipple, while for the other four, only the wire mother had the feeding nipple.

The four infants with the lactating terry cloth mother showed no interest in their wire mother. After a few weeks, the four infants with the lactating wire mother showed an ever-increasing responsiveness to their terry cloth mother, eventually ignoring their wire mother except when they were hungry. In a few months, all eight rhesus infants were firmly attached to their terry cloth mothers. When, in another series of experiments with a different group of rhesus infants, Harlow added heat and a rocking motion to the terry cloth mother, she became a magnet of love. The attachment of the rhesus babies became resolute. They would cling to her for sixteen to eighteen hours a day.

Most academic psychologists agreed that Harlow made his point about the importance of contact comfort in the development of love. To this day, some psychologists cite Harlow's work as proof of the limitations of the psychoanalytic theory of human attachment which, as they see it, minimizes the vital importance of contact experiences and only considers the gratification of oral needs. However, *orality* is a term with vast implications, comprising every physiological and psychological process that gives coloration, tone, and emotional meaning to the earliest interactions between an infant and his caregiver. Orality is about an infant's *dialogue* through his senses of smell, touch, taste, hearing, and motion with a partner, whose every gesture conveys the language of love.

Having accepted Harlow's narrow interpretation of orality as gospel, many psychologists either ignored or forgot that Harlow had overlooked a crucial factor—the vital importance of *reciprocal dialogue* in learning to love. Even the most ingenious, highly perfected imitation mother, however warm, soft, or motherly in appearance and motion, is not truly alive and therefore cannot engage in an animated, reciprocal dialogue with her infant.

When Harlow's infant rhesus monkeys grew up, they were "terry cloth adults." Their repertoire of emotional responses was limited to clinging attachment and destructive aggression. Aside from an urgent and almost continual need to hold onto familiar, soft, furrylike objects, they bit and tore at paper, cloth, their own bodies, and the bodies of other rhesus monkeys as though they had no way of discriminating animate from inanimate. And because they had not been given the opportunity to interact with a mother who was alive, clinging attachment was the only form of love they could express or tolerate. They would clutch and hang onto other rhesus monkeys who had been raised on the same terry cloth mother, but beyond this sibling bond, which Harlow referred to as a "together-together" relationship, the dialogue-deprived adult rhesus monkeys had no desire to be physically or emotionally close to other members of their species. Some carried around shredded remnants of their original terry cloth mothers, some hugged and cuddled with their mirroring together-together sibling, but they could not tolerate any sort of reciprocal, back-and-forth, self-and-other, you-and-I, interactive relationship.

René Spitz, the psychoanalyst who made a detailed critique of Harlow's experiments on the nature of love, had always insisted that *reciprocal* dialogue was the critical factor in the development of human love. A decade or so before Harlow conducted his studies with infant rhesus monkeys, Spitz had described how human infants who have been deprived of this essential life-giving dialogue might continue to live and grow but would nevertheless be unable to relate to other human beings in certain crucially human ways. When he learned of Harlow's experiments, Spitz recognized at once the similarities between the dialogue-deprived human infants he had studied and Harlow's rhesus monkeys.

In a heartrending experiment created by circumstance, the two groups of infants in Spitz's study received two vastly different kinds of mothering. In one group, the mothers were imprisoned delinquent girls, who were encouraged to care for their babies every day in the prison nursery. Most of these girls were not very intelligent and had never mothered a baby before. Yet in their easygoing, spontaneous way, they gave their babies the kind of one-to-one attention and care that human babies thrive on. In the other group, for one reason or another—the mother's death, an illness in the family, financial stress—infants had been deposited for various periods of time, ranging from a few months to several years, in a foundling home. These infants were cared for by intelligent, experienced, highly trained nurses, who efficiently dispensed the food, clothing, and physical care that human children require. But there was only one head nurse and five assistant nurses for forty-five babies. No time was wasted on play or dialogue.

Whereas the infants in the prison nursery were emotionally responsive and animated, and physically flourishing, the foundlings would lie in their cribs in a stupor, staring at nothing, until many of them simply withered away and died. Those who had more physical resilience did not die. They would, however, make their desperate hunger for dialogue evident by spending their waking hours weaving their fingers in front of their eyes, as though eyes and hands were engaged in a meaningful dialogue.

Those foundlings who were reunited with their mothers within three months recovered from their depressive stupors. Most of the infants who had been foundlings since birth and never experienced a human dialogue could not recover even after Spitz arranged to provide them with intimate, one-to-one attention and care. Remarkably, some of the dialogue-deprived infants *were* still able to respond to the invitation to engage in dialogue. But their initial contacts with an animated, responsive caregiver aroused an intense and unmanageable anxiety in the dialogue-deprived infants, who reacted with a violence rarely seen in children. They would tear their clothing and bedsheets into shreds. They would bite the other children in the nursery and tear their own hair out by the fistful.

Spitz described dialogue as "an affect exchange" that was instrumental in developing the libidinal and aggressive *drives*. His point was that human drives are very different from the innate instincts that govern behavior in lower animals. Human drives are not innate—they must be nurtured. In the absence of a reciprocal dialogue, libido withers and never develops. In the absence of a reciprocating partner, an infant's aggressive strivings are simply chaotic and therefore urgently destructive.

Spitz was interested in analyzing external behaviors as clues to the inner life of the human being and, in short, was engaged in pursuits that challenged traditional definitions of scientific method. He devoted his career to the exploration of an invisible inner world—the very world that most so-called "legitimate" scientists avoid talking about in polite society. Since Spitz's day there have been literally hundreds of thousands of "legitimate" experiments on the infant-caregiver relationship. Without setting out to verify Spitz's contentions, these experimental studies have amplified the nature of the reciprocal dialogue he described. Nearly all of them have contributed one or another important detail about the cognitive and emotional intricacies of the nonverbal exchanges between a mother and her infant. Nearly all of them have revealed something new and surprising about infants' active contribution to these communications, and given this better understanding of how an infant initiates and sustains interactions with his caregiver, scientists have been able to design experiments that reveal the inner world of the infant. Infants' self-initiated behaviors—the rhythm and pace of their sucking, their states of alertness, and their capacities to respond in a meaningful way to external events—have provided "windows" into the infant mind and allowed experimenters to further advance their understanding of human love and attachment.

The oversights in Harlow's experiments, in essence, indirectly proved Spitz's psychoanalytic theory on the primal significance of *reciprocal* mother-infant dialogue. Obviously, said Spitz, the inanimate cannot engage in a dialogue. A mechanical mother, like Harlow's terry cloth mother, can lend itself to the child's physical needs for food and warmth and serve as a target for aggression. But a mechanical mother cannot convey emotions or social meaning to an infant. In contrast to the surrogate mother, a living rhesus mother is capable of expressing a wide variety of needs and desires. She searches for food, she plays games, she grooms her baby and is herself groomed by other monkeys. She visits friends. She disciplines her baby by cuffing and scratching him if he bites her or pulls too hard on her fur. She is not always there when her baby wants her. She encourages and stimulates his interest in the world outside the mother-infant orbit. "Therefore she offers her baby, besides food and the opportunity to cling, a wealth of action, shifting over a wide scale from approach to retreat, from embracing to rejecting, from gratification to frustration. . . . Moreover, she is also constantly responding to the baby's initiatives with a whole gamut of different actions."

It is this basic *reciprocal* dialogue between an infant and his caregiver that truly brings a newborn into life. It is this basic dialogue that nurtures an infant and conveys the meaning of love. Perhaps the word *dialogue* seems inappropriate when applied to infancy—a period of life defined by the absence of speech—(Latin: *in + fans,* unable to speak), but Spitz was calling attention to a basic communication process that exists from the earliest moments of life. The basic dialogue is a language of gesture and action. From these nonverbal exchanges between an infant and mother, the infant acquires the emotional language of her species. The basic dialogue is crucial to the learning of love, of hate, of joy, of mastery, of play, and in the human being, the acquisition of verbal language and the symbolic communications of human culture.

The dynamic interplay between a mother, who has an adult social existence, and her still-unsocialized infant is essential to the normal development of *all* higher mammals and primates. A human infant may perish from want of a human dialogue, or he may survive physically but be unable to participate fully in a human society. These days, with our greater sensitivity to the emotional needs of infants, even those babies and young children who must be hospitalized or institutionalized for months or years are held, embraced, rocked, talked to, smiled at, played with and given at least some expression of the reciprocal dialogue that will enable them to become fully human. However, if the person assigned to provide these responses has no genuine empathy for the baby, the baby will still suffer from what Spitz called "derailment of dialogue."

This derailment or breakdown in reciprocal communication between a human infant and his caregiver occurs whenever there is a *consistent* and *prolonged* failure of empathy on the caregiver's part. A narcissistic mother, an insecure mother, a depressed mother, a traumatized mother, or even, as Spitz noted, a mother "bedeviled by the stimulus overload due to urban overpopulation" tends to interpret the actions and gestures of her baby in terms of her need, her confusion, her guilt, her shame, her lack, her trauma, her stress and tension. These emotional derailments are not the effects of abuse and neglect, but the effects of meaningless dialogue, or what Spitz referred to as "interrupted action cycles." The unempathic mother initiates actions that do not correspond to her child's need; she interrupts the child's actions and gestures before the child has completed his side of the communication; she overloads the child with emotional exchanges that have nothing to do with the child's emotional agenda. A mother may love her infant and consciously want to protect him from harm, but if she is overly distracted or preoccupied with her own needs and desires she will be unable to heed the communications of her infant.

The human neonate comes into her world endowed with a diffuse, unfocused lust—a lust for exploring the unknown world that surrounds her. From the very beginning she is reaching out to this unknown world and inviting a dialogue. And because someone is responding to this invitation, from the beginning a newborn has the impression she is entering a world that understands what it is like to be a baby. The new, unknown world seems to be a familiar, caring world that fits in with the baby's inborn gestures and body movements, affirming what she feels herself to be. When she is awake and alert, the baby is always reaching out to something, though her mind is not yet aware of where she begins and ends or where everything else begins and ends. In her moments of tension and need, a helpless baby can be ruthless. She possesses and destroys the breast that feeds her. She devours the arms that hold her. She rids herself of her body products without any concern. A mother's presence in a baby's life absorbs, contains, and tolerates the baby's unruly lusts and thereby tames and humanizes them. Her presence illuminates the contours of the infant's world, making the unknown feel familiar, recognizable, and safe.

The mother's attunement to her baby's crude and inchoate excitements transforms them into socialized human emotions and affects. In the context of dialogue, these confused agitations differentiate into two fundamental types of energy—the aggressive energies of growth, expansion, and exploration and the libidinal energies of attachment, rootedness, and safety. Because the basic mother-infant dialogue endows him with a variety of manageable affects and emotions, the baby will gradually find the courage to extend himself beyond the now-familiar infant-mother orbit and begin to become a participating member of the larger social order. But however far he roams or cleverly he negotiates the challenges of time and space, he is constantly aware of his continuing need for the dialogue that holds him, contains his energies, regulates his aggressions, and makes an unknown world feel knowable and safe.

So let us begin by connecting with the human dialogue. Let us observe a young child at play, as he tries to reckon with the inevitable but often unpredictable ordinary, everyday comings and goings of his mother. It is inconceivable to a child that his mother would disappear forever. When his mother goes away she will always come back. If she is lost she can always be found. Just to be sure, the child plays out a scenario of going away and coming back. Again and again, and then once again.

❧

CHAPTER TWO

LOSING AND
BEING LOST

In 1915, Ernst Wolfgang Halberstadt, an eighteen-month-old boy who lived in the city of Hamburg with his mother, Sophie, and his father, Max, invented a game. For several months he would play this game every day, sometimes several times a day. Though the world would scarcely note the name of the boy, the game he invented, *fort-da* (gone [*fort*] back [*da*]), became famous, cited by experts on child development as an emotionally significant game of early childhood and still referred to by French psychoanalytic philosophers and professors of American and European literature in their interpretations of human culture.

Fort-da, a variant of peekaboo and a precursor of hide-and-seek, is a common childhood creation often invented in the second year of life. At around that age a child experiences his mother's independent comings and goings as a threat to his own identity. She might be going shopping or to meet a friend for lunch, or going to work, or simply disappearing into her bedroom for a nap, but all that the child comprehends is that mother is gone. He worries that she might not come back and, if that calamity were to occur, that he might disappear too. This heightened concern with the mother's whereabouts is an outcome of the child's dawning recognition that he and mother are separate human beings.

The game became famous because it was observed, interpreted, and then used to introduce a controversial monograph written by Ernst's grandfather, Sigmund Freud. Ernst's *fort-da* involved a wooden reel with a piece of string tied around it, and "What he did," explained Freud, "was to hold the reel by the string and very skillfully throw it over the edge of his curtained cot, so that it disappeared into it, at the same time uttering his expressive 'o-o-o-o' [*fort*—gone]. He then pulled the reel out of the cot again by the string and hailed its reappearance with a joyful *da* [back]."

Freud and his daughter, Sophie, agreed that Ernst's "o-o-o-o" stood for the German word *fort*. Indeed, "o-o-o-o" had been one of Ernst's first comprehensible "words." By staging the disappearance and return of the wooden reel, Ernst was representing a mother who might go away but then would always come back. Though the eighteen-month-old Ernst was a boy of few words, he was praised by his family for being "a good boy." He did not wake his parents at night. He obeyed the household rules, and despite the fact that he was deeply attached to his mother, who had always fed and cared for him herself, he never cried when she left him alone for a few hours. He did, however, have one disturbing habit. His favorite game was to throw toys into corners, under beds, and behind chairs while uttering a long-drawn-out "o-o-o-o." His grandfather realized that "the only use he [Ernst] made of any of his toys was to play 'gone' with them." The *da* or "return" part of the games, though obviously more pleasurable, seemed to be less compelling to Ernst than the actions representing loss and disappearance—the very events that caused him anxiety and displeasure. Freud was puzzled by this curious fact.

Another equally expressive game invented by Ernst and also described by his grandfather has received far less attention than the celebrated *fort-da*. In fact, this other game is far more baffling than *fort-da*. One day, after Sophie had been away for several hours, Ernst greeted her return by saying "Baby, o-o-o-o!" The meaning of this barely comprehensible sentence became clear to Sophie when she learned what Ernst had been doing in her absence. He had discovered his reflection in a full-length mirror that did not quite reach the floor. After gazing intently at his image for a minute or so, he would duck his tiny body into a crawl position as though to make himself disappear, and say, "Baby, o-o-o-o." Ernst may have been pleased, even reassured, when he stood up and saw his body once again reflected in the mirror. However, that was not the point of his game. Instead of sulking or throwing a tantrum when his mother left him for a while, Ernst comforted himself by playing "baby o-o-o-o" over and over again until Sophie returned. Instead of suffering passively from the disturbing and worrisome experience of being left by his mother, Ernst took active charge of the situation and made himself disappear at will.

When, three years later, Freud used Ernst's *fort-da* game to introduce his work *Beyond the Pleasure Principle,* he also recalled his grandson's preoccupation with the "gone" aspect of his games. Freud concluded that the first gesture—*fort*—of making the reel disappear might represent little Ernst's vengeance or angry feelings toward his mother: "Go away, mother. You left me, so now I don't need you. You didn't leave me, I am sending you away."

The return of the reel in the *fort-da* game was Ernst's reassurance that his wish to make his mother disappear forever would *not* come true. However, as Freud stressed, common sense dictates that a child would want to repeat a gesture of return, or any other experience that provided reassurance and pleasure. What intrigued Freud were the possible connections between Ernst's repressed hostility and his insistence on a repetition of the unpleasurable and worrisome aspects of his disappearing games. These enigmas were directly relevant to the philosophical questions Freud raised in *Beyond the Pleasure Principle*—a speculative inquiry into the struggle between Eros, the life instinct, and Thanatos, the death instinct.

Freud composed *Beyond the Pleasure Principle* during the closing years of World War I. Of course, he had already written about personal aggression and the personalized aggressive fantasies of his patients in previous papers and monographs, but the large-scale, impersonal horrors of the war, its senseless violence and savagery, seemed to belong to a dimension of human existence that went beyond everyday matters of pleasure and pain.

Two fundamental threads or lines of thought are found in Freud's monograph: the abstract-philosophical and the practical-personal. Freud's philosophical inquiry concerned the abstract forces of Eros and Thanatos. Ernst's games were about the life-and-death matters of a child's daily life. Moreover, Ernst's anxieties about the calamities that threatened his immediate existence and his repetitive manner of mastering these anxieties resembled the psychological dilemmas and solutions of many of Freud's adult patients.

Freud's impersonal philosophical discourse may have, in fact, been masking his more personal concerns. During these four years of World War I, Freud was preoccupied with the possible death of or physical injury to those he loved. His two sons, his grandson's father, and several of his young students and colleagues had been called to fight the Allies. And as the philosophical Freud considered the appalling savagery of a war instigated in the name of humanitarian ideals, he came to believe that the human being must be governed by a destructive impulse more powerful than the strivings for self-preservation and erotic fulfillment. Freud referred to this impulse as the death instinct, or Thanatos. Whereas the life instinct, Eros, binds together and unites, impelling each individual organism toward higher and more complex forms of experience, the aim of this death instinct is to unbind and break down living matter, eventually reverting all living organisms back to their simplest forms and to the inevitable death that awaits them.

Characteristically, according to Freud, the death instinct does its work silently, inside the organism. Conversely, homicide, vandalism, and sexual abuse are manifestations of the death instinct turned outward. Insofar as the death instinct is normally directed toward other human beings and objects of human culture, the full fury of the destruction is defused and balanced by Eros. But in the savage enterprises of war and genocide, erotic aims are lost, and Thanatos could eventuate in a total annihilation of humanity and human culture.

At first, the analytic community and many philosophers, artists, and scientists were captivated by Freud's idea of a death instinct. Today, although the fine points of Freud's philosophical arguments continue to be argued and elaborated, few psychoanalysts consent to the idea of a death instinct. However, the other line of reasoning in *Beyond the Pleasure Priniciple,* which Freud introduced with his grandson's repetitive disappearing games, has become a standard feature of analytic thinking and clinical practice.

Freud's analytic work with adult patients led him to believe that there was a universal tendency among humans to repeat, in one form or another, events and circumstances once experienced as traumatic or life threatening. He called this tendency *the repetition compulsion.* As evidence for the repetition compulsion, Freud cited the recurrent nightmares of soldiers returning from the battlefields. Rather than wish away, block out, or repress the terrifying events they had witnessed and been subjected to, the soldiers dreamed about them over and over again. Even before the war, Freud had noticed the repetition tendency in many of his patients. Some, during the course of their analysis, would repeat over and again the unpleasant experiences of their childhood, acting them out within the analysis itself and living them out in their everyday personal relationships. Other patients would cling to behaviors and attitudes that were self-injuring and self-destructive as though determined to prove that the mere repetition of these acts would gradually diminish their noxious effects.

It is true that the compulsion to repeat ties us to the past, works against analytical cures, and keeps us running in circles instead of proceeding with our lives in more productive and pleasurable ways. However, the compulsion to repeat is not an expression of Thanatos, as some Freudian scholars have insisted. The repetition compulsion orginates in Eros; that is, in the elemental human dialogue that binds each of us to other human beings and to human society itself. Essentially, every trauma poses a threat of loss of dialogue. By repeating the situation of threat, we retain the hope of continuing the dialogue. Any dialogue, even one that entails fear, threat, suffering, and self-punishment, is better than absence of dialogue. The trauma of loss often leads to a repetition of trauma in dialogues with the living. For example, the bereaved may enter into new relationships with the conscious desire to love and to be loved forever, only to behave in ways that insure a repetition of some devastating abandonment. In this way, dialogue is restored and the bereaved retains the hope of refinding his lost beloved.

Games of repetition are a child's way of mastering events which would otherwise overwhelm him. When a child hears a story that frightens or threatens or simply brings her to an unmanageable peak of anxious excitement, she will ask to hear the story again and then again until she has mastered the threat in her own mind. The need to hear the story repeated takes priority over the child's practical life with its ordinary possibilities of pleasure and pain. Whatever menacing feelings have been stirred up and set loose by the images and words in the story must be bound up so that they may be assimilated in a coherent, meaningful way. Then she can resume her ordinary life of milk and cookies.

Soon after he invented his *fort-da,* some extraordinary catastrophes befell Ernst. Every calamity that a child sometimes imagines in connection with his conflicted feelings about his parents and siblings seemed to come true in Ernst's actual life. First, Ernst was told that his father, Max, who had always stayed close to home, working in his photography studio, had been "called up to the front," and would soon be going away. The night before the day his father was to leave, Ernst awoke from a dream, sobbing violently, "Daddy, Daddy, Baby!" Ernst was not an intellectually precocious child, but his dream achieved an ingenious unconscious compromise between his affects and his wishes. His tears acknowledged that his father was going away, while his dream words kept daddy and baby together. Despite Ernst's wishes, his father disappeared and did not come back for a long, long time. When Ernst worried about his father, he reassured himself by whispering "up to the fwont." And when he felt particularly possessive toward his mother, he would throw his toys in a corner and shout, "Go to the fwont."

Max fought in the disastrous battle of Verdun and was nearly killed. After recovering from his wounds, he was transferred to an air force base on the outskirts of Hamburg, where he taught pilots how to use aerial photography in their reconnaissance work. In the evenings, Sophie would take little Ernst with her to stand in line for the bread distributed to the families of pilots. While they were waiting, the huge, low-flying, very loud reconnaissance "Eagles" would return from the front line. Ernst associated these Eagles with his daddy and was impressed with his father's power. He was proud to be his son. His father finally came home, and soon afterward Ernst was presented with a baby brother, Heinz Rudolphe, called Heinerle.

Thirteen months later, when Ernst was five and three-quarters, his mother Sophie, whom he had never entirely forgiven for having Heinerle, contracted influenza. She died a week later. And then, when Ernst was nine, Heinerle also died. Ernst began to fear that he too might disappear—after all, his mother had disappeared and for many years it seemed nothing he did would bring her back.

When Sophie died, Freud lost his favorite daughter. Had it not been for the presence of the enchanting and clever Heinerle, who so much resembled his lost daughter, Freud would have been inconsolable. Then, when Heinerle also died Freud felt that life itself had lost all value.

As for Ernst, he was no consolation to his grandfather, who could not help noting "Now that his mother was really 'gone' ('o-o-o'), the little boy showed no signs of grief." He concluded that his grandson's "violent jealousy" had spared him any feelings of sorrow. Perhaps due to his own bereavement, Freud, who had interpreted the life-and-death struggle implicit in Ernst's *fort-da,* was unable to see beyond his grandson's surface behavior to the desperate emotional conflicts going on inside him. In fact, it was inconceivable to the inventor of the *fort-da* that his mother had actually disappeared forever.

In 1963, a half century after the birth of Ernst Wolfgang Halberstadt, a baby girl named Amy Jeanette Gordon was born in New York City where she lived with her mother, Sally, and her father, George. Like Ernst, Amy invented a version of *fort-da* when she was around eighteen months old.

The *fort-da* game does not emanate from some mysterious instinctual depth "beyond" the child's experiences in ordinary life. Aggressive, even sadistic elements are embedded in the game and eventually become more apparent as the child's mental organization becomes sophisticated enough to express them. But Amy's childhood games were essentially manifestations of the dialogue that binds children to their parents—an expression of Eros.

Sally and George Gordon had decided that one child was all they wanted or could afford, so Amy was never faced with the feelings of being lost that inevitably arise when a mother and father turn their attentions toward a new little baby. When Amy was born, Sally took a leave of absence from her job so she could stay home with her for a few years. As Sally explained, "This is the only time I am going to be a mother. I don't want to miss one second of Amy's babyhood." The fifth of seven children of poor Irish Catholic immigrants, Sally never forgot how she had longed for her mother's attentions. In addition to caring for her children during the day, Sally's mother also had to work at night to help support the family. Sally didn't want Amy to know that kind of longing. Besides, she enjoyed absorbing herself in motherhood and having Amy all to herself.

From the beginning, Amy was bound to her mother's capacity to make sense of Amy's crude excitements and appetites. Each interpretation of her movements, gestures, and sounds gave Amy the sense that she had a mother who knew what it meant to be a baby. By three months, Amy had developed a fierce passion for dialogue with her mother. The predictable excitements of dialogue had become as vital to Amy as being comforted, being rocked to sleep, or sucking in the milk that filled her stomach. Amy had learned that when she directed her crude and formless excitements toward her mother, they were tamed into a meaningful emotional exchange.

After Amy was fed, diapered, and still awake and alert enough to respond to the world around her, she was ready and eager for "conversation." Sally, too, enjoyed their conversations, which for the first two months or so were limited to gazing into each other's eyes, touching fingers, and Sally's loving words, which were spoken in a way that made sense to a baby. Sally's high-pitched voice and long-drawn-out vowel sounds were an adult approximation of an infant's coos and gurgles. As she love-talked with Amy, Sally stretched her mouth, raised her brows, and opened her eyes as wide as possible, transforming her face into an exaggeration of humanness.

Inexperienced as Amy was in the art of conversation, she knew just how to engage her mother in dialogue. Merely by staring into her mother's eye and smiling, Amy could get her mother to love-talk. Then, Amy would listen and look, and when she had enough, she would simply turn her head away.

At three months, Amy had learned enough about human conversations to be a more active participant. She would gurgle and coo in response to her mother's love-talk, and then Sally would become the listener. Finally, Sally would speak, and Amy would cock her head, actively taking in the words. And so it went for several minutes.

As their conversations evolved, Amy and Sally gave up the pretense of alternating the roles of speaker and listener. They spoke simultaneously until their conversation peaked and Sally sensed Amy's readiness to stop. Then Sally would quiet down so Amy could rest, leaving her baby with an impression of having generated her own excitement and having controlled the whole thing. When Amy was ready for another bout of love-talk, she would invite her mother back by kicking, gurgling beguilingly, squinting her eyes mischievously, and smiling.

When Amy was five months old, Sally enriched their conversational dialogue with a game. As Sally's face disappeared behind her hands, Amy's insides would flutter. The fluttering reminded her of how she would sometimes feel when her mother's gestures didn't reciprocate her own needs and desires. But it was only a gentle reminder, for after waiting just so long, Sally would open her palms and reappear, allowing Amy to relax. The peekaboo game gave Amy the opportunity to flirt with the enigmas of disappearing and reappearing, of absence and presence. Instead of experiencing the dread she would feel if her mother disappeared forever, Amy was finding a harmony and pleasure at the core of her body-self. In addition, Sally's reappearing smiling face confirmed Amy's sense that she was very important, something her mother wanted and desired.

"Peekaboo, I see you," said Sally, almost at the second that Amy's body relaxed. Her trilling voice and the animated look in her eyes were telling Amy, "What a beautiful baby you are. How happy I am to see you." Amy looked back into her mother's eyes. A baby gets to know what she is by what is mirrored in the faces of those who look at her. The mirroring admiration of the peekaboo game and the interchangeability of anxiety and excitement contributes to the capacities for optimism and courage. Peekaboo is an introduction to hopefulness.

By ten months old, Amy grew tired of being the passive observer and invented her own version of peekaboo. How would her mother respond to *her* disappearances and reappearances? Amy risked getting lost. She put her special blanket over her face. "Where is the baby?" her mother inquired with mock agitation. "Where is my wonderful baby?" Now that Amy was in charge, she prolonged the tension, and Sally went along with the idea. "Oh dear, my baby is gone. Where can she be?" At last Amy would pull the blanket away from her face, squealing at the look of joyous relief on her mother's face.

When Amy was fifteen months old, Sally decided that she would have to return to her job three days a week. Amy was already having difficulty accepting her mother's absences—a few hours, even a few minutes could be too long. Her mother, on the other hand, came and went as she pleased, or so it seemed to little Amy, who could not know how guilty Sally felt about leaving her in the care of a baby-sitter, or how much she missed her when she was away. From Amy's point of view, Mother had all the power while she had none at all.

By the time her mother's sporadic comings and goings became a serious matter of "going back to work" and being away for a full day, Amy had acquired a certain degree of confidence that she could manage her excitements and fears. Moreover, from her earlier "conversations" with her mother Amy had learned now to imitate her mother's sounds and gestures. She tried to manage her confusing emotions by attempting to imitate her mother's power. Amy wanted to be as powerful and independent as she imagined her mother to be. She did not want to make a fuss and cry every time her mother put on her going-to-work outfits, gathered up her papers, picked up her briefcase, jangled her keys, and walked toward the door.

So Amy invented games that enabled her to feel that she had some control over what she was feeling. At first she was not quite ready to enact these uncertain dramas of losing and being lost on her own. When her mother and father returned from work, longing for some peace and quiet after their often nerve-racking days, Amy would not let them rest until they joined in with her game. She would gather up her favorite toys and throw them, one by one, into corners, under beds, and behind doors, inviting her parents to hunt for them, pick them up, and return them to her. Not just once was this cycle acted out but three times, sometimes four, until Amy was reassured that lost things can be found again.

As she played the game, Amy would call out "o-o-o-o," voicing the pleasure she got from losing her toys and "a-a-a-a" when her parents found them. George would grow impatient with Amy's demand to do it again and again, but Sally, who knew how hard it was for Amy to deal with their separation, understood that the inarticulate "o-o-o-o" was her little girl's way of saying "gone," and "a-a-a-a" her sound for "back."

A few months later, after Amy realized that her disappearing parents always returned at night, she had the confidence to play gone-back all by herself. The baby-sitter reported that each morning, shortly after her parents went to work, Amy would play with a wooden toy wagon on a string. But Amy did not pull the wagon along behind her as it was meant to be used. Instead, she threw it over the edge of the couch and watched it disappear with a mournful but excited "gone." Then she slowly pulled it back toward her and with a joyous "back" watched it reappear over the shoulder of the couch. For a while, the "gone and back" game seemed more important to Amy than food or cuddling or the fun and games her baby-sitter invented to amuse her. As Amy got used to the idea that her loved ones would go away but would always come back, she stopped repeating her gone-back scenario and instead pulled the wagon along behind her in a lighthearted, playful way. She accepted the baby-sitter's attentions during the day and let her parents enjoy some peace and quiet when they returned from work at night—unless she was sick or had had a disappointing day. In that case she would turn away from her father's open arms, greet her mother with an angry frown, and run away to hide herself from them. Before the ordinary life of dinner and conversation could resume, Amy made sure her disappointing parents would search for her and prove to her that they thought she was important.

If we take a more studied look at these ordinary games of early childhood, it is not in the spirit of replacing the charm of childhood with the calculations of psychological functions. We are, in fact, filled with wonder at the remarkable talent and imagination of this eighteen-month-old artist at work, who has enough presence of mind to transform the terrible feeling of losing and being lost into dramas of symbolic complexity. Through her games, Amy demonstrated her conviction that an absence can be transformed into a presence. She also questioned her own value to others. Amy took the risks of hiding and losing because she had the hope and confidence that she could control the outcome.

Let us not forget, either, that there is a vengeance in the *fort-da,* gone-back, hide-and-seek games. As Freud suggested, we must inquire about the aggressive motives in Amy's innocent game. Was the wooden wagon a bad mother? Was Amy getting rid of the bad mother who, she felt, by going back to work had gotten rid of her?

Amy's eighteen-month-old play foreshadowed the complicated identifications and extended emotional meanings she would develop in her later games of losing and being lost. For example, the gone-back game had originated with her desire to be as powerful as her mother. To be like her mother meant that Amy had the power to go away and to leave someone behind to suffer. This identification with the powerful aggressor was one of Amy's first psychological defenses against feeling powerless. At two years old, Amy would return from a visit to the doctor and proceed to give ear examinations and injections to her dolls and stuffed animals. When she was scolded for waking Sally and George in the middle of the night, the next morning she would hit her teddy bear and yell in a gruff voice, "Bad baby." When she felt particularly humiliated by her parents' reprimands, Amy would throw the bear on the floor behind her crib and shout, "Go 'way, baby."

By the time Amy was three years old, she had acquired the symbolic capacities to express the other, more complicated thoughts and feelings that were merely implied in her eighteen-month-old gone-back game. Her favorite new fantasy game made apparent the sadistic pleasure Amy derived from the *fantasy* of making her mother suffer the pains of losing and being lost. This new game coincided with Sally's return to full-time employment and Amy's placement in a day care center.

Amy became a source of consternation to her parents. Her teachers reported that Amy spent much of the day gazing longingly toward the door, clinging to her security blanket, or talking to imaginary friends. She was also intent on obeying the rules and regulations set out by her teachers absolutely. Amy would not move or speak unless she got it "just right." With all her energy going into simply holding herself together, Amy didn't have enough life left over to play with the other children or derive any pleasure from the classroom activities. When Amy was reunited with her mother in the late afternoon, her longing and tension were relieved, but she would not look at her mother, much less hug her. Amy's message to her mother was clear: "You do not exist."

A few months later, the teachers reported that Amy was having a great time at school. She was taking chances. She was too excited to bother with getting everything just right. She was even naughty enough to have to been assigned to the "time-out" chair in the corner of the nursery. At home, Amy informed Sally that her favorite teacher was the most beautiful mommy in the world, and teased George by telling him that her teacher knew more words than he.

No doubt a new game, which Amy had been playing at home repeatedly for several months, had helped her express her hostility toward her mother and also to conquer her frightening feelings of "having been lost." Amy did not play this new game with Sally or George. She required a neutral accomplice, like her baby-sitter, or her grandmother, or her uncle, all of whom she could trust to go along with her directions without taking the drama too personally. She called this elaborate scenario (which had several minor variations on the identical theme) "the talk game." The accomplice would assume the roles, speak the words, and act the actions that Amy commanded, exactly as she commanded. The characters were stored away in a small basket, called "the talk basket." Among them were various babies, a mother doll, a father doll, and a princess doll.

In this game, the princess (talked by Amy) brings to the mother and father (talked by her accomplice) the beautiful new baby (talked by Amy) they had been wishing for ever since they got married. After allowing the mother a few seconds to hold her precious new baby, the princess announces that she must fly the baby up to the sky—just for a little while. "Be back soon," she says.

But instead of returning, the princess keeps the baby for herself. She asks the mother, "Would you like to come for a visit?" "Oh, yes, yes," replies the mother, "I miss my baby so much." "Well," says the princess in a mean voice, "I won't tell you where she is. You cannot visit her. You can never have her back. She is staying with me forever." To make matters worse, the princess grabs the father and flies him away with her. He decides to stay with the princess and the baby. Now the mother is all alone. She calls her baby on the telephone. The baby asks, "Do you want me to come home?" "Oh yes," the mother answers. "Please come back. Mommy loves you so much." "Well, I won't," says the baby. "I am going to stay forever with the beautiful princess and daddy. And you will never see me again." The drama concludes with the mother crying bitter tears and Amy smiling wickedly and repeating, triumphantly, "More, more. Cry some more."

The baby obviously doesn't need the mother anymore since she has the princess—a new, more beautiful, more perfect mother—*and* the daddy, depriving the mother of any pleasure she might have had in the baby's absence. After all, it was the father who was always diverting the mother's attention away from the baby with his endless talk, talk, talk.

The triumph and aggression in Amy's game is obvious. However, to fully understand the complexity of Amy's overtly sadistic fantasy, we must also acknowledge the ambiguity in her apparent triumph. Amy's fantasy of absolute omnipotence and autonomy is inseparable from a repetition of her own pain, and when she deprives the mother of the baby's presence, she also deprives the baby of the mother's comforting presence.

Our little avenger's enlistment of suffering and vengeance is beyond simple innocent mastery yet still emotionally connected to the relatively ordinary life of pleasure and pain. As with any such twisting of pleasure and pain, Amy's masochistic triumph, her scenario of vengeful abandonment, is somewhat perverse, but with all its twisted meanings, the game is still a reflection of Amy's longing for human dialogue. Any dialogue, even one that causes us to suffer, is better than no dialogue at all.

The emotional bond between Amy and her mother was strong enough to allow for fantasy enactments, such as the talk game. The capacity to invent such a fantasy game is a sign that the child is securely attached to her parents. Of course, there are times when the bond between an ordinary parent and child can be strained, and occasionally the positive feelings that ensure the attachment can be reduced to a mutual antagonism and hostility. At such times, a child may forget about games and actually manage to get herself lost.

Most of the time parents do not lose children, and most children, though they enjoy the ritualized games of hiding and being found, don't actually get lost. A child's urgent desire for the parent's comforting presence and protection corresponds to the high narcissistic valuation that the parents place on the child. These two forces of attachment, which are intrinsic to the parent-child dialogue, unite to demarcate the area in which the child roams freely.

Sometimes even the most valued child will arrange to get herself lost—usually in a crowded place—at a picnic ground, an amusement park, a beach resort, a department store. The occasion to get lost is often provoked by feelings of being emotionally lost. Perhaps the child senses that her parents' expressed love for her is mixed with an unexpressed anger and resentment. Or perhaps the parent has been preoccupied with another family member for a few days when the child was lonely, sad, frightened, or simply longing for conversation and dialogue.

When a child actually gets herself lost once or twice, it is only natural to wonder if this exceptional action might be signifying a temporary strain in the parent-child dialogue. When a child habitually and repeatedly gets herself lost, it is safe to assume that she is suffering from the anxiety and humiliation of not being valued, that she is trying to gain control over some pretty frightening and confusing emotions. The passive experience of being abandoned is transformed by the child into the active experience of "getting lost." The child imagines the parent is inattentive because she is not important or is far less important than someone or something else. When the parent makes the effort to find the lost child, she is proving that she missed the child, that she cares and that she would never really abandon her child.

Some children show their reactions to being unloved or insufficiently valued by acquiring the habit of losing their possessions. Cynthia Coles was one of these children, and while Cynthia's parents did love and value her, they also unconsciously conveyed to Cynthia that their thoughts and emotions were invested in someone else—someone more valuable to them than Cynthia could ever be.

Cynthia's everyday life was a perpetual saga of losing and being lost. When she left for school in the morning, she could never find her pen, pencils, and notebooks. In the afternoon, she would leave her homework assignments in her school desk or somehow lose them on the way home. She would lose her hats, her gloves, her sweaters, and even the pocket money for after-school treats or the bus pass to get her home. Cynthia directed the hostility she felt when her parents made her feel like a lost and abandoned child toward the nonliving, inanimate world. As the subject of losing became a constant source of irritation and confrontation with her parents, they would direct their anger toward her, reinforcing Cynthia's feelings of being lost in an uncaring world.

Cynthia's perception of "an uncaring world" developed from the fact that her mother and father still had not recovered from the death of their ten-year-old son, who had been through a long, painful illness. Cynthia was born about a year after the death of their son, almost on the day of the son's birthday. Frank and Eleanor Coles welcomed Cynthia's birth as an opportunity for a new start. But much as they consciously cherished Cynthia, both Frank and Eleanor were still preoccupied with thoughts and fantasies about the son they had lost. Unconsciously, Cynthia's parents were wishing to refind his spirit in the body of another child.

When Cynthia was four, her parents decided she was old enough to know about death. They told her that they had once had another child. They told her about her brother's illness and his death—as gently as they could, shielding her from the name of the illness and the extent of his and their suffering. Cynthia had already begun losing her toys and destroying them before she heard this scary news. But after learning about her dead brother, Cynthia was stricken with painful attacks of a mysterious, undiagnosable illness. Each year, sometimes even twice a year, for four years in a row, Cynthia scared her parents half to death. She was hospitalized twice and once nearly underwent unnecessary surgery. Finally, when Cynthia was nine years old, the family doctor recognized the unconscious motives for Cynthia's attacks.

Cynthia, he explained, sensed that she was less important to her parents than her dead brother had been. She unconsciously reasoned that if she got sick and was taken to a hospital, her parents might value her too. The doctor noted an obvious pattern that would have been apparent if the parents had not been so lost in mourning their dead son. Cynthia's mysterious illnesses always occurred around the anniversaries of the birthday and death day of her lost brother. On those somber days, which were more emotionally compelling to her parents than her own "happy birthday," the spirit of her dead brother was ubiquitous. Her parents' minds were elsewhere. Cynthia punished her mother and father for their lack of attention and hurtful betrayal by refusing birthday parties, losing the presents they gave her, and making sure to forget their birthdays.

But something else was going on—something more drastic than Cynthia losing her possessions and feigning attacks of illness. Soon after the secret of her brother's illness and death had been revealed to her, Cynthia had begun to sneak into the closet where her dead brother's special toys and clothing were still neatly stored away. She had always wondered about those treasured possessions, things she was told she musn't touch or play with. Now that Cynthia had been apprised of her brother's existence and his death, and even felt guilty for having taken the place of her rival, she felt compelled to violate the taboos. She began dressing up in his cowboy hat and jeans and playing with his trucks and pistols, imagining herself as a valuable child. These were the special and extraordinary moments when Cynthia felt loved and wanted.

More usually, when Cynthia had fantasies or daydreams about the person she was or might become, she cast herself in the role of a neglected, ragged, lonely girl who survived many life-imperiling adventures far away on distant planets. She identified with the castaway sweaters and notebooks that wandered the earth in search of a home. However, on those forays into the forbidden closet, when Cynthia donned her dead brother's garments and assumed his persona, she found her safe, beloved self and in her fantasy, the adoring parents she had been longing for. She knew her parents would be horrified if they ever found out, but impersonating her brother was Cynthia's way of loving and being loved. By embodying her dead brother's spirit and bringing him back to life, she was fulfilling her parents' deepest wish.

Cynthia, a chronic loser, was enacting the kind of double identification that Amy exhibited in her games and fantasies. While Amy simultaneously identified with the powerful mother *and* with the gone-away baby doll, a chronic loser like Cynthia simultaneously identifies with the parents who are preoccupied, neglectful, indifferent, or unconcerned *and* with the possessions she has cast away into an uncaring world.

This ingenious capacity for a *double* identification is an outcome of the human dialogue. From the time that a child is capable of wanting to be like a powerful parent, every experience of losing and being lost will be accompanied by a double identification. The difference between a valued child like Amy and a little girl like Cynthia, who was never entirely certain of her value, is that Amy could invent a fantasy game to help her come to terms with her feelings of being lost. Cynthia was compelled to enact her dilemma in the real time and space of her actual life.

Amy took good care of her toys but would also hoard every toy she was given. By the time she was four, Amy's closets and drawers and shelves and toy chests were overflowing with stuffed animals, dolls, broken crayons, pieces of string, and scraps of paper. One day Sally and George decided to throw out the junk and make up neat packages of those toys Amy didn't pay much attention to. These they donated to neighbors and various charitable organizations. And even though they were especially careful to preserve those stuffed animals and dolls and other assorted toys that Amy was especially attached to, Amy was furious with her parents. She didn't want anyone else to have her toys, and the scraps of string and broken crayons they'd deemed garbage were her precious jewels.

Was the four-year-old Amy becoming a spoiled, selfish "overprotected" child, who cared for no one but herself? Could the high value placed on Amy by her parents be transforming her into a child who valued things more than persons?

Amy was not an uncaring child. If anything, she cared too much about certain things. In her possessive attachment to her toys, Amy was identifying with her mother's possessive attachment to her. Apparently there had not been much room for George in the passionate love affair between Amy and Sally, and excluding George meant excluding issues of rivalry, competition, triumph, defeat, and of course aggression. But efforts to eliminate aggression always invite aggression to sneak in through the back door. What might have been a common, everyday outburst of rivalry took on aspects of crime and punishment. Amy feared her father's vengeful anger for keeping her mother all to herself and, at the same time, was afraid to assert her love for George and risk an aggressive rivalry with Sally.

Hoarding was Amy's way of protecting her toys from the hurt they would feel if she excluded them. Amy identified with her toys. She sympathized with their lost and lonely feelings. She empathized with their need to be close to her forever. Like most overprotective grown-up mothers, who also have problems expressing aggression toward their loved ones, Amy was overly concerned with the well-being and psychological welfare of her "babies." She could not throw or give them away because she was sure their feelings would be hurt. As far as Amy was concerned, giving away a broken crayon or a piece of string was no different from abandoning a sick baby.

Amy would tend to her stuffed animals and dolls, covering them with her special soft blanket when they had sniffles and earaches, rocking and singing to them when they were tired, feeding them when they were hungry. This tender concern extended to the broken crayons and the trucks without wheels that Amy could not bear to part with.

When Amy was in day care, and later on in school, she tried to care for some of her playmates. She was particularly kind to those children whom she sensed were having a hard time managing on their own. In the playground, she would share her pails and shovels with the younger children and teach them how to dig a proper hole. When Amy was ready to leave the sandbox and move on over to the swings, she would retrieve her pail and shovels but graciously donate the hole to her little pupil. Amy would not hit another child, but she was quite capable of enjoying the misery of a child who had either been hit by another child or scolded by a parent. She would stare at the scene with unabashed glee, her eyes lit up, her cheeks flushed with excitement. Amy was equally capable of identifying with the hurt feelings of a lost and needy child as with the aggressor who was causing the child to hurt.

Amy Gordon and Cynthia Coles, though different, are representative of most human beings in that the emotions they invested in their possessions were offshoots of the human dialogue. Our attitudes toward material things reflect the value we place on our own selves and the persons who are of value to us. The attachments we form with other human beings and the complicated mix of emotions aroused by those attachments are frequently displaced onto the inanimate objects we call our own.

Adults who have in childhood lost a parent through divorce, desertion, or death are, like Cynthia Coles, susceptible to the habit of losing things. The scenario of losing and finding becomes a daily event, and it doesn't much matter what is lost. Often it is something significant—a passport, a manuscript, a key to the bank vault, a will—but just as often it could be anything at all—a hair clip, a coffee cup, a glove. Losing a possession may also be a solution to an emotional conflict. The "thing"—whatever it is—represents and symbolizes the conflict, and losing it is very different from folding it up, donating it to charity, and never thinking about it ever again. To lose something means we entertain a hope and possibility of refinding it. Losing, therefore, is a device for prolonging the value of something that provokes mixed sentiments. Losing the object signifies as much our longing and desire for it as our disappointment in it. The hope of finding the object again and the act of looking for it and trying to find it recharges a devalued something with emotional importance, value, and desire.

The glove lost in the park was a gift from a friend whose intellect we once greatly admired and idealized. Soon, though, that admiration turned to envy because her intelligence was far superior to our own. We purchased a graceful, long-stemmed pen, with a fantasy that this writing tool would endow us with the graceful wit of some famous writer. Now, several months later, perhaps we are disillusioned by his latest book but still want to believe in the ideal he represented. We don't simply toss the pen in the trash or bury it the back of our desk or give it away to a friend. We lose it in the library after an entire week of failing to write even one graceful sentence. By losing the pen we are expressing our loss of faith but also our hope of refinding it.

A lost possession is something we have personified in one way or another—a representation of our own self or a representation of some other person. Some possessions, like a child's security blanket, which is simultaneously imbued with the smells and textures of his own body and the smells and textures of the mother's body, seem to embody the essence of everything we value and cherish. Because our most treasured possessions are charged with a high degree of emotional intensity and are also personified, when we lose one of them, we feel especially upset and guilty, almost as if the thing were a person we had hurt or abandoned. We imagine the glove or the pen as lost and frightened, alone in some lonely place with no one to care for it.

We keep on expecting that maybe one day our treasured possession will turn up again somewhere. We keep longing for it. In contrast to an object that has no emotional charge, a lost object seems to retain its value indefinitely. After a long while we decide finally to give up the search and hope of refinding it. But we never really give up. We can't comprehend that something which is "lost" is *really* gone forever.

CHAPTER THREE

✳

THE DEATH OF A VIRTUOUS FATHER

When the parent of a young child dies, the child has lost her safety net. She dutifully repeats what she is told: "Daddy is gone. He is never coming back," but these words of "truth" don't make sense to her—they fill her with a sinking feeling and make her want to withdraw from the world. She avoids those who might try to console her. She doesn't allow her mother to pick her up or hold her. She thinks, feeling both sad and angry, "I don't need anybody." The thought is temporarily comforting, but within a few days or weeks this thin shell of self-sufficiency will yield to the pressures of longing and desire. "Where are you?" she will wonder. "I need you. I want you back."

The child knows her daddy is gone and will never return, yet she experiences a sense of certainty that he is only hiding, or maybe lost. Her hopefulness manifests itself in her effort to continue the dialogue with her lost father. Any dialogue, even one that brings its own form of suffering, is better than no dialogue at all, and the need for dialogue, the compelling urgency that is the heartbeat of a human life, mobilizes the child's emotional energies and psychological resources. Her mind is alerted. Perplexing sensations are pulsing through her body. She wants to understand what has happened and even more to give shape and voice to the inchoate fantasies that assail her mind. If only there were someone who knew how she felt.

Adults often mistake a child's imperfect way of showing her feelings as an indication that she has no feelings at all. Since death, like sex, is often treated as an obscene secret, it is assumed that death *should* not (and therefore *does* not) trouble the mind of an innocent. The surviving parent, the grandparents, the uncles and aunts are consumed by their own grief. The very sight of the child of the dead parent is a painful reminder of the awful truth that everyone would prefer to deny. When they wish to reassure themselves of the child's innocence, the adults pay no attention to the signs of the child's confusion, or her yearnings to be helped. They say things like: "Oh, he barely noticed she was gone," "She was sad at first, but now she seems quite well and happy," or "I don't think she misses her mommy at all." "She's not sad but she sure is grumpy and mean." How easy it is not to notice the child's attempts at communication, when deception is a salve and truth only stings the aching wound.

The child has been told that her father is dead, and sometimes she utters the words "dead," "gone to heaven," or "lying asleep in the earth." But these words of obedient reason are simply cover-ups—as far as she is concerned, her father is merely lost. Her entire being is possessed by a longing to get her father back.

A child does not deliberately hide her confusion. She *is* sending out signals and cues, but usually nobody reads them. The child concludes that her thoughts and fantasies must be crazy and shameful and that it's better to silence them and dissemble a happy face. No one will be the wiser, least of all herself, until one day, in the distant future, some other loved one will die, or a precious possession will be stolen or some cherished ideal will be violated. It is then, as she comes face-to-face with the later loss, that the adult who lost a parent in childhood is overwhelmed by the feelings and thoughts she was not allowed to feel or think when that first calamity struck.

The child who is trying to come to terms with the death of a parent is not passively submitting to fate. She is actively attempting to restore the parent, and these determined efforts to reestablish a connection with the dead parent are signs of the child's resourcefulness and emotional vitality. Nevertheless, the child's ingenious methods of reconstituting the dialogue with her lost parent may befuddle her imagination, skew her development, and warp her image of who and what she is. Crucial to the child's development will be the support given by the surviving parent or some other adult who can empathize with the sufferings of a grieving child.

It is not easy for adults to empathize with children under any circumstances, but empathy is especially difficult when a child is suffering. Left to her own devices, a child will take the shortest route from feeling pain and disappointment to feeling better again. Adults do *sympathize* with the child's wish to short-circuit pain, and the adult's first thought is to rush to the rescue and quickly bring the child's suffering to an end. But sympathy—to feel what the child is feeling—is not the same as empathy. Empathy is sympathy *plus* an understanding of how best to help a child make sense of her experience.

True empathy for a child begins with listening to a child and not acting until it is clear what the child is trying to communicate. Parents and grandparents are intimately and passionately involved with a child's emotional state and therefore apt to be immensely sympathetic. However, they are not always empathic. Sympathy occurs in an instant. Empathy requires time and energy and thought. Sometimes parents and grandparents are too emotionally caught up in a child's anger or fear to empathize. They feel the anger. They feel the fear. Then, when the emotional climate cools, they are relieved to let sleeping dogs lie.

Much of the time, they are too busy trying to earn a living or prepare dinner or read the newspaper to pay close attention to the everyday concerns of a child. They say, "Uh-huh," and "OK," and "That's nice, honey," figuring that a child's problems have a way of sorting themselves out whether or not the grown-ups listen. And usually they are right. However, a few minutes of an adult's thoughtful attention can go a long way.

One afternoon, a four-year-old boy and his grandmother were taking a leisurely walk through their neighborhood. Both were wrapped up in their own thoughts. Suddenly, the boy tugged on his grandmother's hand and told her that yesterday—or maybe it was tomorrow—he had lost a picture postcard. Without skipping a beat or bothering to detach herself from her musings, the grandmother smiled benevolently and offered a string of her customary niceties. "That's all right, dear. Don't worry about it. I'll buy you another one." The grandmother felt her grandson's hand tighten. She looked down at his face and saw a sad-eyed, wistful expression. At that, she decided to give a moment's thought to what her grandson was trying to tell her. He wasn't seeking reassurance that he hadn't been bad, nor did he want another postcard. He was wanting something else.

Taking her cue from the expression on his face, the grandmother said, "Oh, you must be so sad thinking about your poor lost postcard." The little boy sighed and gave his grandmother a tentative smile. His mood remained sober as he contemplated what she had said. Then he spoke: "But it's only lost, right? So it must be somewhere, right? It didn't disappear. That would be scary if it disappeared."

Because society tends to idealize childhood, adults are perpetually bewildered by what children know and don't know. On the one hand, we like to believe that children are endowed with a native wisdom and can intuit everything. On the other hand, we like to think that children are innocents, and therefore we try to shelter them from knowledge that could be disturbing if revealed too early on. The question of what to tell a child about death stirs up extraordinary bewilderment in most adults and, as one might expect, much controversy among experts.

The controversies center on the theoretical issue of whether mourning is possible for young children. Some psychologists assume that because children demonstrate signs of protest, grief, and withdrawal—in other words, the acute stage of bereavement—they are also capable of the longer, more complicated process, the full *work* of mourning. Others contend that the full work of mourning is beyond a child's intellectual and emotional reach. Another controversy concerns the extent to which mourning represents a detachment and giving up of relationships and the extent to which mourning also encompasses a way of continuing the dialogues of life after a person is deceased.

Despite these theoretical disagreements, there is a consensus that the death of a parent is potentially traumatic for a child and that it is crucial to help the child come to terms with this calamity. Experts also agree that the decisive factors in a child's responses to the death of a parent are the current family configuration, the personality of the surviving parent, the child's personality, the child's ongoing conflicts, and the stage of her development. And while some psychologists stress the therapeutic aim of helping the child to grieve and to acknowledge death, and others feel it is more important to help the child with the immediate conflicts and anxieties aroused by the parent's death, fortunately most therapists who specialize in work with orphaned children get around to both sets of issues sooner or later. The bereaved child will reveal to an empathic adult what his concerns are and make sure he gets the kind of help he needs.

It is very likely that children are incapable of sustaining the long and emotionally complex process of mourning, which is difficult enough for an adult. Children do have certain emotional and intellectual limitations that must be respected. Nevertheless, they *are* capable of grappling with the contradictory thoughts and perplexing fantasies aroused by the loss of a parent and can even acknowledge how sad and lonely and angry they feel. While a child's silent grief and longing must eventually be brought out into the open, what the child needs most is some relief from his ongoing emotional dilemmas, many of which represent long-standing conflicts that are exacerbated as the child tries to cope with the loss of a parent. By helping the child work through these dilemmas, one also helps him to acknowledge death in a way that makes emotional sense to him. When a parent dies, one can best console and comfort the child by simply helping him to express and voice what is on *his* mind—the confusion of thoughts, the fantasies and feelings that such a catastrophic event inevitably evokes.

The death of a parent is always accompanied by fantasies of abandonment, except in a tiny infant, whose emotional states are not yet regulated by fantasies. And because being abandoned implies a judgment of not being valued, a child is easily confused about the issues of goodness and badness.

In early infancy, a mother's death can only be experienced as an absence—not as a loss, not as an event with moral reverberations. An infant's sense of time is limited to the immediate present—the here and the now—and the infant's attachment to the parent is governed *primarily* by need. When a state of need—like hunger, for example—arises and the parent is not there to feed, the child's first response is a physical sensation of unease and discomfort. Any prolonged delay results in a frustration that induces a diffuse, unfocused rage and a feeling of being surrounded by a bad, unfriendly environment. If a young child's attachment to the parent is still determined *primarily* by need, anyone that can gratify the need with a bottle of milk will do. A gratifying presence can erase the child's sense of foreboding absence. When the need is satisfied, the child's entire being relaxes into a calm relief, which is why a very young infant of, say, two or three months will accept a substitute if her mother should suddenly disappear. The longing for dialogue, profound as it will soon become, is not yet as powerful as the need for physical care. So, even if the substitute caregiver is not very good at interpreting the world, even if she doesn't engage in talking games and conversation and dialogues, if she gives milk, feels soft, rocks back and forth, and every once in a while looks into the baby's eyes, she will do nicely for the time being.

The *fort-da* games invented by Ernst and Amy were signs that they had acquired a capacity for emotional attachment that went beyond simple physical need. Ernst and Amy missed their mothers and longed for them even when they were not hungry, tired, tense, or in need of a comforting embrace. They wanted their mothers for their dialogue. However, should mother stay away for too long, the child might then turn away when she returns or greet her with an angry frown or want to bite her or, now that she has reappeared, wish that she would disappear forever. For a child under the age of three, too long can be an hour or a day or a weekend. The older the child, the better he can retain an internal image of the mother in her absence. The older the child, the better he can invent active means of coping with his mother's absence. For Ernst and Amy, their mothers' absence was experienced as a loss. The mother had become a valuable person in her own right, someone who was worth having around whether or not she fed or comforted them. The fact that a child can miss his mother and long for her is a sign of the strength and permanence of his attachment.

Chronological age is not the only factor by which to measure the depth of a person's emotional attachment, nor is it the most reliable. An older child, an adolescent, even an adult who has been unable to make a secure attachment to a parental figure will respond with frustration and rage when the person who attends to his needs is absent. Usually, however, from the time a child is two, the death of (or desertion by) a parent is accompanied by profound disappointment, a loss of self-esteem and fantasies of abandonment. These emotional devastations are compounded by attributions of fault and responsibility, good and evil, and other complexities of conscience which, in a young child's mind, are always reduced to "Who is to blame?" "Who is the bad one?" "Who made Daddy disappear?"

In the process of trying to make sense of the calamity that has befallen her, the child reaches a point where she begins to feel angry with the parent for leaving her unprotected. She blames the parent for abandoning her. She reasons that if the parent had valued her, he never would have gone away. She even sometimes wishes he could feel as bad as she does. But despite this confused angry-hurt, the child does not really want to destroy the image of the parent, which is still very much alive inside her. What she really wants is to refind the lost parent and resume their dialogue.

Eventually, the child transforms her anger with the dead parent into disappointment—that is, the parent's disappointment in the child. She reasons: "If only I hadn't been so grumpy and mean, my daddy would still be here." "If only I had not thought of chewing my mommy into little pieces, she might come home tonight and hold me in her arms." "If I had not been a dirty, worthless nothing, my father would not have abandoned me." In keeping with such primitive logic, the child unconsciously makes up her mind to transform herself into the kind of human being she imagines her dead parent would have wanted her to be. And this identification with the parent's ideal of a good and valuable child becomes *one* of the primary methods by which a child might reinstate a dialogue with the lost parent. By internalizing the parent's ideals and making them part of her own self, the child refinds her lost parent and in doing so resolves some of the conflicted feelings she had about that parent before he disappeared.

When two children in the same family are trying to cope with the death of a parent, it becomes clear how each child's response depends partly on her age and level of emotional maturity, on the surviving parent's personality, but also, most crucially, on the quality of her previous dialogues with the dead parent.

The voice of the dead father can be heard clearly, yet its sound is distinctly different, depending on the child. Each child strives to uphold the dead father's ideals—but only those that were crucial in his or her own dialogue with him. Each child has identified with a selected aspect of the father; not with the father in all his emotional fullness and rich moral complexity, but with some narrow ideal.

Charles Evans was killed in a car accident while driving with his wife, Marilyn, and his two daughters, Winnie, age five, and Wendy, age eight. Although he died instantly, his head and arms had burst through the windshield and he had bled profusely. Each girl's reaction to her father's death would be shaped and influenced by her personal interpretations of the mutilation she had witnessed. But each girl's attempt to resume the dialogue, to refind her father, would depend on the differing ideal of a "good girl" conveyed to them prior to his death.

Charles Evans was a good-hearted, generous man who was devoted to his wife and children and was a perfect master to his dog, Rusty. He didn't subscribe to any formal religion but instead devoted his energies to political causes and taught his children to value all living things, especially animals and particularly Rusty. While most of his college friends had gone off to graduate school, Charles had set about to fulfill one of his childhood dreams—to own a sporting goods company. His freethinking spirit and independent mind were crucial to his self-esteem, as were his good looks and charisma. Charles was rather vain about his handsome face, strong, muscular body, and his ability to charm other people. He was an ardent surfer and captain of the neighborhood baseball team. He was gregarious and liked to be liked.

It was altogether in keeping with *one* aspect of his narcissism that Charles Evans would have adored his younger daughter, Winnie, who was pretty, vivacious, and coquettishly adorable. Winnie was well aware that her helpless, dependent behaviors appealed to her father— Charles Evans was easily flattered by the attentions of a female who needed his care and protection, and Winnie sensed this early on.

Wendy, on the other hand, identified with her father's pride of independence long before Winnie was born. Wendy had always been able to win her father's love and approval by being as self-sufficient and smart as a little girl could possibly be. Wendy had been blessed with a temperament and intellect that pleased her father, and from birth, she had been thoughtful and persistent. She learned everything quickly and easily. She was patient, even tempered and easy to console. In short, Wendy embodied everything her proud, independent father valued *and* also everything that would make her neat, well-mannered, orderly, intellectually gifted mother proud. When Charles came home from work at night, Marilyn would give him a detailed report of Wendy's new words and deeds of the day, listing and describing each and every marvelous feat. He would then admire and praise his daughter for all that she was and all that she did.

Wendy was especially happy to be, in her mind, her mother's "everything." As many little girls (and boys) like to imagine—particularly those who are the only child—Wendy imagined that she was her mother's only true love. After spending all day performing the many feats that amazed and delighted her mother, it seemed not unreasonable to Wendy to assume that her mother must consider her even more charming and smarter than her father.

Marilyn's pregnancy when Wendy was two years old might have immediately shattered this fantasy. For a few months, however, Wendy was able to console and delude herself by stuffing her pajamas with a pillow, pretending she could make a baby too. With the birth of her baby sister, Wendy's exclusive love affair with her mother ended. Marilyn was now enthralled with her new baby, and she had much less time for Wendy. Wendy, of course, had not given birth to anything except misery and a profound sense of loss.

Wendy was too proud to show her sadness and loneliness. And certainly she could not admit, even to herself, how much she longed for her parents' attention. She had always been precociously independent, and she responded by becoming angry, messy, dull-witted, helpless, and dependent. Previous to Winnie's birth, the two-year-old Wendy had been able to dress herself, brush her teeth, wash her hands and face, and rinse out her breakfast dishes. After her sister's birth she could do nothing at all for herself. Though Wendy, who wasn't much of a charmer, had never appealed to her father's vanity, her cleverness and self-sufficiency had made him proud. But now that Winnie—who seemed to her sister a dependent, helpless crybaby—got all the attention, Wendy became cheerless and sullen and made a huge commotion whenever she didn't get what she wanted. Nothing her mother or father gave her was good enough. She developed a habit of losing or breaking the toys they bought for her. Wendy let her parents know, in no uncertain terms, how dissatisfied she was with them.

Marilyn, always the good, patient, even-tempered mother, remained loving and tender despite Wendy's provocations. But Charles, who couldn't tolerate unhappy faces around the house, got fed up with Wendy. He let her know how disappointed he was with her helplessness. When he felt guilty about rejecting Wendy, he would become affectionate and try to hold her on his lap. Wendy refused to acknowledge his love. She wouldn't let him cuddle and pamper her. She'd figured out that that sort of baby stuff was for Winnie. On her best days, Wendy acted as though she were indifferent to her father. On her worst days, she did everything she could to annoy him. And she enjoyed nothing so much as tormenting the little sister whom her mother and father made such a fuss over.

When Wendy started nursery school, she wandered around daydreaming and made friends with no one. In first and second grade, Wendy maintained an obedient surface, but she lost her pencils and notebooks, never did her homework, and got test marks that were far below her level of intelligence. In short, she displayed every behavior that would be an affront to every one of her father's ideals.

Then Charles died. Despite the shock of her sudden loss and her profound grief, Marilyn tried to stay closely attuned to her children's reactions. Winnie seemingly acknowledged her father's death. She dutifully recited the litany she had been taught, "Daddy is dead. He's never coming back." But Wendy worried her mother, for several reasons. She would not speak to anyone about her father or his death—not even her mother who encouraged her to express what was on her mind. Suspiciously, however, a remarkable change had occurred.

Two months after her father's death, Wendy's personality had changed completely. This incompetent, sullen, demanding eight-year-old suddenly became efficient, independent, and cooperative—as she had been as a toddler. She began to get the high marks she was capable of and, for the first time ever, made friends with her classmates. The teachers reported that she had lots and lots of friends and was quickly becoming the most popular girl in the entire third grade. She cared about her appearance, took care of her possessions, finished every homework assignment perfectly, and carried herself like a proud, confident young woman. As far as her teachers were concerned, Wendy was finally liking herself and becoming a likable little girl.

Marilyn was proud of Wendy's school behavior and wished her husband could see what a socially popular and independent child she had become. But Marilyn sensed that something was not quite right. She had the eerie feeling that Wendy was trying to woo her by imitating Charles's behaviors and attitudes.

Although Wendy was now a miniature incarnation—actually a caricature—of her father's ideals, she would still never mention his name or his death. In one respect only did she defy her father. She was meaner than ever to her little sister. Now that Winnie's protector was gone, Wendy was free to invent new and better ways to torment her. She would drive Winnie to tears by claiming that she was Rusty's rightful owner. If Winnie dared to pet him, Wendy gave her a sound smack on the hands. Most of the time, Wendy took great pride in feeding Rusty and playing with him in the same way that her father had done. But sometimes she would whack Rusty on the head with her schoolbooks and pull his ears till he howled.

One day Marilyn discovered Wendy poking a fork into the soft shell of her sister's pet turtle. The next day she saw Wendy running over a wounded bird with her bicycle. At this, Marilyn confided her concerns to the school psychologist, who recommended therapy for Wendy and parent counseling for Marilyn.

Initially, Wendy refused to enter the therapist's office unless her mother came with her. She clung to Marilyn as though her existence depended on her mother's presence. In a few weeks, Wendy overcame these humiliating, "babyish" fears of separation. She was a big girl, and proud to manage on her own. Besides, she wanted so much to understand what was happening to her. She let her mother go, but she still wouldn't let the therapist help. After many months of listening (with hands over her ears) to the therapist's tactful comments about Wendy's efforts to be as good as her father had been, Wendy decided that the "enemy therapist" might be able to help her, after all.

She took her hands off her ears and shed her facade of restraint and self-sufficiency. Her terrors and sadness tumbled out in a jumble of confusion. She wanted to play games that involved the disjointing of toy animals but was afraid she might destroy them, so assigned the role of disjointer to her therapist. Wendy repeatedly hit herself on the head, saying she hated her head. Then she said, "My mommy should not love me. I am bad and no good," but later that week Wendy changed her mind, saying, "I hate my mommy." "My mommy hates me and wants to throw me out of the house." She shot at male puppets with a toy gun and when she imagined that one of them retaliated by shooting back, she fell on the floor and screamed, "Now I am dead. The guy killed me."

At home and in school Wendy suddenly became accident-prone. Over the course of one month, Wendy had cut her hand several times, sprained her ankle, and fallen off her bicycle, bruising her chin and her knees. She drew pictures of bicycle crashes and told stories of airplane crashes where only the mother and child survived. She was obviously trying to understand how her powerful, independent father had not been immune to death. After all, Wendy explained to her therapist, "Mothers can never be killed."

It was clear that this little girl who had lost her father was suffering, not only from a grief she could not acknowledge, but also from feeling lost and confused about who she was or what sort of person she was supposed to be. If she was independent like her father, she assumed she could be killed. However, if she adopted her mother's power—that is, if she became omnipotent and impervious to injury or death—that seemed more dangerous still. She could become a killer. She could maim and mutilate others. Furthermore, competing with such an all-powerful mother was too terrifying for Wendy to even consider. Marilyn Evans, the "perfect" mother, the strong, sensitive, caring mother who rarely got angry, was a lot for a little girl to live up to.

Wendy's worrisome and confusing identifications with her parents were not an outcome of her father's death. His death, and specifically the physical mutilation that accompanied the death, had forced deep-seated dilemmas to the surface. Like many little girls who are so good and so smart that they imagine themselves to be their mother's everything, Wendy always had an exaggerated view of what her parents needed or wanted from her. She thought she'd be letting them down if she showed any weaknesses or limitations. She thought they expected her to be invulnerable and omnipotent. She thought she had to be everything to everyone. Many children experience the birth of a sibling as a wound to their self-esteem, but most usually find a way to recover and go on with life. Wendy's extreme response to Winnie's birth lasted nearly three years. Since she could not admit how miserable and sad she felt, she transformed these humiliating, powerless feelings into an omnipotent rage that demolished everything about her that her parents had valued. Wendy could have used some help before her father died. Perhaps, if her father had lived, he might have realized how much Wendy loved him and needed his protection. He might have seen that it was this exaggerated pride, the pride of independence that was so important to him, that had undone his young daughter.

After her father died, Wendy's method of resurrecting him by becoming exactly like him afforded her a good *temporary* solution to some of her ongoing conflicts and fears—until her mother caught on that something was seriously wrong. Had it become a permanent way of life, the "good Wendy" solution would have constricted Wendy's emotions and narrowed her life choices. But in the short run, it was an ingenious solution that served quite a number of diverse psychological functions.

The radical transformation from bad Wendy to good Wendy certainly helped her to like herself a little bit more. Her pride in her school accomplishments and the many new friends she acquired also provided some immediate relief from the grief and loneliness she could not express. Perhaps the most remarkable aspect of the solution was the way it helped Wendy to cope with the guilt that had been aroused by the death of her father.

As a toddler, Wendy did everything and anything she could to woo and win her mother. Most of all, she had tried very hard to be just like, or even better than, her father, the man her mother seemed to value so highly. However, because of this fierce and altogether impossible rivalry, Wendy also had wished her father would disappear. Before the fatal car accident, Wendy had had conscious fantasies of cutting her father into little pieces and poking holes into his body. Now that he was gone, the good Wendy could win her mother's love by becoming a perfect little "husband." The good Wendy was also the bad Wendy's way of trying to atone for the mutilation fantasies that seemed to have come true when her father's car smashed into the tree.

Then there was the secret "love affair" with her father, a secret so well kept that Wendy herself barely knew about it. Wendy's intense rivalry with her father and her desire to get rid of him had been, in part, a clever masquerade that alleviated her fears of competing with her all-powerful mother. Wendy dared not acknowledge how much she adored her strong, handsome, charming father, and much of the noisy show of negativity and indifference toward him, which Wendy had freely expressed after her sister was born, was a way of hiding her passionate love for him. The more Wendy feared her mother might notice this passion, the more she had to feign indifference. But then, when he died, Wendy was bereft to think that her beloved father had really disappeared. She had wanted so much to be able to show her love. This unacknowledged love for her father was another unconscious motive for embodying his ideals. By becoming socially popular, independent, smart and likable—just like him—Wendy was saying, "I love you," to her lost father.

As Wendy was increasingly able to express her angry, rivalrous feelings toward her mother and her loving, possessive feelings toward her father, she became less good and also less bad. She was able to talk about her father's death and to acknowledge how much she missed him, and even to voice a regret that she had not been able to show him her love when he was alive. The end of therapy was not the end of Wendy's conflicts. It would take a few years for her to absorb and integrate what she had learned. Not until adolescence would she arrive at more full and wholesome identifications with both her parents. But her therapy had succeeded in tempering these rigid identifications with their narrow versions of good and evil.

Empathy, for a child who has lost a parent, is not entirely or in fact necessarily a matter of helping the child confront the fact of death. The child should simply be invited to express what is on *her* mind, so that the fantasies of abandonment, the attributions of fallibility and blame, the distributions of goodness and badness, all the conflicted desires and longings that the child has enlisted to reinstate and continue the dialogue with the parent can be brought out and clarified. The idea is not to terminate her inner dialogue with the lost parent but to transform that dialogue into something more generous and flexible.

This is not to suggest that every child who loses a parent must be brought to a child therapist. Perhaps if parents understood more about how to listen to children's thoughts and fantasies, the surviving parent could help the lost child to find her way. However, even a sensitive parent like Marilyn Evans is generally preoccupied and conflicted herself. When one parent dies, it is too much to expect that the surviving parent can cope with her own grief as well as the confused emotions of her children. The surviving parent needs some guidance and support from someone.

Marilyn's insights into Wendy's behavior helped her to perceive that things were not going well with Winnie either. But she still did not have the emotional wherewithal to take things into her own hands. Besides, Winnie was so different from Wendy, Marilyn sometimes joked that they might have come from different families. Ironically, there was more truth to that thought than Marilyn realized. In fact, Winnie and Wendy each had their own version of Charles Evans inside them.

When Winnie was nearly six years old, Marilyn brought her to the same child guidance clinic where Wendy was now busily engaged in shooting at male puppet dolls. Winnie had no trouble at all saying good-bye to her mother. She blew her a kiss and waved good-bye. She held out her hand to her therapist like a perfect little adult and said cheerily, "How nice to meet you." After the first session she greeted her mother, "I love you. How nice of you to wait."

Winnie loved therapy and most of all she loved preening herself at the mirror, admiring her pretty clothes and praising her extra long "Barbie" ponytail. She was always asking for compliments and coaxing her therapist to report to Wendy's therapist that she was much better at therapy than her big sister. Each day she mixed up a fresh batch of pink paint. Each day she dipped her brush carefully into the paint and outlined a neat square house with neat square windows and a tall chimney "as tall as my ponytail." Then she'd color inside the pink borders with more of the bright pink paint and say, "This is my lipstick palace. Isn't it pretty!" and "I wish my mommy would go away and leave me here with you and never come back."

After her father died, Winnie immediately turned her charm on her mother's father, who was only too happy to hold his cheerful little granddaughter on his lap and tell her how pretty she was. "Your daddy would be proud of you," he'd say. When the postman handed her the mail in the morning, he'd ask, "How is my pretty girl today?" When she went to the dentist, he winked at her and told her that she was his best little patient. And Winnie kept saying, "My daddy is dead. He is never coming back."

As Winnie's trust in her therapist grew, she expanded her horizons in the therapy room. The lipstick pink palace and the mirror became items of the past. She became absorbed in a dollhouse and dollhouse family. Her artifical mannerisms were replaced by a sober thoughtfulness. She flew the daddy doll over the house saying, "Daddy flew away in a plane and soon he will come back." "Daddy is the sandman flying around the house putting everyone to sleep. When the morning comes he flies away over the treetops." Through her doll-play, Winnie was confessing that her obedient litany of "Daddy is dead" was a sham. She was sure her daddy was "only hiding" and at last she could tell someone. Perhaps, she thought, she could even ask her therapist to help her find him.

After admitting to the therapist that she "sometimes" believed her daddy was lost, Winnie's behavior in the therapy room changed dramatically. She started to shoot at the daddy puppet. She shot at her therapist. She smeared brown and black paint over the therapist's desk and put a few dabs on the walls, trying to find out just how far she could go. She was determined to find out which toys her sister played with and shrieked that she was a witch who would smash her sister's favorite toys to bits and pieces.

One day, as she was splashing water and smearing paint in the therapist's office, Winnie suddenly remembered being in the hospital the night her father died. In a flurry of excited words, she told her therapist what had happened and how she had felt. While the nurses were attending to her mother's cuts and bruises, they had put Winnie into a crib all by herself. She had wet her pants and messed up the crib with an attack of diarrhea. Then Winnie confessed to the therapist that she had peeked when her mother screamed that she and Wendy mustn't look at their father's body. She had pretended to be asleep but, in fact, had been wide awake the whole time. She recalled how the car kept turning round and round before it smashed into the tree, but Winnie didn't mention the sight of her father's mutilated body. The therapist didn't go any further than Winnie wanted to. She simply listened. Yet Winnie protested anyway just to make sure that she wouldn't have to see again what her mother had told her she wasn't supposed to see. "Don't ask me any more questions," she snapped at the therapist. "Stop it. Stop it."

Winnie never did speak about what she had seen. She didn't have to. She knew that her therapist understood. The next day, however, Winnie began to reveal how much she hated her father for leaving her. After several weeks of angry shrieking (directed toward her mean, disappointing father), Winnie began to attack herself, saying how worthless and dirty she felt inside. "If I had been a good girl, he wouldn't have gone away." "I am always so dirty. I'm nothing but a dirty little thing." Because Winnie's attachment to her father was primarily based on having been a mirror to his vanity, she had been unable to find a place in her mind for any of her less than ideal feelings and thoughts. Her narcissistic view of loving and being loved restricted the range of her emotions and stood in the way of her arriving at a more generous assessment of goodness and badness. Winnie had learned that if you are a clean, cheerful, pretty girl, you are valuable. If you are messy, or sad and lonely, or angry, or your hair is too short and your dress isn't pink and fluffy, you are worthless. As her mother and her therapist worked together to help Winnie, she began to understand that she could be loved and valued even if she weren't a picture-perfect Barbie doll. Winnie began to assemble a more complete father inside her.

Wendy and Winnie, each in her own way, had attempted to resurrect their dead father by internalizing their own childlike versions of his ideal of a good and valuable child. These narrow identifications, if they go on without any modification, will narrow the child's possibilities. Nevertheless, it is one of the more benign methods of continuing a dialogue with a lost parent. For desires and motives that are personal and unconscious and not entirely virtuous, the child has taken into herself a benign image of the parent. Such a child does not trouble the adults in her environment with irritating and unpleasant behaviors. She is lovable and everyone praises her. However, the child is hoping someone will read the signs. She tries, as best she can, to make people notice and question.

Wendy's destructive behavior with animals was her way of helping her mother to notice that under the halo was a very confused and frightened child. Winnie, who was even less conscious of her lost, angry feelings, wanted her mother to notice that she was always provoking her big sister to torment her. When Wendy tormented her, she had an excuse for tears. She had someone there to be angry with. Unconsciously, Winnie believed she should be tormented and punished for her angry feelings toward the father who had abandoned her. Since she didn't know how to be a bad child, she assigned that nasty role to her big sister, who was obviously a master at that sort of thing. Yet all along she had been wishing for someone to rescue her from the scary dungeon of her pretty pink palace. Finally her mother read the signals.

If no one recognizes a child's efforts to express her less than virtuous feelings, she may never arrive at a more complete version of her lost parent. Luckily, Marilyn Evans noticed what was going on with her two little girls. If Charles Evans had not died, his daughters would have had the time and opportunity to modify their narrow, childlike impressions of who he was and what he valued. In the average course of a daily life with their good-enough father, Wendy and Winnie would have come to know a good-enough man, with ordinary strengths and weaknesses.

The most significant outcome of Wendy and Winnie's therapies was the modification of their constricted ideals. A few years after Charles Evans's death, both Wendy and Winnie, each in her own way, restored within her a fatherly presence that encompassed the complexities of the person Charles had actually been.

CHAPTER FOUR

THE RED THREAD

"The loss of my mother runs like a red thread through my life."

W. Ernest Freud (Ernst Wolfgang Halberstadt), 1992.

A child may respond to a mother's (or father's) death by accentuating his own unlikable qualities and transforming himself into the kind of child that he imagines no one can love—no one but a mother. By demonstrating how bad he can be—since, after all, he doesn't have a mother to teach him how to be good—the child is trying to coerce his mother to return. In his desperate attempt to continue the dialogue with his mother, the child manages to make himself and everybody else suffer from his badness. "You see how much I suffer," he is, in effect, saying. "You see how bad I am without you? Come back and make me feel good and whole again."

This tactic of bringing back the lost parent by becoming a bad and disappointing child is not the total madness it seems. Suppose that a mother's death came at a moment when her child was disenchanted with her. If, then, the child suddenly becomes disappointing to everyone (including himself), his mother is redeemed as faultless. Or the child may reason that if he continues to be bad, the parent will come back to coax him into goodness. Thus the idealization of the dead parent is maintained at the expense of a devaluation of the self—an emotional tactic that also helps keep hope alive.

In 1913, not quite a month after Sophie Freud married Max Halberstadt, her father sent a postcard to her husband, signing it "Cordial regards from a wholly orphaned father." On March 11, 1914, the day after Ernst Halberstadt's birth, Freud sent off another postcard, this one to his friend and colleague, Sandor Ferenczi. "Last night . . . around 3 o'clock a little boy as first grandchild! Very remarkable! An elderly feeling, respect before the wonders of sexuality."

Ernst, Freud's first grandchild, the inventor of the *fort-da,* was soon to be replaced in his grandfather's heart by Sophie's second child, Heinz. When Sophie died in 1920, the five-and-three-quarter-year-old Ernst and the thirteen-month-old Heinz responded very differently to this catastrophic event in their lives. They also met with distinctly different reactions from the adults who loved them dearly.

Sophie was pregnant when she died, so in addition to losing his wife, Max also lost a child. His faith in his capacity to protect his children, already somewhat fragile, was shattered. Max Halberstadt was a well-intentioned man—kind, decent, and hard-working—but since his own father had died when he was an infant, he did not have a reliable internal model for fathering. He worried about Heinerle, a physically delicate infant, who after his mother's death seemed to become even more susceptible to the typical childhood fevers and illnesses. Convinced that his little son would not receive the best possible medical attention in Hamburg, Max was grateful when Sophie's sister Mathilde and her husband, Robert Hollitscher, who had no children of their own, brought Heinz to their home in Vienna and informally adopted him. Heinz Halberstadt was a lovable child with a sunny disposition—anyone would have wanted to adopt him. Ernst, on the other hand, reacted to the news of his mother's death by gradually becoming a more unappealing child. No one in the family seemed to understand what he was going through—no one except Sophie's sister Anna Freud.

Anna, who had suffered during childhood and adolescence from her unsuccessful rivalry with her beautiful and charming sister Sophie, took on the rescue of Ernst. Before her sister died, Anna had noticed how Ernst, once an imaginative and exceedingly obedient little boy, appeared to become dull-witted and mean-spirited after his little brother's birth. To make matters worse, Sophie and Max had put him into a school where the two elderly headmistresses would beat the children every time they misbehaved. Anna arranged for her nephew to attend a small private school run by a warmhearted, middle-aged lady whose assistant, her kind and patient niece, managed to win over the confused little boy.

Anna understood how much Ernst's rivalry with Heinz was affecting his responses to his mother's death. While others in the family lost patience with Ernst, Anna was able to empathize with him. Even Sigmund Freud, who, a few years earlier, had been perceptively attuned to the myriad unconscious meanings of his little grandson's disappearing games, mistook Ernst's apparent heartlessness for his true feelings. He said that Ernst did not miss Sophie or feel sad because he was still so angry with her for having given birth to Heinz. Ernst was probably still hurt and disenchanted with his mother for what he considered her betrayal, and these feelings might have compounded his misery. It is very likely that his little mind was a maelstrom of illogical and contradictory feelings and thoughts: It was all his fault—his anger must have sent his mother away . . . Now he would punish her by showing her how much he was suffering . . . If only she would come back, he would make things up to her.

Ernst was lost. As always happens when a child loses a parent, the loss becomes intertwined with the ongoing conflicts and dilemmas the child is trying to work through. When Sophie died, Ernst was already suffering from the turmoil of Heinz's birth. The hurt and humiliation of his mother's third pregnancy (which he tried to deny) were more than Ernst could tolerate. When his mother was pregnant with Heinz, he could pretend that it was *his* baby in his mother's belly, but this time he was old enough to know better. He often appeared to be overcome with angry thoughts and, as his grandfather interpreted, he had at times wished his disappointing mother would go away for good. And then his mother died.

Ernst was so desperate and confused that he nearly alienated his devoted aunt Anna. More than once Ernst disappointed his aunt. More than once she despaired of carrying out her rescue mission: "For the first time in my life I am glad that I do not have any children, for if he were my child and behaved like he does, I could hardly bear it." But Anna did not give up. She decided it would be best for her little nephew to live with her in her own home. When Anna proposed that Ernst come to live with them in Vienna, Freud protested, explaining that he feared Ernst would be "too much" for his wife, Martha, who had been physically ill and heartsick ever since the death of Sophie.

In late May of 1923, a few weeks after a tonsillectomy, Heinz was stricken with tubercular meningitis, a childhood form of the influenza that killed his mother. Anna rushed to the aid of her sister Mathilde, who was trying desperately to nurse her adopted child back to health. Despite the efforts and attention of his two aunts, this inevitably fatal illness took its course. Heinz wasted away, slipped into a coma from which he occasionally awoke, and then died on June 19, 1923.

After the war, thousands of other children contracted tubercular meningitis and died. According to Freud, Heinz had always been "very weak, never free of a temperature, one of those children whose mental development grows at the expense of his physical strength." Yet it is possible that Heinz's susceptibility to this illness and his rapid decline were, in part, responses to his mother's death. For all his determined efforts to continue to be a clever, agreeable child, Heinerle must have been suffering silently from the loss of his mother. Perhaps heartbreak hastened his own death.

In the midst of her grief over this sudden loss, Anna wondered what Heinz's death would mean for Ernst, who seemed to be responding in his customary sullen manner. Moreover, as if he hadn't gotten his fill of betrayals, Ernst was soon betrayed by his former nursery school teacher. After his mother died, the pretty assistant teacher at his private school had been especially kind to him. Not realizing that her attentions had something to do with her attraction to his widowed father, Ernst thought "it was like having found a mother again." He wished that one day he might marry her. However, just like his real mother, the teacher found his big, strong father more appealing and interesting than little Ernst. When she became his stepmother and took over the household, her easygoing, tolerant attitude toward Ernst changed. Though not quite a "wicked stepmother," his father's new wife was, at any rate, more preoccupied with her household routine than with paying attention to her troublesome little stepson, whose very presence constituted a challenge to her need for law and order. Later in life, Ernst would recall, "I felt very excluded. I was a lonely small boy who suffered a lot under the regimentation of my stepmother, which was well-intentioned but lacked imagination." Shortly after Ernst's tenth birthday, his stepmother became pregnant, and he promptly developed a respiratory illness. He was sent away to a sanatorium-spa in Switzerland for seven months. When he returned to Hamburg, he was greeted by a little half sister.

Again Ernst was lost. Again Anna came to his rescue. She prevailed on her father to invite Ernst to spend the summer holidays with them in Italy. Three months of sunshine with an empathic, imaginative aunt and a doting grandmother gave Ernst a much-needed respite from his unhappiness. But when the holiday was over, Ernst had to return to Hamburg—to a father who did not know how to father him and a stepmother who had her own little baby to attend to.

Once back in Hamburg, Ernst spent a great deal of time daydreaming, wanting to create a world that was new and better, wanting to invent a perpetual motion machine and become a famous scientist. When he tried to explain his marvelous imaginary inventions to his father and stepmother, they told him his notions were "out of this world," unrealistic and impractical, and that he'd do better to pay attention to his schoolwork.

Ernst only daydreamed about the perpetual motion machine, but he actually invented another gadget. A grown boy—nearly a teenager—he was still playing *fort-da*. It seems the terrace at the back of the Hamburg apartment overlooked a common backyard shared by several other buildings. Every day there was a new assortment of interesting objects that had either fallen down or been discarded by one of the tenants across the way. Ernst constructed a large hook out of a thin piece of metal and fastened it to a long thread. By using two thread reels as weights for his homemade fishing rod, Ernst could trawl the bottom of the yard, fishing for the treasures that lay there. When he wasn't daydreaming, Ernst was fishing back and forth, over and over again.

The thought that his aunt Anna was accessible when he needed her gave Ernst some hope of surviving: "I did not have much self-assurance and she was always very encouraging. She tried to imbue her conviction in me that one could achieve something if one really tried, and she seemed to actually believe it." Despite his considerable and ongoing provocations, Anna continued to defend her nephew, arguing that his disappointing behavior belied his inner substance: "In reality, he is such a nice and highly decent person that I would not wish my own son to be any different." Her empathy with Ernst's self-destructive responses to loss and his ways of getting himself lost to everyone who might have loved him contributed to her famous essay "About Losing and Being Lost."

Anna Freud had started thinking about loss when she was a troubled adolescent, bitter about her unsuccessful rivalry with Sophie and struggling to win her father's approval. Conflicted about her father, she lost a hat he had given her. She personified the lost hat, imagining it as a lonely soul wandering the earth in search of love. When her sister died and she undertook the rescue of her lost and lonely nephew, Anna began to write about her thoughts on loss. Over the years she composed many drafts and revisions of this essay, but it was not until 1963, after more than two decades of mourning her father's death, that Anna Freud felt ready to claim her authority on the subject of loss.

In 1927, when he was thirteen years old, Ernst Halberstadt began to discover what it meant to be *happy*. His aunt Anna had invited him for an extended summer vacation, both in Vienna and at a fashionable resort in the Austrian Alps. There he met Bob, Michael (Mikey), Mary (Mabbie), and Katrinka (Tinky) Burlingham, the children of Dorothy Burlingham, the Tiffany heiress who would become Anna Freud's most intimate friend, professional colleague, and lifetime companion. The Burlingham children became Ernst's unofficial foster brothers and sisters; they even nicknamed him "Ernsti." Eventually, the Burlingham family became "the idealized family which he fantasized as substituting for his own."

Ernst idolized the tall, handsome twelve-year-old Bob Burlingham, who knew how to wink and flirt, had his own gramophone and records "direct from America," a Leica camera with accessories, and a darkroom. The Burlingham kids also had a Pathe Baby film projector and an assortment of Walt Disney films including *Mickey Mouse* and *Felix the Cat*. They were permitted to play hide-and-seek for hours and to hide anywhere they wished—under furniture, in the pantry, in closets. In addition to all this, Ernst was given special treats by his aunt. Understanding her nephew's unrequited love for his Eagle father, Anna took him on a circular flight over the city of Vienna.

All the while, Ernst was aware of a "dark cloud hanging over this marvelous existence." He could not forget that "it would all have to end after the holidays." But this thirteen-year-old boy who had no self-assurance had learned some important lessons from his aunt. Had she not taught him that anything was possible? That one did not have to submit to fate? That a person could always *do* something to avoid a catastrophe? He recalled his aunt's visits to Hamburg after his mother had died. Anna had showed him that if the small figures he made out of clay had not turned out quite the way he had imagined, he had only to knead the clay into a lump again and out of that brand-new lump came another chance to transform his visions into a reality. Anna called this "the plasticene miracle"—and of course, it always worked. Things always come out a little better if you believe in yourself.

Ernst decided to believe he could do something to preserve his new-found happiness. He mustered up the courage to confess to his aunt his wish to stay forever in that dreamland. Within twenty-four hours, his grandfather invited Ernst to join him and Anna for a discussion in his sanctuary.

Sigmund Freud was worried about his grandson's eagerness to part company with his father and his childhood home. He wondered if Ernst might not have loyalty conflicts that would be troubling to him later on in life. When he told Ernst to think carefully about the consequences of leaving his family, Ernst grew queasy and almost lost heart. But Anna's "plasticene miracle" worked again. Freud said he understood how unhappy Ernst had been. He agreed that a boy his age who had been so lonely and endured so many losses deserved a chance at happiness. Freud took another puff on his cigar and gave his permission—Ernst could stay in Vienna as long as he wished.

Max Halberstadt was surprised to learn that his son did not want to come back to Hamburg. But, after a while, as he noticed how content and relaxed Ernst was, Max seemed to understand why Ernst preferred living in Vienna. When Max's photography assignments brought him to Vienna or to Berlin (near the Freud country home in Grundlsee), he would visit with Ernst. Father and son began to get along a little better and, after a few years, actually enjoyed the time they spent together. Whenever Max came down from Hamburg he would take photographs of Ernst's new family. It was not exactly a traditional bourgeois family, what with two grandmothers, two mothers, five children, several dogs, and no father to speak of—except for a very important grandfather who seemed to be everyone's father.

As a member of this family, Ernst discovered a form of happiness that would bring a whole new dimension and meaning to his existence. To his amazement, Ernst realized that he was not only capable of learning but that he derived enormous pleasure from the process of learning—in a nurturing educational environment. Ernst became one of the fifteen or so students in the private progressive school that Dorothy Burlingham had originally set up for her own children.

Anna Freud's humanistic psychoanalytic ideals inspired the school. Dorothy Burlingham financed it. Eva Rosenfeld, who between 1924 and 1930 was one of Anna Freud's closest friends, donated half of her idyllic suburban garden as the site for a two-story log cabin school and playground. In fact, the so-called Burlingham-Rosenfeld, or Matchbox, school was a monument to Eva's fifteen-year-old daughter, Rosemarie (Mädi), who had died in a mountain-climbing accident on July 8, 1927. As Eva would later recount in her memoirs, "I wanted to find comfort for my own sad heart in being with the young ones; it was as if I postponed the time of realizing that I would not find *her* among them."

Though Eva Rosenfeld did not teach or direct the educational activities, she assumed personal responsibility for the physical and emotional well-being of the students and their teachers. As a former student would recall, she was "a divinely inspired housemother who 'breathed life' into the school." The children, particularly those like Ernst who had suffered a deprivation of mothering, considered Eva their foster mother. During the school months most of the students lived with the Rosenfeld family.

The Matchbox school's educational principles were modeled on the so-called Project Method that had been developed in America by the philosopher John Dewey. For Ernst Halberstadt this unique educational experience was decisive. As he would put it many years later, "In no other place was I taught with so much sensitivity, understanding and openness. . . . We were neither 'taught' nor 'educated' but given the opportunity to acquaint ourselves with fascinating knowledge. It was a kind of 'self-help learning buffet.' " As he explained to one of his former classmates, "Education, it seems to me, is a form of feeding, and learning an extension of mothering."

In 1931 Eva Rosenfeld left her husband and returned to her childhood homeland, Germany. For nearly two years she managed the housekeeping of the Tegler psychoanalytic sanatorium in Berlin, where she also gained practical psychoanalytic experience "for her future career as an analyst." When Eva left, the Burlingham-Rosenfeld school lost its emotional center. Many of the students, including Bob, Mabbie, and Tinky Burlingham, were ready to go on to high school, and many of the supervising teachers were training to be analysts. When the school's doors closed in 1932 the remaining students, including Ernst, had to complete their fundamental education elsewhere, because the educational program had never been accredited.

Anna Freud felt that it was vital for her nephew to be in an educational environment that held out "an ideal of what kind of person one should become." She found Ernst a school on the island of Scharfenberg in Berlin's Tegeler Lake. Scharfenberg was an experimental school run by the city of Berlin, a boarding school for one hundred inner-city boys, which was "cheap, democratic, and very Spartan." After nearly two years of a semiprogressive education in this semi-agricultural school, Ernst began to hear about the Nazis. His fellow students, many of whom came from working-class families in Berlin, would return from visits home to report about Nazi activities. They told of arrests and of torture and of lead coffins full of ashes delivered to the parents of those who had disappeared. Ernst also heard terrifying stories about Jews being grabbed on the streets and carted off to unknown places in transport trains.

Ernst decided to return to Vienna as soon as possible. He would be escorted by Eva Rosenfeld, who was willing to assist her friend Anna despite the potential danger to her own life. Ernst packed a suitcase and took a subway to the center of Berlin, where Eva had arranged to meet him. As he stepped out onto the street, he heard a shout: "Oneway street to Palestine!" When next he saw a policeman wearing an armband with a swastika, it became clear to Ernst that if he should run into any trouble, the police would be of no help. On the eve of April 30, 1933, the day the Nazis instituted their official boycott of Jewish stores and offices, Ernst and his foster mother, Eva, boarded a train for Vienna.

Once back in Vienna, Ernst had to go back to an ordinary school, and it was a struggle to keep up with the ordinary students who had not been exposed to the luxuries of a learning buffet. Despite considerable time out for sore throats, headaches, stomachaches, and so on, Ernst finally matriculated in 1935. But since he had no hobbies, few interests, and was not exactly a devoted student, he did not know what to do or what to become. He tried a kibbutz in Palestine. He studied photography, thinking he might become a photographer like his father. He couldn't decide. And then the Nazis decided for him.

On March 11, 1938, at four o'clock in the morning, the twenty-five-year-old Ernst was awakened by the hum of low-flying German air force planes. His horror was mixed with a childhood curiosity about planes and flying Eagles. He rose, took out his binoculars, and recognized the Luftwaffe planes and Luftwaffe pilots wearing their large glasses. Because of what he'd heard from his friends while in Germany and what he'd witnessed in the streets of Berlin, Ernst knew exactly what was about to happen. He turned on his shortwave *Kristallset* and heard that the Germans were invading Austria. He realized he must act quickly. His first thought was of the immediate danger to his best friend and Viennese classmate, Leopold Bellak, who had never made a secret of his socialist convictions. He rushed to Leo's home and burst into the apartment, explaining to the family that they must burn certain books at once, before the Nazis could find them. After helping his friend to sort out his books and cast the "suspicious" ones into the woodstove, he dashed back to his own studio apartment and packed up. He moved in with his family on the Berggasse where he thought he would have the protection of the foreign friends of the Freud family—the Burlinghams from America, the Princess Marie Bonaparte from France, and Ernest Jones, the British psychoanalyst.

But there was no safety for anyone. Ernst had grasped the extent of the nightmare that was about to descend on the Austrian Jews several months before the rest of his family or their foreign protectors. Jews had been just barely tolerated in Austria, and it did not take the Austrians long to collaborate with the German persecution of them. Many of the Viennese actually welcomed the Germans with open arms, particularly because of their mutual hatred for Jews. Soon SS men who had been trained in Dachau were standing on every street corner. For Ernst it was like 1933 in Germany. He feared, since he was a Jew *and* an illegal alien, that he would be one of the first to be taken and carried away. He thought, "I could disappear without a trace and be counted as missing." He confided his fears to Ernest Jones. Jones was steely. "You are neurotic."

Soon afterward, Ernst's neurotic fears that he or perhaps someone in his family might "vanish without a trace" almost became a reality. One day he was walking down the street and there, in an open car, sitting between two Gestapo men in black uniforms, he saw his aunt, Anna Freud. The Gestapo let her go after a few hours of questioning. But Anna's capture finally made it clear to Freud that the entire family was imperiled. With a heavy heart and many misgivings Freud decided to leave Vienna. However, once the decision was made, the only thing the Freud family could do was wait patiently for their foreign friends to get them the proper exit and entry papers to make their escape from Vienna.

A few years earlier Max Halberstadt, together with his wife and daughter, had emigrated from Hamburg to South Africa, and Ernst planned to follow them there, thinking that perhaps he would fulfill his earlier ambition of becoming a photographer. However, fate intervened to keep Ernst attached to his mother's family. The only entry permit Ernest Jones could obtain was for England, and there Ernst Halberstadt was welcomed by his uncle, Ernst L. Freud, who invited him to stay for a while with him and his family in London. A few months later, when Anna, Martha, and Sigmund Freud settled in London, Ernst decided to stay in England permanently.

Ernst knew that he could always count on his Freud family to help him out, but he also recognized that sooner or later he would have to be on his own. The first few years he spent in England were discouraging, and he frequently felt like giving up. Thinking that his photography experience might prove valuable, he worked for a film company doing odd jobs and transporting film reels. Before too long, he realized that if he were to get anywhere in England, he would have to advance his education. Shortly after England entered the war, he began to prepare for the entrance exam that would qualify him to enter a British university. But this activity was interrupted when Ernst, along with his uncle Martin and many other other German aliens, was imprisoned on the Isle of Man. When, many months later, he was allowed to return to London, his physical health had deteriorated. After recuperating, he resumed his preparatory studies and finally, in 1944, passed the necessary exams and was admitted to the University of London.

Since Ernst did not have the qualifications for medical school, he studied for a B. A. degree in psychology at night while working at a clerical job during the day. Soon he found academic psychology sterile and began to toy with the idea of becoming an analyst. At the encouragement of his analyst, Ernst entered psychoanalytic training, "albeit late in life." He consoled himself with the thought, that he "had always been a late developer, knowing this would give one more scope toward the latter part of life." Along the way, he married and became a naturalized British citizen. The unpopularity of German-sounding names in England gave Ernst Halberstadt a rationale for changing his last name to the famous name of Freud. Then, since everyone kept confusing him with his uncle, Ernst L. Freud, he changed his first name to Ernest, added a W. (possibly from his middle name, Wolfgang), and became W. Ernest Freud.

During his analytic training he interned at a teaching hospital, where he worked with mothers and infants and did research on nursing failures. Later in life he would recall that these were some of the happiest years of his life: "At last I found I had a real purpose in life." Though he would become an adult analyst and then a child analyst, at this early moment in his psychoanalytic career he must have intuited that his true calling would have something to do with infant development.

As he neared the completion of his analytic training, he and his wife joined Anna Freud's child study center in Hampstead, London, where he eventually became dean of the Well-Baby Research Group. In 1956, the centennial of Sigmund Freud's birth and the year when he himself was accepted into the British Psychoanalytic Society, W. Ernest Freud became the father of Colin Freud, a charmer, who immediately endeared himself to his great-aunt, Anna.

W. Ernest remained "in touch" with his idealized childhood father, the reconnaissance air pilot, by taking his son to air shows and reading him the biography of Charles Lindbergh, the American aviator who made the first solo nonstop transatlantic flight in his plane *The Spirit of St. Louis*. Despite Ernest's great love for Colin and his strong conscious wish to protect his son from the painful separations he had suffered as a child, he was emotionally remote and unable to be an entirely dependable father. In 1981, after more than three decades of marriage, W. Ernest Freud divorced his wife and took up permanent residence in Germany. Colin remained in England with his mother.

As it was, things did not turn out too badly for Ernst Halberstadt. However, had it not been for his aunt's devotion and her capacity to empathize with his feelings of loss, Ernst, the inventor of the *fort-da*, might have been emotionally crippled by the deaths of his mother and little brother. Ernst, like so many other children who get lost in the wake of the deaths of their loved ones, might have succumbed to a severe depression or turned out to be a dreamy malcontent, a hypochondriac, a destructive or violently self-destructive adult.

On February 10, 1992, W. Ernest Freud was awarded a Doctor of Philosophy degree by the philosophy faculty of the University of Cologne, Germany, for his unique contributions to the study of the psychology of premature infants and their families. In his acceptance speech, Ernest Freud stressed the intimate connections between his special psychoanalytic interests and the loss of his mother and brother in childhood. Later that year, Dr. Freud also acknowledged that the same traumatic events that had inspired his professional accomplishments might also be exerting a disruptive influence on his personal life. Indeed, his responses to certain life situations reminded him of the *fort-da* game. He explained, "Naturally, the loss of my mother runs like a red thread through my life."

When Ernst Halberstadt's mother died, the thread of his life was broken. He would never become the person he might have been if she and his brother had lived. But when he was sixty-three years old, he finally found his true calling. His psychoanalytic training, and the well-baby clinic at Hampstead, both of which were direct outcomes of his emotional connections with Anna Freud, turned out to be the preludes to an even more personal psychoanalytic enterprise.

As in the past, he seemed to have drifted into something; each phase of his professional life seemed to happen to him quite by accident. This time, however, W. Ernest Freud had a profound conviction, a compelling inner motive—a calling. In 1977, while he was on a visiting professorship at the University of California, the director of the Department of Psychiatry invited him to take a look at the Neonatal Intensive Care Unit. Freud was fascinated. He vowed to return to California during his summer vacation, and once back there, he persuaded the director to give him the run of the neonatal unit, even though he was not a medical doctor.

"I got to know what it was all about. . . . I got 'hooked' on it." The idea that he'd hooked onto a treasure reminded him of the fishing rod he had invented when he was a lonely boy in Hamburg. The image of himself throwing out the reel and pulling it back then reminded him of his original disappearing game. He concluded that "It was basically an umbilical-cord game, and maybe this is a reason why I felt at home in the vicinity of the many tubes and wires to which the prematurely born are connected."

W. Ernest Freud knew that those who chose to work in NICUs were not there by chance. He noted that a few staff members were twins or related to twins. More to the point, a large number of them had been premature themselves, or had a prematurely born family member. But he was none of these. What, then, he asked himself, was his motive for wanting to devote the rest of his life to the care of premature babies? One day a thought came to him: "I owe it to my little brother." Upon further reflection, he realized that he wasn't thinking of Heinz, the brother he lost when he was nine years old, but rather of the unborn child who died when his mother did.

W. Ernest Freud embarked on this new venture, wanting to understand the psychological life of the unborn child. Upon learning that some couples experience a dramatic alteration in their bodily states at the moment of conception, and that some scientists were touting this magical moment as the earliest stage of the parents' attachment to the infant, W. Ernest Freud argued that the emotional bond between parents and children began even earlier than the moment of conception. He proposed that when the mother and father were children and played at making and having babies it was then that they began bonding with their unborn children.

While a woman is pregnant, her entire family is bonding to the unborn child. Even the siblings, who dash into the bedroom the minute they wake up, are making their presence known to the fetus by bouncing up and down on the mother's bed. As for the fetus, the unborn human, W. Ernest Freud claims that he also is bonding to his family, if not from the moment of conception, most likely within a month or so. He is certainly bonding to his mother, whose body touches on his body, whose body rumblings he can hear at all times of the day and night.

Not every psychologist would agree with W. Ernest Freud's attributions of postnatal sensibilities such as touch and hearing to a fetus. The fetus probably senses the mother first through the fetal ear, which matures very early. And no doubt the fetus experiences many sensations. However, only as he engages in a human dialogue in the world outside the womb can he identify himself as a self, or make any sense of the various sensations and sounds that impinge upon him. The mental organization of the fetus is not, in fact, as fine-tuned as Freud claims. Bonding does not have to take place in the womb or even immediately afterward for there to be a powerful and lasting attachment between parent and child. Doubtless his own traumatic experiences of separation had made W. Ernest Freud particularly sensitive to the issue of maternal bonding. As he has said, "Deprivation made me inventive. . . . the passively experienced situation of loss became a driving force."

In support of his beliefs, W. Ernest Freud cites the work of other psychologists and biologists who also contend that the fetus "hears" the mother's heartbeat, and is "aware" of the rhythmical swooshing sound of the mother's blood flow, the noise and rhythm of her breathing, the rumbling of her stomach, her sleep patterns, and the pace at which she lives her life—hectic or lethargic. Moreover, these scientists claim that the fetus bonds to his liquid environment and can "touch" and "know" his own body as well as its extensions into the mother, the wall of the uterus, the umbilical cord, and the placenta. What seems more likely in W. Ernest Freud's contentions about the unborn child is that life inside the womb exposes the fetus to the essential patterns of human existence outside the womb—"interaction, continuity, regularity, movement, rhythm, and stimulation." But these patterns are applicable to other animals as well. For an attachment along specifically *human* lines to develop, the infant requires a reciprocating dialogue with another human being, and this can occur only after birth.

With all of this information about the early and still earliest moments of bonding between the unborn child and his mother, W. Ernest Freud could not help but be impressed with the momentous and potentially lifelong traumatic effects of separating a premature, low-weight baby from its mother. Many of his later papers are really an impassioned plea for these babies, who are routinely separated from their mothers and then subjected to massive medical interventions with machines. He relates the story of a premature baby born in Brazil who was incubated by being "bound between the breasts of his Portuguese wet nurse." This dramatic story illustrates W. Ernest Freud's conviction that a newborn always be "in touch" with a nurturing, caregiving, responsive person, preferably its own mother—but not a machine. Obviously, a machine cannot bond to an infant, and therefore an infant who is bound to a machine loses touch with its humanity.

As he studied low-birth-weight infants in neonatal and postneonatal intensive care units in the United States and England, W. Ernest Freud became increasingly concerned with the psychological welfare of mothers, who would become depressed, withdrawn, uncertain, and emotionally frozen when they were not allowed to hold their newborns or touch them. All too often, the mother was given the message that her baby belonged to the doctors, nurses, and technicians who ministered to the child—but not to her. W. Ernest Freud also observed how the mother would unconsciously collaborate with this transfer of maternal authority as she felt guilty about having produced a damaged child. Freud would frequently ask NICU personnel, "Whose baby is this?" He urged that the competition over who "owned" the little patient be replaced by considerations of how the hospital staff and family members could complement each other in the care of a fragile newborn. Each member of the staff was asked to put aside his or her own personal interests and territorial claims so that the welfare of the premature baby and its parents became the primary consideration.

His observations of the "Whose Baby Syndrome" in NICU wards alerted Freud to similar disturbances in the wider social environment. As he reflected on these psychosocial issues, Freud might have recalled the words of the psychoanalyst Erik Erikson, his former art teacher at the Matchbox school: "Trustworthy motherliness requires a trustworthy Universe." W. Ernest Freud would probably agree that an infant's failure to thrive is not the fault of the mother who has failed to bond to her infant but the result of an indifferent society that does not protect and nourish mothers. Despite all the commotion about "family values," society generally does not support parents in their efforts to parent. When help *is* offered, the helpers often forget "whose baby" the child is. Instead of collaborating, family agencies compete with one another and with the parents. As a result, mothers and fathers are robbed of their dignity and authority and made to feel guilty for not being good-enough parents—which certainly doesn't help them bond to their children.

W. Ernest Freud also recognized that there was some question about "whose baby" *he* was. In his funeral tribute to Anna Freud, in 1982, he first reminded the audience of his privileged relationship with his aunt and then reminded them of *whose baby* he must always be.

> When my mother died, Anna, who was the sibling next to her in age, assumed the role of foster mother, and not infrequently conveyed to me that a unique and superb aunt such as she could fill it better than any mother. As an unmarried and unattached woman she was perhaps in competition with my mother and may have sought the experience of vicarious motherhood throughout her life.

In fact, there was never any question about the lost boy's gratitude toward the aunt who restored his hope and imbued him with the will to live. However, there was also that ever-present red thread that inevitably bound him to his mother.

Three years after Anna Freud's death, W. Ernest Freud, who had finally found himself by helping parents to stay in touch with their children, lost his twenty-eight-year-old son, Colin. The thread of life had been broken again. Colin was killed while riding a bicycle, when he was hit by a truck.

It seems the profound anxieties stirred up by this devastating event caused W. Ernest Freud to question his own identity. It was as though he had been set adrift in a dark sea without any familiar landmarks. Colin's "disappearance" also brought to mind Freud's own childhood fears of disappearing and his adult fears of being captured by the Nazis.

Shortly after Colin's death, W. Ernest Freud was invited to give the keynote address at an International Psychoanalytic Conference held in Vienna. Many members of his audience were the sons and daughters of Nazis or Nazi sympathizers, and Freud wanted to remind them of the not-too-distant Viennese past: the Nazi occupation of Vienna, the collaboration of the Austrians, and the fate of the Viennese Jews who had simply disappeared. His address, "Personal recollections of the Anschluss of 1938," might also have been an unconscious memorial for Colin, as the opening paragraphs forge a powerful emotional link between the family of his own childhood and Colin's childhood relationship with him.

W. Ernest Freud began his recollections with a tribute to home. "To me coming to Vienna is always a homecoming . . . since Vienna to me means my mother, Sophie Freud—my 'alma mater' in the fullest sense." And then through his words, he painted two pictures. First, there was little Ernst with his mother Sophie standing on the breadline during World War I, looking up to catch a glimpse of his father, the brave Eagle reconnaissance pilot. Then there was young Colin listening attentively as his father reads to him, over and over again, from *The Spirit of St. Louis.*

Perhaps Colin's death also reminded W. Ernest Freud of all those he had lost in the course of his long life. Further on in his address, he spoke of his other loved ones: his friend Leopold Bellak, his foster mother, Eva Rosenfeld, his great-aunt Minna, his aunt Anna, his uncle Martin, his grandmother Martha, his grandfather Sigmund, and Bob and Mabbie Burlingham. Except for Bellak, who emigrated to the United States and became a well-known psychoanalyst, every one of the persons Freud mentioned was now gone.

Though his address evoked images of loss and disappearance, Freud did not refer directly to the deaths of his loved ones or to the millions of other deaths caused by two world wars. His recollections stressed the various ways in which living people manage to go on living and caring for one another in the midst of the horrors of war. The contrast between W. Ernest Freud's reticence and the catastrophic world events he was alluding to brought home forcefully the unimaginable violence that had taken place in his "alma mater."

As for Freud's Viennese audience, it is very likely that many of them were struggling with a conflict between their family loyalties and an unconscious need to make reparations for their parents' crimes. They themselves were still coping with a version of death that had not—and possibly could not—ever be reconciled or mourned. One by one, every Jew, every Gypsy, every Socialist, Communist, and homosexual had disappeared from Austria. Those who had not been able to hide or escape to another country simply vanished without a trace. This apocalyptic reign of death, the work of Thanatos, is tantamount to an annihilation of human dialogue and thus beyond the language of pleasure and pain.

CHAPTER FIVE

BROKEN PROMISES

The loss of a parent during adolescence is qualitatively different from the loss of a parent earlier in a child's life because in adolescence this loss derails and interrupts the essential task of mourning childhood. In saying farewell to childhood, an adolescent evolves through the developmental phases that lead to psychological adulthood, among them a new appreciation of selfhood and identity, an accommodation to genital sexuality, and a critical alteration of moral priorities. Before adolescence, moral authority is invariably invested outside the self in the almighty and powerful parents. The awakening of genital sexuality demands a dramatic shift in the quality of moral authority. And if for one reason or another this shift does not take place, the person grows into physical adulthood but remains arrested with the conscience and moral aims of a child. If a parent should die or otherwise "disappear" due to severe depression, divorce, or desertion during the critical life juncture of adolescence, the child's opportunity to integrate sexual passion with moral authority may be lost forever.

An adolescent is aware that her childhood is over and that she will never be a child again. She knows she must say farewell but she dreads a of loss of dialogue. A black cloud of hopelessness settles. Every now and then, the adolescent becomes vaguely aware that she has lost something. She is suddenly overcome with a bewildering sense of grief. She senses something has disappeared, but what? Will she ever find it again?

The anxiety reactions of adolescence, depressive moods, and profound grief are manifestations of an inner emotional struggle that is akin to mourning. An adolescent does look forward to acquiring the sexual powers of an adult. But genital sexuality and reproductive capacity carry with them moral responsibilities that are frightening. As much as the adolescent wants to lunge straight ahead to the future, she also clings desperately to the past. Hence the bittersweet mood of nostalgia is born.

Nostalgia is one of the more visible manifestations of adolescent mourning. Along with a growing conviction that time is finite and irreversible comes a longing to refind the lost past. Childhood is remembered by adults and adolescents alike as a time of innocence and purity, a time for wishing, for hoping and dreaming. In a nostalgic mood, we may say that "heaven lay about us in our infancy," or that infancy was "the happy highways where I went / And cannot come again."

The fantasy of childhood as the "golden age of goodness" emanates from the adolescent glorification of a time when the child was the center of the universe and his parents were the most noble and beautiful of beings. In arousing these memories of childhood, nostalgia mitigates the heartbreak and grief, the disillusionments of the adolescent present.

Bittersweet longings for this lost state of perfection serve to heighten the adolescent's awareness of social injustice and evoke some musings on how to improve the lot of humanity. Nostalgic idealizations of a past goodness are being slowly transformed into adult social ideals that might realistically be accomplished in an adult world—if not now, then at least perhaps in some foreseeable future. However much the adolescent may silently mourn the past, the inclination to advance keeps thrusting her toward the future. In order to find out who she really is (and who she is not), the adolescent fervently engages parents, friends, lovers, cohorts, peers. She extends herself, reaching out to her environment, commanding from it responses that will rectify the disappointments of the past and help ease her way into the future.

These alterations in the experience of self are accompanied by a profound change in the quality of parent-child dialogues. As the adolescent reconciles the illusions of her childhood past with the realities of the adult world she is about to enter, she attains a clarity of vision she did not have before. She begins to view her parents from a new perspective. Her childhood eyes are opened to the historical realities and tragic dimensions of her mother and father. She discovers that her mighty parents, those omnipotent gods of her childhood, are flawed, undone by the very traits she once regarded as saintly and heroic. This new awareness of her parents' fallibility instigates a reordering of moral priorities.

A child always exaggerates and misconstrues the parents' powers. What she internalizes is still a child's version of power—of desire, of reason, of aggression, of virtue. The child has not yet established her own character, the reliable and steadfast inner compass that will eventually guide her actions. In order to develop her inner compass, the adolescent must first loosen her moorings to the secure but narrow moralities of childhood. She must cast out to an unknown sea which at times can be perilous. The familiar markers that used to guide the way are gone, and until the new moral order is established, a variety of new idealized figures are adopted as role models. The adolescent's walls and closet doors are papered with the posters and photographs of her current superheroes and heroines. Some idols are pure and saintly types who represent the adolescent's longing to be virtuous. Others are ruthless and seductive men and women who represent the temptations the adolescent is struggling against. These new idols are appealing because they are glamorous; they exhibit sexual prowess, wealth, and power, or prominence in politics, religion, art, films, or science. As the parents watch their child adopting what might seem to them exotic or peculiar new values, their own moral values and virtues are brought into question. They hold their breath and pray.

Whenever moral priorities are reordered, whenever a passion must be deployed from one realm to another, there is a revolution. Revolution always begins with a variation of violence. The question is whether the revolution that takes place will be a revolution of annihilation or of transformation. Adolescence itself is tumultuous and unpredictable. But once a person survives the loneliness, despair, hopelessness, intoxication, even madness of adolescence, generally a full-blooded adult emerges from the chaos and declares herself her own agency and authority.

What happens when a parent disappears during a child's adolescence? Often, the quest for moral authenticity is deflected into a perverse sexual scenario. The person may spend the rest of her life trying to resurrect the lost parent through a displaced erotic connection with other men or women. These fruitless quests to refind and resurrect the lost parent through sexual activity squander genital vitality and devastate the moral life.

Milly Wolfenstein was born in America on a sunny, bright Sunday morning in April of 1952. It was the era of family togetherness, when a middle-class child could still assume that every child had an intact family and a home just as she did. When Milly was a little girl, she lived with her parents, Harold and Rosalie Wolfenstein, in a gracious two-story house in an affluent Jewish community on the South Side of Chicago. She went to the best nursery school, where the student-teacher ratio was three to one. After that, her parents had planned to enroll her in the progressive public school that her older brother Tom had been attending for several years. But when blacks began to move in to the predominantly Jewish middle-class South Side and the neighborhood public school began to fill up with "bedraggled hippies" and "the shabby poor," Harold Wolfenstein decided to follow his business colleagues and friends to the suburbs. He packed up his family and moved them to Highland Park, on the North Shore of Lake Michigan, into a six-bedroom Tudor just two blocks behind the mansions that lined the lakefront. And there the Wolfensteins stayed. The neighborhood was safe. The public schools were intellectually enriched and secure from the intrusion of children who might drag down the intellectual and moral climate.

Milly was blessed with many advantages. She was pretty, smart, and talented. She adored her brother Tom, who was five years older than she. And her parents loved her dearly. She was never physically or mentally abused by either of them.

Every parent promises his child that he will protect her forever. Every parent becomes a parent in the belief that he has the power to keep this promise. And every child believes it. However, sometimes a parent will make other promises that, like the promise of eternal protection, simply cannot be kept. And this results in a confusion. In the parent's mind, the words are meant to reassure the child. In the child's mind, a parent's promises are deeds to be fulfilled.

Harold Wolfenstein was a well-meaning parent who was always rushing to his children's rescue so they would never have to suffer frustration or disappointment. He was full of *sympathy* for his children, but like many men who equate manliness with power, domination, and virility, Harold equated his children's helplessness and weakness with the so-called feminine longings. His exaggerated version of manliness made it impossible for him to *empathize* with a child's need for understanding and guidance. Harold believed that a good father does not waste precious time listening to his child's worries or trying to understand the feelings behind these confused thoughts; a good father simply takes charge and banishes worry by demonstrating his powers to fulfill his child's every wish and desire.

In his misguided view of how to be a good father, Harold Wolfenstein made all kinds of foolish promises to his daughter. And Milly, who wanted to believe in her father's omnipotence, embraced these promises as though they were gospel. Once, as Harold listened to his little daughter chant a nursery school rhyme she had committed to memory, he applauded her squeaky, uncertain voice and told her she would grow up to be a great musician. When the next year Milly asked for a piano and piano lessons, Harold promised that he would get her these gifts when she was ten years old. The magical date came and went but there was still no piano. One afternoon, when Milly was eleven, she came home to discover a piano and a piano teacher. But the piano and the lessons were for her sixteen-year-old brother.

When she was five years old, Milly proposed marriage to her father. In response, Harold whispered that they would be "secret pals forever." When she asked if he loved her more than mommy, Harold would tell Milly that she was smarter and prettier than her mother rather than hurt his daughter's feelings or damage her self-esteem. Since Milly's mother was a helpless and dependent woman whose entire identity depended on keeping a good house and setting a proper table, dressing her children in the latest styles, and looking up to her husband as the lord of the castle, Milly had good reason to believe in the fairy tale her father told her. Nevertheless, like all family myths that are meant to protect a child from the painful truth, the truth eventually came out.

Despite her father's promises, Milly could not help noticing that he adored his wife, and that they shared an emotional life that excluded Milly. Each time her father reneged on a promise, Milly unconsciously chalked up another mark against him. But in order to remain secure, Milly kept on believing in her father's ability to grant her every wish. Whenever she got low marks in school, whenever her friends made fun of her, whenever her brother bullied her, whenever she fell off her bicycle and scraped her knee, whenever her mother made her dust and wash the dishes while her brother was practicing the piano, whenever things went wrong and her father was not there to protect her, Milly blamed herself, thinking, "What is wrong with me?" and never "What is wrong with my father?"

There was another confusion in the Wolfenstein household about the way the father conveyed his ideals of virtue. Milly and her brother Tom were brought up to believe that their own self-interest and safety were more important than anything else going on in the world around them. Like many other good Americans, Harold Wolfenstein's soul had been scarred by the Joseph McCarthy hearings.

Before Harold was born, his own parents had escaped from the Russian pogroms. Soon after arriving at Ellis Island, they did what many Jewish immigrants at that time did—they settled in on the Lower East Side of New York. Harold's mother stayed home to raise the children and do piecework on men's shirts while his father worked fifteen hours a day, six days a week selling odds and ends from a pushcart. After a decade of day-in-day-out drudgery, Harold's once unassuming, patient mother was transformed into a loud-mouthed suffragette who every now and then got carted off to jail. His father became a union organizer who occasionally got his head or limbs bashed in by the union busters. As a proper young Jewish boy, Harold had been ashamed of his parents' "antisocial" activities, but later in his youth he began to see the virtue in it all. Instead of studying and memorizing his textbooks, Harold daydreamed about joining the rebel Spanish army. He had been too young to fight then, but he got his chance to fight "the just cause" in World War II. On April 29, 1945 he was among those brave American soldiers who liberated the inmates of Dachau. He vowed never to forget this sight of evil incarnate and to always have the courage to stand up for his beliefs.

During the Alger Hiss–Whittaker Chambers trial and the two years of Joseph McCarthy's witch-hunt, Harold Wolfenstein was starting a family, and like many other good Americans, the moral aims he had aspired to as a youth were transformed into the virtues of fatherhood. Five years after the liberation of Dachau, Harold's interests centered on his wife and children. The larger ethical principles Harold had once held as precious were now of secondary importance.

Whether Harold had been intimidated into silence and obedience by these shameful years in American history, or whether goodness is inevitably a fragile bloom that withers when the social climate is degraded, or whether what he saw at Dachau was too devastating to think about for very long, or whether some disenchantment with his own father had weakened his moral resolve, we do not know. We do know the conscious moral values that Harold conveyed to his children: There is only one way to survive in this world—keep to yourself and protect your own. Keep your mouth shut about social injustice or moral corruption. Work hard to support your family. Pay your taxes without questioning where the money goes, and ignore what is happening to others who are less fortunate.

When President Kennedy escalated the Cold War into the Cuban Missile Crisis of 1962, Harold Wolfenstein's first and only thought was how to protect his family. He assured his wife and children that he would find a place in the world where there was no threat of nuclear fallout. This obedient, hardworking man who never had time for reading more than the front page and financial news now spent every evening reading scientific papers on the effects of nuclear radiation. He scrutinzed the Rand reports, the Congressional Record and the Senate hearings on nuclear warfare. On the basis of his investigations, Harold Wolfenstein decided that Uruguay, a citadel of law and order, would be a safe haven from the nuclear menace. When the Soviet ships turned around, Harold Wolfenstein sighed with relief. He was, in fact, wise enough to realize that his plan of finding a safe haven from nuclear fallout had been highly unnecessary, as crazy an impossibility as the nuclear possibility itself.

Highland Park and the other affluent communities on the North Shore were insulated from the marches led by Martin Luther King during the mid 1960s. These protests were aimed at the segregated housing within the ghetto neighborhoods of the southern and western sections of Chicago, but nevertheless, Harold spent many a sleepless night calculating the potential threat to his suburban home. He also worried about the riots that the mayor kept promising would never happen in Chicago and decided that if ever there was rioting anywhere in Chicago, he would pack up his family and bring them to his brother's country house in Wisconsin until the trouble blew over.

There were obviously limits to Harold's power, and this fact was brought home to the entire family when Tom, the boy whom Harold tried to protect from all harm, refused to heed his father's advice about going to college to escape the draft. Tom was called up for a tour of duty in Vietnam. The Tet offensive had just begun and the family lived in dread of what might happen to their son. Tom was among those young men who survived with his physical body intact. But the horrors he witnessed and participated in changed him into a alien. This young man, who just barely overcame the psychotic culture of Nam, never forgave his father for the lies he had told. His father had not protected him from evil. And because of his father's moral temerity, Tom had come to view him as an accomplice to evil.

When Harold died six months after Tom returned from Vietnam, Tom was already out of the house and living on a commune in New Mexico. On the basis of a half-pretended, half-true post-traumatic stress disorder, Tom was able to refuse his second call of duty in Vietnam. When his mother called to tell him that his father had died, Tom was organizing a Vietnam protest march with some of his Nam buddies. He came back to Chicago for the funeral and sat Shiva with his family but then resisted his impulse to stay at home to protect his mother and sister. He knew he could never take his father's place, and he knew that he would be lost forever if he did not find his own way of life. He had to save his tormented soul. Tom eventually became a lawyer and a leading figure in the civil rights movement. He became the kind of man his father had once wanted to be instead of the frightened man his father had become.

In the end, Tom fared better than his sister Milly. By the time his father died, Tom had already gone through and survived his adolescence. He had also survived the moral calamity of Vietnam. For all that he would suffer from his disenchantment with his father and with his country, Tom was able to arrive at a sense of his own moral authority. Milly, on the other hand, went on believing in her father's power. She went on believing that she could be safe forever if she put her life in the hands of an all-powerful protector.

A vivid memory of childhood, which came to Milly's mind on the eve of her father's death, dramatically encompassed Milly's confusions about her father—confusions that were characteristic of her entire childhood. When her father was whisked away to the hospital in an ambulance, the fourteen-year-old Milly suddenly recalled a car trip she took with her father when she was four years old. The two were on their way to a country fair, and Milly was all excited about collecting the prizes her father was promising to win for her. As the car pulled up to the entrance of the fairgrounds, Milly could not wait a moment longer. She opened the car door, leapt out into the busy traffic, and was hit by another car, which fortunately was moving along very slowly. Milly escaped with only a few bruises and a tirade about self-control from her father. The adolescent Milly vividly remembered that the four-year-old Milly berated herself for being such a bad girl, for being so excited, for upsetting her poor father.

The events Milly remembered in adolescence had actually occurred. However, the fact that she evoked them at that specific moment suggests that the memory had been created in order to hide some emotional truths that Milly preferred not to know.

Even as the thirty-year-old Milly recounted this childhood memory to her therapist, it still did not occur to her that a protective father would have made absolutely certain that the car door was locked when driving with a young child. Milly's childhood memory both exposed a still consciously unacknowledged truth and yet effectively screened it out. The "truth" recreated by Milly, as she thought about her father's crumpled body lying on a stretcher, was reassuring. The memory said, "My father was the strong one. I was weak. My father protected me." For the adolescent Milly, this memory was magical. After all, a father who protects his child forever is both omnipotent and immortal.

When Milly's mother returned from the hospital consumed by the tears and wails that spoke a truth Milly could not bear to hear, Milly had a fleeting thought: "He broke his promise." Her father would not be there "to protect her forever"—not ever again. As this thought was incomprehensible, Milly unconsciously devised a way to bring her father back.

Milly's way of resurrecting her father was inspired by his last promise of protection. Harold had been alarmed to see his little girl's body changing into the body of a woman. To him she was still a helpless child in need of protection. He, whose self-esteem depended on constantly proving his fatherly omnipotence, interpreted his daughter's emerging sexuality as a threat to his power. After all, he thought, she might go off and find a new "prince charming" to replace him. She might succumb to the seductions of a man who promised to protect her forever. In his characteristic way of managing his anxieties and regulating his self-esteem, Harold decided to have a "heart-to-heart" with his fourteen-year-old daughter. He warned her to beware of the false promises of the opposite sex. He spoke of her mother's virtuous life and informed her that her mother had been a virgin when he married her. He instructed her to control her appetites and excitements and not to let her sexual passions prevail. "Don't you worry, little cookie. No guy is ever going to take advantage of you. If some boy ever does anything mean or nasty to you, you just come and tell me. I'll take care of you."

Two months after her father died, Milly made up her mind to "lose her virginity." This was a decision she made consciously. To insure her wish, she picked one of those "bedraggled hippies" that her parents had always warned her against.

Milly got more than she bargained for. Despite her knowledge of this sixteen-year-old boy's well-earned reputation of "love 'em and leave 'em," Milly believed in his whispers of eternal love. The next day, after their encounter, when Milly's "prince charming" did not even look at her or say hello, she was bewildered. She waited for the promised phone call. Each time the phone rang, her heart skipped a beat. But it was never him. Milly continued hoping, and she suffered an agony of belief and disbelief. After several months of this preoccupying torment, the truth of the young man's desertion could no longer be denied. Milly was mortified. "What is wrong with me?" she wondered, blaming herself for her small breasts, her fat thighs, the "unsightly" beauty mark on her forehead. "What did I do wrong?"

Perhaps she hadn't smiled the right way. Perhaps she was too excited. Perhaps she wasn't excited enough.

Suffering in love became Milly's way of continuing her dialogue with her lost father *and* punishing him for deserting her. She kept falling in love with men who would break their promises to her. Each love affair ended in disappointment and humiliation. In her early teens, Milly had chosen lovers who were ruthless, often as angry and vindictive as she was, just the sort of young men who would be sure to disappoint her. As she grew older and somewhat more self-protective, Milly would choose men who were more suited to the task of satisfying her demands for eternal protection. She put her body and her soul in the hands of older fatherly types, usually "decent" family men just like her father. These devoted family men, of course, would never desert their wives or children in exchange for Milly's hot passions. But whether the men Milly selected as lovers were self-centered and uncaring, or protective and kindly, their efforts to please and satisfy this frightened and desperate young woman were doomed to fail. No matter how promising a love affair's beginning or how consciously well-intentioned the man, each new love was destined to end in a repetition of the father's broken promises. Nevertheless, these repetitions were also Milly's attempts to rewrite her tragedy with a happy ending.

She would ignore the obvious signs of imminent disaster, signs that her friends could detect at once. The unconscious wish that this time her father would come out of the shadows where he was hiding to save and protect her blinded Milly to the reality of her lovers' intentions. And though she wanted to rectify the past and change its ending, unconsciously she recreated with her lovers every disappointment she had experienced in her childhood relationship with her father. Instead of working through the complexity of feelings and fantasies directly with her father, Milly spent her adolescent years and much of her young adult life repeating the hurt and perpetuating the confusion in her self-destructive sexual encounters.

If Harold had been around long enough for Milly to work out her conflicting feelings and confusions, Milly might have been able to recover from her disenchantments with him and move on to a promising future. Most adolescents behave as though they'd like to be rid of their parents. At times they may wish that these bothersome, nagging creatures would simply disappear and give them a little peace. They act as though they want to work out their dilemmas without any interference from their parents. And while parents may not be able to say very much or do very much to directly influence the decisions and behavior of their adolescent children, their steady and reliable presence is absolutely essential to an adolescent's sanity and well-being. Though she may ignore or disparage them, an adolescent counts on her parents to be there as she is undergoing the internal process of mourning her childhood past. She also depends on her ongoing relationships with members of her own generation.

Every adolescent goes through phases where she reenacts the dialogues she once had with her parents by treating her peers as though they were merely new editions of her parents. For example, many adolescent girls who are working out their disenchantments with their fathers will choose self-centered and inevitably disappointing young men as their first lovers. Everything that could be new and different is immediately translated into something old and familiar. These peer dialogues are a distorted reflection of the parent-child dialogues—which of course consisted of much more than disappointment and disenchantment. The stereotyped scenarios of loss and disappointment in adolescence have been written with the express purpose of rectifying the childhood past. To serve their purpose, they must be shadow plays and repetitions of the childhood past, coupled with the unconscious aim of rewriting and reevaluating that past.

Every adolescent assigns these exasperating roles from the past to her peers. However, while such repetitions are necessary to revise her inner life, the ordinary adolescent also has an ordinary life, with some down-to-earth ordinary friends who continue to respond to her in terms of the present realities. Side by side with her desperate reenactments, the adolescent is also involved with the more genuine peer relationships we are accustomed to think of as characteristic of adolescence. Usually she has one or two special girlfriends with whom she shares her passions, secrets, and anxieties. Then there are the outsiders, whom she and her friends regard as stupid, mean, hostile, and ugly. She belongs to a group of friends from school or the neighborhood, which she regards as her home base; to this group of friends she is loyal, and she counts on them to be there for her as she returns from her lonely excursions into the past.

Milly was so entirely engrossed in reliving and rectifying the past that she had no time or room left for the ordinary exaltations and let-downs of an adolescent present. Milly's daily existence was a soap opera of excited drama, fraught with lots of intense social interaction, but all in the service of trying to bring her father back from the dead. It was as though Milly's entire development had ground to a halt when her father died—she was arrested in that moment of time and could never move forward. She did, however, move backward. Many of Milly's behaviors were more childlike than adolescent. When her frantic love affairs did not succeed in keeping her worries at bay, she would become anxious and her anxiety would quickly escalate to panic. At these moments, Milly was quite capable of a full-blown two-year-old temper tantrum.

Milly's mother was no help. In fact, her reactions to the loss of her husband exacerbated Milly's dilemmas. Rosalie Wolfenstein was in a panic about her own survival. Since she had always looked to her hus-band as her only means of getting along in the world, she had never developed her own emotional and intellectual resources. When her husband died, she fought constantly with the teenage Milly about money. She berated Milly for anything she bought. She fell into a tantrum of disorganization whenever the bills and bank statements arrived. Since Rosalie now saw her daughter as her competitor for food, clothing, and shelter, she was totally incapable of sympathizing with Milly's lost and frightened feelings. Nor could she empathize with the sexual dilemmas that preoccupied Milly. Milly's mother did not have any real cause to worry as she did about money. Harold Wolfenstein had left her with plenty of money and assets to live on. Milly's mother was in a panic because she had lost her omnipotent protector and guardian. Milly identified with her mother's panic, which closely resembled her own, and these feelings only intensified and complicated her emotional distress.

On the surface, Milly's childhood had been ordinary—not at all de-serving of the term *traumatic*. However, when Milly lost her father, she also lost her adolescence. The decisive factor that transformed this unexceptional childhood with its common moral dilemmas into something traumatic was that the father lost his life just as Milly was entering the springtime of hers. The pattern of attempting to rectify the humiliations and disappointments of childhood through a repetitive acting-out is typical of adolescence. The question is whether these repetitive enactments that attempt to rewrite the past will eventually advance an adolescent into adulthood. Unfortunately the death of a parent is an exceptional event that all too often leads to an arrest in development. Unless there is someone who can empathize with the sexual and moral dilemmas set in motion by this loss, an ordinary disappointment of childhood can become an adolescent trauma that preoccupies the present and blocks any movement into the future.

Milly was not the innocent, passive victim she appeared to be. She actively, albeit unconsciously, contrived her fate. She consciously wished for a protector and comforter, yet Milly's impossible demands that her lovers restore to her what she had abruptly lost when her father died drove them away. When her demands were not met, Milly reacted with a fierce rage. If her tantrums did not scare her lovers away, she would escalate her demands or invent a more frightening form of emotional blackmail, such as passing out drunk in public places or threatening suicide. Eventually she always succeeded in getting the man to desert her.

The final scene in the last act of Milly's unconscious sexual scenario invariably had to be a broken promise, a disappointment, and a reawakening of the question, "What's wrong with me?" With that question, Milly's self-doubts resurfaced to haunt her, and the cycle of looking for love and losing love would begin again.

From Milly's point of view, her lovers were never separate persons with their own separate identities, individuals with wishes and desires of their own, but merely the instruments for carrying out her fixated sexual scenario. Milly cared nothing at all for the many men she had intercourse with. The man's erect penis was proof enough to Milly that she was a safe, valued, and loved person. The man's erect penis was a reassurance about her own body. Milly devoted herself assiduously to making sure her lover had an erect penis. She regarded the penis as a trophy, designed to fix her own inadequate body and to make her feel less depressed and anxious. Thus it was not erotic fulfillment that assuaged Milly's anxieties of abandonment, separation, and castration, but the fantasy that she had the power to make any man fulfill her unconscious scenario. Because she was a lovely looking young woman who bleached her hair to a scintillating platinum and wore slinky skintight dresses like her childhood idol, Marilyn Monroe, Milly had no trouble attracting men. However, also like her idol, Milly's demands for constant admiration and eternal protection made it impossible for her lovers to love her for very long.

Milly Wolfenstein's responses to the loss of her father are reminiscent of Ernst Halberstadt's, who lost his mother when he was five and three-quarter years old. Like Milly, Ernst deflected the rage and disappointment away from his dead parent and toward himself. Like Milly's, Ernst's behavior was governed by a vindictive need to prove how mistreated he was. And like Milly, he clung to the unconscious wish that his demonstrations of suffering would force his mother to return and care for him.

However old or young a person is when a parent dies, the response to this traumatic event will always reflect the developmental issues and conflicts the person was struggling to resolve and work through when the calamity struck. Questions of moral authority and virtue will always be raised. However old or young a person is when a parent dies, an effort is always made to resume the dialogue that was interrupted and to make it come out right.

The difference between the fourteen-year-old Milly and the six-year-old Ernst, *and it is an essential one that makes all the difference,* is that Milly was old enough to employ genital sexuality as her means of rectifying the traumas of childhood. Her perverse sexual scenario was fixated and ritualized, leaving no room for the enigmatic and unexpectable gestures that enable sexual intimacy and sexual pleasure. The aim of Milly's sadomasochistic enactments was not pleasure through pain but a repetitive cycle of losing love and finding love, of castration and restitution, of abandonment and reunion, of death and resurrection.

Because the teenage Milly had no one to empathize with her confused feelings, she rushed into the first solution that came to her mind. Her adolescent trauma became instantly charged with an erotic excitement that bound her more and more firmly to the disappointing past she was trying so hard to rewrite. The *fort-da* game that a child plays out with a spool of thread, or a toy wagon on a string, an adolescent or adult plays out with genital organs. And that was Milly's undoing. For once a scenario of losing and being lost is eroticized, it becomes a perverse preoccupation that is in itself self-perpetuating and fixated.

Until Milly was nearly thirty years old, she was deceived by the noisy elation of her sadomasochistic enactments. She did not recognize how alone she was. She certainly did not think she needed therapy. She was convinced that she was still looking for Mr. Right, a man who would keep his promises to protect her from every harm. All along, however, she was unconsciously seeking an accomplice who would participate in her lifelong scenario of broken promises. Her life was dominated by her perversion, and because she was so entirely possessed by the drama and intoxication of her love affairs, she kept at bay the depression and anxiety she might otherwise have experienced. Her father was gone. Her mother seemed to fear and despise her. Her brother was off saving his own soul. The few friends she had of her own age were valued only insofar as they participated as "witnesses" to her reenactment scenarios. Milly had lost her inner moorings as well as her moorings in the world of reality. Left to her own devices, Milly kept herself only tenuously connected to the real flesh-and-blood world through her endlessly doomed love affairs.

For an adult to transform the sexual and moral priorities that remain untransformed during adolescence requires a long time and an enormous expense of spirit. When adolescence is over, who we are and what we might become are not as open to change. We are never as flexible again.

Fortunately for Milly, Harold and Rosalie had been protective and caring, good-enough parents despite their emotional limitations and moral fallibility. As a result, Milly had just enough trust to believe that someone might be able to help her. Despite the turmoil of her adolescent and young adult years, she managed to attend high school and eventually graduate from college. She wanted to go on for an advanced degree but had no idea of what she might do. A history professor who had been assigned to Milly as an advisor recognized at once that she was a lost and lonely young woman. Although he knew nothing of her disastrous social life, the professor learned from Milly's record that her father had died several years earlier. He could see beyond the platinum glitter to the aching sadness in Milly's eyes. He recommended therapy.

Milly's first therapist lasted less than a year. As so often happens when the repetition compulsion is more powerful than any conscious desire for pleasure or self-fulfillment, Milly repeated the trauma of broken promises with her therapist. Intially, she idealized him as an all-powerful guardian who would protect her from the heartless men who only wanted to seduce her with their false promises. Unfortunately the therapist accepted the role assigned to him and then had to suffer the destiny that came with it. He was a disappointment. And one day, without any word of warning or good-bye, Milly deserted him. A similar fate awaited the second therapist. She had not accepted the role of guardian angel but nevertheless became too intent on curing Milly's "sexual aberration" and rescuing her from a life of promiscuity. Her moralistic attitude blinded her to the underlying meanings of Milly's sexual behaviors. After a few months, Milly abandoned her.

Then Milly found someone whom she could really trust. This third therapist, who had the benefit of being able to appreciate the pitfalls in the previous "disappointing" therapies, realized early on that Milly's self-destructive sexual scenarios were a symptom of something even more desperate. She did not make the mistake, as the other two analysts had done, of focussing on Milly's unfortunate sexual life and trying to save her from it. Instead, she paid immediate attention to Milly's underlying depression and interpreted her suffering in love as a response to the loss of her father. Milly was then able to see for herself how she had recreated the drama of broken promises with her other therapists. Milly had enough common sense and sense of self-preservation to understand exactly what her therapist was talking about. And that understanding, of course, was only the first step of Milly's new beginning.

Despite the fixity of her perverse solution Milly was able, after a long time and a great expense of spirit and energy, to use her therapy as a way to create a new kind of ending. By gradually internalizing the life-enhancing dialogue that was offered to her, Milly was finally able to say farewell to her dead father. As she finally mourned the loss of her father, she also mourned her lost adolescence. She came to understand that if there was promise in her life, she alone was the agency of its fulfillment.

A perversion, the stereotyped preoccupation that squanders a life and prevents any possibility of intimacy and sexual fulfillment, is still more connected to living dialogues than a psychosis—the break with reality that a perversion holds at bay. For those who *were* repeatedly and severely traumatized as children, a perversion can serve as the safety valve that prevents or at least minimizes the torments of outright madness.

Like perversion, psychosis is often a response to loss. In contrast to a perversion, however, where the afflicted person is still partially attached to the world of reality and still engaged in a human dialogue of sorts, in a psychosis the afflicted one is so entirely undone by his loss that he responds by divesting himself of any attachment to everyone and everything in the real world.

The immediate occasion that instigates this extreme withdrawal from reality may not be the death of a parent. The parent may have died long ago. The parent may still be alive but so much a reminder of trauma that he or she can no longer be a reliable source of human dialogue. The actual loss that brings on the break with reality may be a high-minded abstraction or a seeming triviality. Whether it be a job, a calling, an ability to paint or write, fame and success, a home or a homeland, an ideal of justice, sexual potency, an arm or a leg, a mole on the cheek, a tattoo, to the loser—to the potentially psychotic one—the "thing" has come to mean everything. The unifying factor in all these varied losses is that the lost "something" symbolizes a narrow aspect of the person's childhood relationship with a parent. The lost ideal, the fame, the sexual potency, has become the measure of one's own value, the embodiment of the human dialogue, which is what makes life worth living.

CHAPTER SIX

✻

A WOMAN
SUCCUMBING

When a parent dies during a person's adolescence, the traumatic effects may not become evident until much later, during some other juncture in life's passage. Marriage, parenthood, middle age, the arrival at the time of life when procreation is no longer feasible, the attainment of celebrity or professional acclaim are turning points that may bring a burst of vigor, new opportunities, a whole different way of interpreting one's life history. However, at these critical junctures, the traumas, disappointments, and unfinished business of childhood and adolescence, which until then had not impeded the person from living a relatively peaceful, even productive, successful life, may reemerge to stir up a cataclysmic disruption of the person's identity.

Daniel Paul Schreber was ten years old when his forty-four-year-old father, Dr. Daniel Gottlieb Moritz Schreber, suffered a massive cerebral injury after a heavy iron ladder fell on his head. From then on, he was tormented by excruciating head pains, chronic insomnia, and a terror of bodily disintegration. This man, once a pillar of strength and wisdom, a veritable god to his children, often could not eat, bathe, or dress without his wife's assistance. He would speak to no one but his wife and showed no interest in any of his five children. In his humiliation and despair, in his lapses of speech and memory, in his irritability and uncontrollable rage he was unrecognizable to himself and to his loved ones. On those few occasions when the children were permitted to visit their father, what they saw was a familiar face—a face they knew and loved. But their father's ways of responding to them were peculiar; he was both an intimate and a stranger. Dr. Schreber was indeed physically alive; however, his personality had long since died. On November 10, 1861, nine years after the blow to his head, Dr. Daniel Gottlieb Schreber died of an intestinal obstruction. He was fifty-three.

Sixteen years after his father's death, when Daniel Paul was thirty-three, his thirty-seven-year-old brother, Daniel Gustav, shot himself in the head shortly after his appointment to a judgeship. The following year, at age thirty-four, Daniel Paul married a beautiful, charming nineteen-year-old woman from a famous theatrical family. He became a judge. He seemed to be thriving. However, it is likely that his brother's suicide—coupled with the loss of his father, which, at the time, Daniel Paul seemed to take in stride—contributed to his own psychotic illnesses.

Survivor's guilt may have been a factor in Daniel Gustav's suicide and in Daniel Paul's eventual psychological demise. But such severe guilt reactions in the sons, both of whom achieved prominence in the legal profession, would suggest an unusual degree of severity in the father. Had Dr. Schreber been a different sort of man, his two sons might have internalized a friendlier, less judgmental, fatherly presence.

Dr. Schreber was not an intentionally cruel father. In fact, he viewed himself as a savior of children. He himself had been a frail, sickly child, an undersized adolescent of very poor physique. When the growth spurt of his youth was over, he just barely topped the five-foot mark. His humiliation was complete when he was pronounced unfit for military service.

Lest his short, slender frame be mistaken for an unmanly soul, the young Dr. Schreber determined to overcome his physical shortcomings. He set up a rigorous course of calisthenics which he pursued daily—rain or shine, sick or healthy. Within three years, out of frailty there emerged a manly physique, an excellent gymnast, a powerful swimmer, and a sturdy horseman. He proved his strength of character in other ways as well. He graduated with some honors from medical school. He wrote the 1831 edition of *The Book of Health*, the first of his many home medical advisors. In 1838, he married the lovely and cultivated Louise Henrietta Pauline Haase, the daughter of a well-known physician, and the very next year became the father of his first son, Daniel Gustav, called Gustav.

Dr. Schreber's personal salvation was not enough to rectify the traumas of his childhood. Having proved on his own body that nature's cruel mistakes can be corrected, Dr. Schreber determined to save all children from the mortifications of physical imperfection. Early in his career as a child saver, Dr. Schreber realized that the mechanical devices he had designed to straighten the muscles and bones of crippled children could benefit the average child, whose habits of sloth and lackadaisical posture could damage even the healthiest of bodies. It was not long before Dr. Schreber's regime of gymnastics, body care, and moral hygiene would be adopted by wealthy and middle-class German parents and rigorously imposed on any boy or girl whose body or soul might otherwise "stray" from physical or moral perfection.

Dr. Schreber asserted that a child's body must be kept straight at all times—when he stood, sat, walked, played, lay down, or slept. He invented a chin band for ensuring the proper growth of jaws and teeth—a simple strip of leather fit snugly under the chin and was held firmly in place on the head by a helmet of crisscrossing leather straps. He invented the *Kopfhalter*, which prevented the child's head from falling forward or sideways—a suspenderlike leather strip was buttoned onto the child's underwear at one end, while a metal fixture at the other end was clamped onto the child's hair. A child wearing Dr. Schreber's head holder would get a sharp tug on his hair if his head was not held absolutely straight. Then there was the *Geradehalter*, a T-shaped metal bar that could be screwed into a desk at school or at home to prevent a child from slumping while doing schoolwork. The horizontal bar pressed against the child's collarbone to prevent forward motion while the vertical bar which supported it pressed hard against the child's crotch to prevent leg crossing, thigh pressing and other "immoral" acts.

In his *Book of Health,* Dr. Schreber assured his readers that he always tried his devices out on his own children before marketing them to the public. Yet while he believed it was imperative for his two sons to be free of weak, childish, or effeminate traits, Dr. Schreber was tolerant of—and even subtly advocated—physical delicacy, childishness, and feminine mannerisms in his three daughters. It was enough for them to simply walk straight, sit upright, and fall asleep in a straight posture. They were never to touch their genitals and, above all, *not* grow up to become emancipated, masculine women. The Schreber girls, who identified primarily with their brilliant, talented, aristocratic mother, seem to have survived the father's medical devotions without obvious mental anguish. The two sons did not survive.

The traumatic effects of Dr. Schreber's actual death were exacerbated by his personality death nine years earlier. As with any loss, and particularly with the loss of a venerated parental figure, the *full* work of mourning encompasses the gradual restoration of a inner presence that is benign and comforting. Dr. Schreber's two sons were unable to rediscover a friendly fatherly presence within themselves.

Surely, Daniel Gustav and Daniel Paul had been emotionally traumatized by having to accommodate their father's stringent standards and ideals. And surely the epigraph to Dr. Schreber's *Book of Health,* which went through several printings, was indelibly engraved on their bodies and souls: "Always bear in mind, that a god resides in your body and that the temple must at all times be spared desecration." However, until a blow on the head reduced the mighty "god" of the Schreber nursery to a state of infantile dependency, the two sons had compensated for the severe trials of body and spirit imposed upon them by identifying with their father's power and authority. When the massive cerebral injury virtually demolished their father's personality, the sons, no longer certain of who their father was, began to doubt their own reality and identity.

The personality death of a parent can be devastating to children, more traumatic in its own way than actual death. An actual death can be mourned. The bereaved can say farewell to the beloved and even find a way to reinstate a dialogue with him. With a personality death, the person and everything he once represented has effectively died, but his body is still alive, still recognizable. There can be no mourning.

Now and again, a flicker of the person who once was arouses the family's hope that the lost personality will soon be restored. Yet within an hour, a day, or sometimes scarcely a second, the familiar is once again lost, consumed by the alien force that has possessed the physical presence the family knows and loves. But who is the real person?

In contrast to other serious injuries and illness, where the victim can still express how he feels about the calamity that has befallen him, severe brain injury renders the survivor incapable of sharing intimate experiences with his loved ones. As the wife of a man suffering massive brain damage explained:

> It feels uncanny because the potential to share it [intimate experiences] seems to exist in certain ineffaceable remnants of the previous personality, lying in scattered pieces like a puzzle that's been kicked around on the floor. The face, the voice, the gestures are familiar, but there is an eerie barrier, or scrim: no answering sensibility comes back.

If the person whom you had once counted on for an intimacy of shared responsiveness still looks familiar but has been transformed into an unrecognizable personality incapable of emotional reciprocity, the effect on the beholder is uncanny—in a terrifying way. But why should this absence of reciprocal dialogue evoke fear?

Until 1906, when Dr. Ernest Jentsch published his groundbreaking study, *The Psychology of the Uncanny,* the phenomenon of the uncanny, while a source of fascination for centuries, had not received attention in a scholarly journal. Jentsch's study did not reveal anything surprising or remarkable—but he was the first to give the human experience of the uncanny a respectable "scientific" explanation. Essentially, he attributed the uncanny effect to an uncertainty about the distinctions between animate and inanimate. He described how waxwork figures, mechanical dolls, and hand-operated puppets—all of which are, of course, inanimate—can seem uncanny, particularly when they are animated or moved by some unseen force. He then explained why human beings suffering from epileptic fits and certain manifestations of insanity often evoke a *fearful* sense of the uncanny in an observer. Unlike inanimate dolls or puppets, these tormented persons are living, but like the puppets, their gestures and body postures make them look as though they are being animated by unseen mechanical forces. Jentsch's paper was limited in its explanatory power because he focused on the characteristics of the objects or persons that induce uncanny effects. Since Jentsch did not address the psychological forces within the observer, he was unable to answer the more difficult question of why such ambiguities between animate and inanimate, real and not real, alive and dead are sometimes a source of fear and anxiety for the beholder.

In his 1919 paper *The Uncanny,* Freud credited Jenstch's seminal contributions but finally insisted that the blurring of distinctions between animate and inanimate, while essential to understanding the uncanny experience, was not sufficient to explain its emotional intensity. The uncanny experience, Freud proposed, has as much to do with the emotional turmoil aroused in the beholder as with the mystifying characteristics of the observed object. The confusion between animate and inanimate is usually a source of playful fascination and benign excitement to the observer of waxwork displays, mechanical dolls, and puppets. However, a living person who appears to be governed by some alien force evokes terror, or at least a momentary apprehension that something awful is about to occur. *The devastating emotional effects of the uncanny come from the hostile forces inside the observer which resurface when a loved one is transformed into an alien incapable of reciprocal emotional dialogue.*

Freud's paper begins with a long etymological dissection of the word "uncanny." Briefly, in German, "uncanny" is *unheimlich;* meaning unfriendly and alien, the inverse of *heimlich,* meaning friendly and familiar. Linguistically, however, these two apparently opposite words oscillate and blend into one another—just as they often do in actual life. Thus, the uncanny is not something entirely new and strange but rather something old and familiar that has become alien.

As the familiar representatives of the outside social order, and as living models for the child's conscience, the parents encourage the child to hide, disguise, keep secret—that is, to repress any reminders of those impulses and desires that are unacceptable or foreign to society. Thus any wishes, fantasies, and thoughts that are *unheimlich* within the child are made *heimlich* by keeping them out of conscious awareness.

In his efforts to convert his potentially hostile impulses into behaviors more amenable to social life, the child identifies with both parents' social behaviors and also with the ideals of perfection they convey. A parent who is no longer able to engage in human dialogue will stir up all kinds of emotional havoc within the child. Confronted by the strange appearance of a parent suffering from personality death, all the alien impulses that the child had repressed in the interests of gaining the parent's love and protection threaten to leap out of the hidden recesses of the child's mind.

Ordinarily, the reciprocal dialogue between child and parent gives direction and meaning to the child's otherwise chaotic impulses and desires. In the absence of reciprocal dialogue, anything might happen. The old demons the child thought he had banished forever might reemerge. His secret forbidden wishes might come true. His worst nightmare—of vanishing without a trace—might actually happen. His conscience, which is sometimes harsh enough during the daylight hours when it can at least be placated and cajoled by the rituals of cleanliness, obedience, or orderliness might also regress to its ruthless, primitive origins.

That aspect of the child's inner life we call superego or conscience represents the high moral aims and lawfulness of the social order. However, much as this lawgiving agency is invested in the future and in all that is highest and most noble in human nature, it also harks back to the archaic *unheimlich* past with its threats of annihilation, absence, separation, castration, and mutilation. As if eternally beholden to the erotic and aggressive impulses it aims to regulate and control, the superego devours, scrutinizes, tempts, torments. If we are dreaming, for example, and have not sufficiently disguised the unfriendly, forbidden wishes that emerge in our dreams, soon enough our dreams are visited by punishing voices, accusatory eyes, chastising hands, demolishing claws, fiery tongues. At this, of course, our forbidden wishes scurry back into hiding, and we wake up relieved to find ourselves in our sweet, familiar bed.

Conscience represents both the protective and punitive aspects of the parent. When the protective aspects predominate, the child feels loved and loves himself. When the punitive aspects come to the fore, the child feels deserted by the forces of goodness and protection. Having lost these most precious aspects of his own identity, the child feels lost. In his desperate confusion, he may even surrender to the harsh presences that have taken command of his inner world and cause himself to die—by accident, addiction, or suicide. More usually the child goes on living but then squanders his life trying to appease a conscience that is ungiving and merciless.

In a personality death, the regression of the father's personality threatens everything that has become sacred to the child. In Daniel Paul Schreber's case, when his father's personality disintegrated, Daniel Paul's conscience, his ideals of perfection, his dreams of becoming strong and powerful like his father also threatened to disintegrate. When a father, the almighty powerful father who was the original source of a child's moral sense, now seems animated by forces that are inhuman and out of his control, the child's own superego, a capricious and corruptible agency of mind to begin with, may lose its protective function and become savage and sadistic.

As a wife beholds the personality death of her husband, the wife is also confronted with everything alien within herself. In her sympathy for him, she often feels that she also will disintegrate and fall apart. But as an adult, she can at least recover her sense of who and what she is by framing the logical thoughts or words that will give some recognizable shape to the fragmented, shapeless presence that sits opposite her at the dinner table. A child, who has few ways of expressing, much less comprehending, what is now so strange about his once-familiar father, is liable to experience the father's bizarre personality changes as a commentary on his own imperfections. The father's eyes, which once mirrored all that was strong and beautiful in the child, are now dull and stony. His expressions are now interpreted by the child as accusatory. The father's stilted gestures and halting phrases are perceived by the child as criticisms and condemnations; he also senses the father's rage and deep humiliation, which he begins to embrace as if he were the hurt, humiliated one. Moreover, since the child's identity is still being verified and shaped by the parent, the child feels alienated from his own self and often concludes that he is not worth anything at all. But instead of giving up and letting himself die, the child will, in fact, work ten times harder to improve and advance himself. This uncanny experience of a parent's personality death makes the child infinitely susceptible to being overwhelmed by ordinary defeats, losses, and disappointments.

The traumatic effects of his father's personality death did not become evident until Judge Daniel Paul Schreber, at age forty-two, suffered a humiliating defeat as a candidate for a seat in the Reichstag. The vote was 14,512 to 5,762. A local newspaper headlined his ignominy: WHO, AFTER ALL, HAS EVER HEARD OF SCHREBER?

After he learned of the newspaper report on the election results, Daniel Paul became severely ill, and his symptoms uncannily resembled his father's responses to brain injury: insomnia, excruciating head pains, and delusional fantasies of bodily disintegration. He attempted suicide twice. Then, after eighteen months in the Leipzig *Nervenklinik* hospital, he lived in relative contentment for eight years. Judge Schreber described those years as rich in worldly honors "and marred only, from time to time, by the repeated disappointment of our hope of being blessed with children." The couple had difficulty conceiving from the start. But when the judge did manage to impregnate his wife—at least six or seven times—she suffered miscarriages.

Daniel Paul Schreber's second illness, a full-fledged paranoid psychosis, emerged after his fifty-first birthday and immediately before the thirty-fourth anniversary of his father's death at age fifty-three. But tremblings of the disaster to come had begun four months earlier, in July, when the judge realized that he might never be a father. This possibility that he might fail to attain the pinnacle of manhood provoked a fantasy that he was turning into a woman. While in bed one morning, still half asleep, he felt a peculiar sensation wash over his body. The sensation was accompanied by the half-conscious thought that "it really must be so lovely to be a woman succumbing to intercourse."

The feminine sensations came just as he was about to be named chief judge of the highest court of Dresden. In October, his appointment as a *Senatspraesident* was confirmed. Judge Schreber was a bit apprehensive about assuming authority over the gray-bearded father figures, many of whom were twenty years older than he. He was also ashamed of his inability to produce a child and was consciously fearful that the senate might mistake his childlessness for a lack of virility.

When he assumed his duties, he worked day and night, sometimes without sleeping, to prove himself a worthy moral authority. On November 9, the evening before the anniversary of his father's death, he pleaded with his mother to let him end his life. The following day she had him recommitted to *Nervenklinik*. Schreber's behavior was so unmanageable that he soon had to be transferred to the Sonnenstein mental asylum, where he could be observed every minute of the day and night.

Suicide seemed the only way to end the torment he suffered at the "hand" of his own psyche. However, he lived, and for the next seven years resisted the voluptuousness that was overtaking his body. He barked and bellowed. He enlisted every form of manly virtue. And still the voluptuousness was getting its way with him—especially in the mornings while he was still in bed.

The imaginary god within Schreber was ingenious—each invention he devised to transform Daniel Paul into a woman brought a new form of torment. The compression-of-the-chest device crushed Daniel's ribs and squeezed the air from every cavity of his body. The "abominable" head-compressing machine operated from within Schreber's skull by the god's little devils, who methodically pulled his skull apart, sawed it into pieces, and occasionally squeezed it into an elongated pear shape. Another of the god's specialties was his "coccyx miracle" machine, which created excruciating pains in Daniel Paul's lower vertebrae. The pains would prevent him from sitting up or lying down or standing up or walking. When, for example, Schreber was walking about, the god's rays penetrated his body and forced him to lie down. Ah, but the moment he was lying down, the rays would attack his vertebrae and force him to stand up. And so it went.

This bodily conversion to femaleness seemed so real to Schreber that he could feel his male organs retracting and softening. And every day *somehow* a few more hairs from his beard and mustache would disappear. He could feel his vertebrae, thigh muscles, and bones contracting. He was sure his stature was shrinking to female size. Then the voluptuousness overtook his bosom, shoulders, and neck. At last, Schreber's mind achieved its final victory. He finally realized what the god wanted—to enter him and bless him with motherhood. He *would* succumb completely to the voluptuousness that was invading his body.

Daniel Paul imagined that his internal organs had somehow been converted into female reproductive organs. At this, as if by magic, Daniel Paul Schreber was suddenly relieved of his torments. As he would later recount in his *Memoirs*, "It was *common sense* that nothing was left but to reconcile myself to the thought of being transformed into a woman. [From then on] I wholeheartedly inscribed the cultivation of femininity on my banner." Once he had succumbed to the voluptuousness of his womanly inclinations, he believed that the rays of god would soon penetrate and fertilize him.

By the time Schreber was capable of composing his *Memoirs of My Nervous Illness* in 1900, he was convinced that his wishes to be impregnated by god would soon come true. He was certain he had a womb and on two occasions he even felt the quickening of an embryo. "By a divine miracle, God's nerves, corresponding to male seed, had been thrown into my body; in other words," he explained, "fertilization had occurred." It was only a matter of time before Judge Schreber would bless the world with god's child.

In *Memoirs*, Daniel Paul exposed the paternal inspirations of his mental torments. Inscribed on the pages of *Memoirs* were all the virtues recommended in *The Book of Health*, as well as descriptions of the mechanical devices that controlled the body and prevented rebellion. *Memoirs* is Judge Schreber's memorial to his dead father, a record of the anguished experience of a son whose soul was crippled by the inflictions of his father's severe and uncompromising ideals of virtue. It is also a fantasy intepretation of his treatment at Sonnenstein. The tormenting therapies he was subjected to for seven years were transformed by the judge's tormented mind into bizarre replicas of his father's straightening devices. Thus the mechanical restraints devised by his doctors and imposed on Daniel Paul collaborated with his unconscious wish to be reunited with his dead father. *Memoirs* is also an embodiment of Daniel Paul's primitive identifications with the father whose brain injury had made him act like a puppet manipulated by seemingly alien forces. As Judge Schreber also became a helpless puppet controlled by seemingly alien presences, the spirit of the father gained entrance into the son, as though the dead father became the living son's puppeteer. This fatherly inner presence was not the loving, protective, and noble savior of children's souls Dr. Schreber had tried to be, but a savage god who demanded nothing less than absolute submission.

• • •

With the psychosis, there had been only humiliation, torment, and terror. With the perversion, Judge Schreber found his way to filial love. What had been, for so many years, *unheimlich* and alien to his soul was transformed into something *heimlich,* something familiar and friendly. How did Judge Schreber, whose father's ideals of virility ruled his family, get permission from his conscience to become a woman succumbing? To gain permission to substitute the pleasures and exaltations of a perversion for the torments of psychosis, Schreber had first to convince his conscience, the almighty god-father within him, the very father that he had both feared and adored as a child, that he was living up to his moral responsibilities. Judge Schreber figured out that his most sacred duty was to satisfy the god's need for constant sexual enjoyment. If he could satisfy him in this way, he could rest assured that the god would never abandon him, that the god would never again attempt to mutilate his body with torturous devices.

As a child, Daniel Paul Schreber had intuited in the hot vehemence of his father's warfare against femininity the father's desperate need to prove his masculinity. As a transvestite-transsexual, Judge Schreber was submitting to the almighty one just as a woman would and thereby granting to his father the indubitable virility he had so desperately sought. With Daniel Paul playing the role of woman succumbing, the father was confirmed as the dominating male. Judge Schreber loved his father and knew (at least unconsciously) what he secretly desired. By "becoming" a woman, the judge seduced the alien presence within him into becoming something familiar.

In 1902, after having completed the writing of his *Memoirs,* Judge Schreber was rational enough to convince the Royal State Superior Court of Dresden that he was capable of taking care of his own interests and managing his own affairs. He contested a judicial order of 1900 placing him under permanent medical supervision (tutelage). In addition to formulating the legal grounds for his case, he several times appeared personally before the court to plead for himself. Though the judges agreed that Daniel Paul Schreber was still delusional and even cited *Memoirs of My Nervous Illness* as proof of his lingering illness, they were impressed with his thoughtfully reasoned arguments and intellectual acumen. On December 20, 1902, the order of tutelage was rescinded and Daniel Paul Schreber was released from Sonnenstein on his own cognizance. In 1903, to the consternation of his family and his doctors at *Nervenklinik* and Sonnenstein, he arranged to have his *Memoirs* published. Four years later, when both his mother and his wife died, he was committed for the third and final time to a mental asylum. Judge Daniel Paul Schreber died in the Leipzig-Dosen mental hospital in 1911.

The psychotic break with reality that is sometimes a response to loss never succeeds entirely. The need to reestablish a dialogue with the lost parent and resume relations with him cannot be relinquished, and the hallucinations and delusions are attempts to restore what has been lost. The world annihilation fantasy of the psychotic, for example, is always countered by a world reconstruction fantasy. Over the ashes and bones of the dead the psychotic always attempts to erect a citadel of renewal and hope. However, once reconstructed and resurrected, the hallucinated presence of the lost person or thing often comes back in bizarre forms—forms that torment and torture and cause the psychotic to howl, tear out his hair, and mutilate his body. If we listen to the delusional voices of the psychotic, we hear the voice of the accusatory, tormenting parent he has internalized. If he turns away from the internalized presence, he is doomed to an unbearable emptiness, an abyss of nothingness, the equivalent of a living death. If he turns toward the presence and resumes their dialogue, he suffers the torments of hell.

A break with reality forestalls the possibility of dialogue with the parent. To come back to reality means enduring a dialogue of unspeakable atrocities. As Judge Schreber explained in *Memoirs,* "God Himself was on my side in His fight against me." By offering a moral compromise, a twisted form of virtue, Schreber's perversion offered him a way out of psychosis.

Of course, the death of a parent need not affect a child so traumatically. Dr. Schreber's own childhood traumas, the compensations he enlisted to overcome them, the emotional tenor of his relationships with his children, his personality death from brain injury, and perhaps even his wife's total absorption in his self-esteem and well-being to the detriment of her children's welfare had consequential effects on Daniel Paul. And then, as in any response to loss, there were also those unpredictable life circumstances that might either have evoked the loving and protective aspects of the inner paternal presence or his punishing and condemnatory ones. The psychotic is a person predisposed by a concatenation of nature, nurture, and circumstance to suffer loss by a brief or eternal descent into hell.

In examining Daniel Paul's terrifying solutions to the loss of his father, it is reassuring to think that we are psychologically less vulnerable than he and therefore capable of recovering from the death of a parent in "saner" ways. However, the *full* work of mourning always entails a certain degree of unconscious madness. The stages of the normal process of mourning are not all that different from the stages of torments suffered by Judge Schreber.

We all "annihilate the world of reality," so to speak. We retire for a while into an inner world that seems to have crumbled and been emptied of all pleasure. Then, as we begin to recover from this acute illness of the soul, we gradually regain access to reality. We reconstruct our inner world. We restore our dialogues with the lost parent—who often enough starts out by accusing us of not having been a good-enough child. However, unlike Daniel Paul Schreber, most people's dialogue with their dead parent goes beyond self-accusations and torment. Unlike Schreber's father, the average parent has not been internalized as a malignant, alien presence who demands an absolute perfection of mind and body. The differences between the mourning process of a "sane" person and the delusional melancholia of Judge Schreber are derived from the different identifications established with the parent before he died. If our earlier identifications with the dead parent were founded on humane and flexible versions of desire, reason, aggression, and virtue, eventually the restoration of the lost parent brings peace of mind and the return of a sense of bodily well-being.

CHAPTER SEVEN

A PARENT'S
GRIEF

Grief fills the room up of my absent child,
Lies in his bed, walks up and down with me;
Puts on his pretty looks, repeats his words,
Remembers me of all his gracious parts,
Stuffs out his vacant garments with his form;
Then, have I reason to be fond of grief.

SHAKESPEARE, *King John*, ACT 3, SCENE 4

At the end of the nineteeth century in New York City, scarcely a day passed without an abandoned child being discovered live on a doorstep or dead in a garbage pail. Now, as we are nearing the end of the twentieth century, the Century of the Child, each day brings news of a mother who has wrapped her infant in a plastic bag and dropped her down the trash compactor or a father who has beaten his child to death with a coat hanger.

Evidently, for some parents—not only in the United States, but around the world—there is nothing sacred about their bond with their child. Merely the appearance of a helpless little child or the cries and whimpers of a needy child can evoke rage and violence in a parent. And if a child's neediness poses a threat to such a parent's existence, it seems that the parent can simply sever the bond—lose the child, get rid of the child, destroy the child, often without second thoughts, guilt, or remorse.

However, *most* parents will tell you that the death of a child is the worst calamity they can imagine—and imagine it they do. They imagine it when a child goes into convulsions from a high fever, when a child is an hour late returning from school, when a child is out with a boyfriend who drives his car at eighty miles an hour, or when, for one moment, the parent thinks she might strangle her child if he wakes her one more time, whimpering that he is afraid of the monsters hiding in the shadows.

When you speak to a parent who has actually lost a child, who has actually lived her worst nightmare, you hear the words again: "Nothing worse can ever happen." These are the words of someone who wears the mask of living but will never be fully alive again. And if you probe deeper, you will hear of a grief that is never ending, a grief that is nourished by the parent as she once nourished her child. Grief becomes her child. It is as though grief fills the child's vacant garments, as though grief lies in the child's bed and speaks his conversation.

When a child dies, the parent loses a vital aspect of her own self. The flesh-and-blood child, his tangible presence in the world, is evidence of the parent's meaning in life. When a child dies, the parent longs for actual conversations with an actual child. Unlike the child who, when a parent dies, finds some way to reproduce the parent within her own self, when a child dies, the *palpable* presence of grief is all that is left for the parent. A child can no longer talk with her dead father in the morning when she has her breakfast, but she can carry on an internal dialogue with him. The presence that held and protected is gone, but the dead parent's comforting and discomforting presences have been assimiliated into the child's own self. A dead child can only be memorialized in the parent's grief.

How can a child, with his underdeveloped emotional and intellectual resources, recover from grief and find some way to continue the dialogue with his dead parent, whereas the parent of a dead child is vulnerable to suffer a never-ending grief? The reasons for this inequity have to do with the motives that induce a parent to beget a child.

The eternal bond between parent and child means one thing to a child and something quite different to a parent. It is easy to understand why a child, once brought into the world, needs a parent. But what accounts for an adult's desire to have a child? What explains an adult's eagerness to undertake this demanding, time-consuming, frustrating job of parenting?

A child does not choose to be born. Presumably, the child is brought into the world because an adult has chosen to become a parent. But parents become parents for various reasons, not all of them in the best interests of the child. All too often, an adult chooses to engage in the sexual activities that might produce a child without any conscious desire to become a parent. Other times, an adult chooses to become a parent, but the motives for wanting a child are ambiguous. Young men who doubt their manhood sometimes try to prove their virility by choosing to become fathers, but only for the proof—the penetration, the ejaculation, the pregnant belly, the birth, the baby photos they can show off to their pals. Some young women who were deprived of love and protection as children choose to have a baby because only a baby can give them the kind of unquestioning, adoring love they so desperately crave.

Even in the best of circumstances, where both parents have made a conscious and responsible decision to bring a child into the world, the desire to beget a child has little to do with the compassion, empathy, altruism, or selflessness that it requires to raise one. The compelling urge to parent is more about gratifying the parents' need for self-love, self-esteem, and power. At the start, even the best-intentioned parent has some unconscious motives that are not all that different from the young man who needs a child to prove his virility or the young woman who needs a baby to love and parent her.

Every child is a proof of some ideal in the parent. Even after the attachment to the child has been firmly established and the parent is willing to sacrifice her own interests and her own life to insure the safety and life of her child, this altruistic surrender is a transformation of the original narcissism that compelled her to beget a child. The human dialogue that brings a newborn into a human existence includes an exchange of narcissistic gratifications between parent and child.

The parent mirrors the child. The excited pleasure in the mother's eyes outlines the child's body with pride. Her look of joy makes the child feel that he is a grand and valuable creature. The parent's mirroring presence is like an electric charge that induces the child to want to live.

The child also mirrors the parent. A thriving, satisfied and happy child mirrors an image of a good parent. A toothless grin of delight, gurgles of satisfaction, upraised arms inviting a hug, the proper "thank you," the school prizes, the graduation speeches compensate for every moment of sacrifice and every sleepless night.

The parent becomes attached to the child because of the self-enhancement that comes from being able to satisfy, protect, and comfort a needy creature. Each time the infant says yes to the parent's gestures of parenting, the parent feels larger than ordinary life, better about herself. Later on, when the child is older, each time he fulfills a wish or dream of the parent, the parent has a sense that her own value has increased. Conversely, each time a child disappoints a wish or dream of the parent, the parent feels lessened in value. The urge to generate a new life that is a reflection of one's own life stems from a profound desire to extend one's own existence, to be and to become something more and better than one actually is. When a parent loses a child, this mirror of her own value and power is gone forever.

The child receives the image that the parent projects. The child embraces the whole history of needs, desires, longings, and ideals that the parent communicates. Initially, an infant absorbs this vast history within the narrow framework of a primitive mental organization based on physiology—innate predispositions and congenitally acquired dispositions, erratic mood states, and crude, untamed appetites. Therefore, what an infant is capable of receiving from the parent is limited and capricious. If, for example, the infant is overwhelmed by a devouring hunger, he may, for that moment in time, interpret the breast that feeds him as a devouring mouth. The boundaries between self and other, tenuous at best in these earliest stages of life, dissolve entirely in the lust of hunger. But after he is satisfied, the infant restores his mother as a friendly and comforting presence that he can trust. As time goes on, little by little, the framework of the child's mental organization enlarges to encompass more generous and constant images of the parent. Where once there was only appetite and need in the child, conflicts and desires of various kinds will gradually enter into and bear upon what the child is able to receive of the parent's agency and desire. However, from the perspectives of narcissistic exchange, the child is, until adolescence at least, fundamentally a receiver and absorber of the images the parent projects.

The child wants to be what the parent is—he wants access to the parent's powers, and he wants to fulfill within himself the values and ideals that the parent projects. Each parent projects a whole set of personal ideals; the ideal self she saw mirrored in her own mother's eyes, the repudiated self her parents could not tolerate or permit, the parental ideals that she strove to emulate, all the conscious and unconscious ideals of her own parents that were once transmitted to her.

There is a profound difference between the child's narcissism and the parent's narcissism. The child wants to absorb and internalize the parent—he gets to love and admire in the parent what he would want to become. The parent has no such motives. She wants the child to be and to become not only what she *is,* but also what she *wanted to be* and could not become in her own life. The parent loves in the child the tangible presence of her virtues and ideals. Should a child die, the parent loses an aspect of her ideal self, her hopes of a new chance to fulfill her unfulfilled dreams and those of her own parents.

Several other factors help to explain how a child can mobilize certain emotional resources when a parent dies, while the parent who loses a child is susceptible to never-ending grief. For one thing, a child is protected by her inability to comprehend the larger meanings of death. She has no knowledge of the tragic implications of her calamity, nor any foreknowledge of its long-range consequences. For all that she does suffer, the child does not suffer from knowing that her parent's death may cast a shadow over her own adult existence. Moreover, the young child or adolescent who loses a parent is just starting out in life. Beyond her immediate despair, there is hope. The child can fill the empty space of longing and desire by turning to other people. She can forget her pain and sorrow by immersing herself in the pleasures and excitements of everyday life. The child can fantasize about desiring another person, falling in love, perhaps marrying and having children of her own.

Every child—whether or not he is faced with the loss of a parent—finds alternatives to his parents. As soon as a child goes to school or enters the social world outside the family, he begins to acquire other figures to admire and emulate, and eventually the child's dependence on the parent for actual dialogue and self-enhancement comes to an end. Childhood concludes with adolescence, a social and psychological process that enables the child to leave her home and family. As she goes out into the world to create her own home and family, her parents remain with her as an internal presence. Whether or not the child remains in close proximity to them, the dialogue goes on, with the parent existing as a source of authority, a model, an ideal to fulfill or an ideal to reject, an intangible guiding force.

A child is *supposed* to outlive his parents. The death of a child is a reversal of the natural course of events. Unlike childhood, parenthood does not reach a natural conclusion where an internal presence can substitute for an actual presence. For a parent, the child—even when she reaches adulthood and is herself a parent—will always represent to the parent a possibility of fulfillment, a range of hopes, wishes, and dreams. Whereas a parent is destined to be replaced by a loved one from the child's own generation, a child is irreplaceable. The parent's sense of self and self-worth is eternally bound to the actual presence of the living child.

When a child loses a parent, she does not think of her loss as a break in generational continuity. Generativity is merely a tentative wish and a fantasy in the life of a child, but it is a major psychological issue for an adult. A dead child is hard evidence of the parent's failure to generate new life. Quite literally, a portion of the parent's genetic inheritance, which might have been transmitted to another generation, is now lost forever.

In June of 1923, as his grandson lay in a coma, Freud was already speaking of him in the past tense. "He was indeed an enchanting little fellow, and I was aware of never having loved a human being, certainly not a child, so much as him." Heinz was frail and skinny, nothing but eyes, hair, and bones. There was no hope of survival, yet Heinz would occasionally open his eyes and act and talk just like his old charming, clever self, making it hard to believe he was really dying. Freud said, "I find this loss very hard to bear. I don't think I have ever experienced such grief."

Three years later, in a letter of condolence to a colleague, Ludwig Binswanger, who had recently lost his eight-year-old son to tubercular meningitis, Freud does not immediately tell him about his grandson's death from the same illness. Instead he begins by recounting his reactions to the death of his twenty-seven-year-old daughter, Sophie. "That was in 1920, when we were crushed and miserable, after years of war, during which we had steeled ourselves against hearing that we had lost a son or even three sons. We had been resigned to fate in advance." Freud was trying to explain to Binswanger, and to himself, why Sophie's death had not affected him as profoundly as the death of his little grandson.

It was not Freud's previous resignation to fate, however, that had made the death of Sophie bearable. In telling Binswanger about Heinz, Freud said, "To me this child had taken the place of all my children and other grandchildren." The presence of Heinz had consoled Freud and helped him to recover from the death of his favorite daughter. As so often happens when a parent dies, a part of him or her seems to survive in the child who is left behind. The clever, enchanting Heinz embodied those precious aspects of his mother that Freud could not bear to lose. If Heinz were alive, Sophie was not altogether dead.

The full emotional impact of Sophie's death did not register with Freud until Heinz dragged what remained of his mother into the grave with him. In August of 1923, three months after Heinz's death, Freud was aware that he might never recover from this loss. To his colleague, Max Eitingon, he wrote, "I am obsessed by impotent longing for the dear child." He confessed to his cherished friend, Oscar Rie, "He meant the future to me and has taken the future away with him."

There is a fundamental sense in which the loss of a child always represents the loss of the future. The grief experienced by an individual parent corresponds to a tragic grief that is universal.

Throughout human history and in nearly every human society or cultural group, a living child has always signified regeneration and moral renewal. In ancient societies, the child, especially the male child, was the symbol of fertility, and in the guise of Eros or Cupid *he* was a symbol of sexual desire. On the other hand, a dead or unborn child has always signified the degeneration and moral decay of a social order. This has been so even in societies that condoned and practiced infanticide or required the sacrifice of a child to the mighty gods. In ancient Carthage, parents would willingly offer up their own children as a gift to the gods; those who had no children would purchase them from the poor. Abandoned children would be adopted by citizens who mutilated their bodies and trained them in the art of begging. Yet with all this rampant ambivalence toward childhood itself and *some* children personally, parents would show great concern for the welfare of the fortunate child who was selected to go on living. Such a valued child was always viewed as the hope and possibility of generational transmission. For the parents, that chosen child was the future.

As the Greek philosopher Democritus said, "To raise children is an uncertain thing. Success is attained only after a life of battle and disquietude. Their loss is followed by a sorrow which remains above all others." The loss of a child is a disruption in the orderly succession of generations. In Western European tragic drama, from the Greeks to Shakespeare to Ibsen and O'Neill, themes of parental sterility, child sacrifice, infanticide, or child murder and genocide are enlisted to represent degeneracies in the individual moral life, in the society and in the universe. Or, as in the *Endgame* of Samuel Beckett, an existence bereft of the pleasures and responsibilities of generational tasks is represented by degradations in the human dialogue.

Consciously or unconsciously, the idea of generational continuity influences an adult's desire to beget a child. An adult's failure to create and sustain the life of a child is taken as a sign of her own degeneration and decay. From the perspective of generational continuity, sterility, miscarriage, even a voluntary abortion undertaken consciously can have tragic implications. Insofar as they convey a sense of threat and hopelessness with respect to the succession of generations, such losses are no less tragic than the fatalities resulting from illness, accident, medical incompetence, murder, or kidnapping a child.

Thus in the larger context of the inevitable disruption of generational continuity, the death of a child has a universal psychological significance. However, in terms of the more ordinary, everyday life, a parent's narcissistic investment in a child is subject to variations and fluctuations that are more individual and personal.

Each lost child—the dreamed-of child that remained only a dream, the miscarried child, the aborted child, the stillbirth, the lost child of any age—will signify the loss of some vital aspect of the parent and with it the loss of the future. At each stage of a born child's emotional and intellectual development, she reflects back a different facet of her parent's hopes, dreams, and wishes. As the child grows and develops, her changing image and presence will correspond to different aspects of her parent's self-image. And it is the aspect of the parent that the child was reflecting at the time of her death that can have a direct effect on the grieving parent's emotional equilibrium. The stage of life of the child will sometimes indicate which aspect of the parent came to grief when the child died.

For example, the miscarried, aborted, or stillborn child who was still physically attached to the mother's body when the death occurred awakens fantasies in the potential parent of her own bodily decay and degeneration. When it is an infant who dies, there is a tendency for the parent, the mother especially, to interpret her baby's death as a commentary on her caregiving capacities. A healthy, thriving infant is the equivalent of a good mother, a good self. So the bereaved mother imagines that if only she had held the child differently, or fed him healthier foods, or had not left him alone so much, or not been so impatient when he said no, or wanted to do things his own way, the child might have lived. And then she cannot help recalling the hatred she sometimes felt for her baby. Was it her inner violence that killed the baby? If only her heart had not beat so wildly when her baby screamed and raged with frustration, maybe he might have lived.

The death of a young child forces the father to question his manhood. Even these days, in the most gender-enlightened or nontraditional household, the father of a child will measure his own value by his capacity to provide for his family. If his child dies, he thinks, "If only I had been wiser, stronger, and more powerful I could have prevented this disaster. If only I had spent more time at home, paid more attention to the child and had not been a driven workaholic, the child might have lived. If only I had been a real man, able to earn a proper income, I might have provided the child with the substances and goods that cure illnesses and prevent accidents."

The death of a school-age child evokes other fantasies in parents. They blame themselves for having been too strict or too lenient. They should have cautioned him more thoroughly and firmly about lighting matches or speaking to strangers or crossing the street. If the child dies just as she is learning to read and write, the parent may lose his own intellectual ambitions. If it is an adolescent child who dies, the mother and father may interpret the death as a commentary on their moral and ethical laxities. They berate themselves, "knowing" they should have stood by the authority of their beliefs when their son began to take cocaine and cruise the bars searching for erotic fulfillment. These fantasies of how they might have or should have prevented the death of the child are the surface manifestations of the parent's deeper grief. The *core* of every parent's hopes, wishes, and dreams is the fantasy and fixed belief that she has the power to protect the child from accident, illness, and death. A parent measures herself by her capacity to offer this lifelong protection to a child. When the child dies, the parent's fantasies of omnipotence go to the grave with him.

A parent who has lost a child will often continue a dialogue with that child, pouring his juice in the morning, folding his clothes, rearranging his books, pretending to comb his hair as she rakes the autumn leaves away from the grave. This is not the same as a child's internal dialogue with an internal parental presence. For a parent this is a dialogue with grief, but it is nevertheless a dialogue that facilitates certain transformations that bring comfort.

The hopes, the wishes, the dreams, the ideals that the child had once embodied can be resurrected and revived as an aspect of the parent. The urge to parent a child begins in a narcissism that is slowly transformed into compassion, empathy, altruism, and self-sacrifice. For a parent to recreate in herself the possibilities and hopes that her child embodied requires a further transformation of narcissism. If the parent can find a way to reflect back to the world the ideals and hopes her lost child had represented, she may be able to regain some portion of her power to generate life, to nurture it and protect it. The future is not lost.

What, though, are the circumstances that would enable this theoretically possible transformation of narcissism to become an actual possibility for a bereaved parent? How can the death of a child, an event that always signifies a loss of the future and degeneration, become a source of hope and moral regeneration?

In the natural course of events, an adolescent or young adult begins to want to influence the ideals and values of her parents. Some parents are actually willing to listen, giving their children the opportunity to transmit to them a new kind of moral vision.

An adolescent's visions of the future can become a source of moral regeneration for the parents. The situations of narcissistic transformation in this and the next chapter involve parents whose lost children were adolescents and young adults.

When George Gordon's only child, Amy, died at nineteen years old, George felt he no longer had any reason to live. He blanketed himself in a rage and despair that were relieved only by his desire to protect his grieving wife, Sally. After a few years, George and Sally Gordon were actually able to get beyond their grief because Amy had left them a legacy. George and Sally found a way to enrich the world by resurrecting in themselves the hopes and ideals of their lost child. Eight years after Amy's death, George was able to explain this transformation of grief to his brother, Amy's uncle.

Amy's death—I can talk to you about it now without trembling. For a long time, merely saying her name caused my voice to shake. Most of the time, now, I feel proud and relieved that I can tell my friends what happened. Sometimes, though, I am ashamed of myself for not trembling, for being able to speak. At first I didn't dare say the words—not her name, not what happened, especially not how I felt. I couldn't look in the eyes of those who came to the funeral, and when they touched me or spoke words of consolation, I thought my heart would burst. I know how much you loved her too. But I couldn't let you near me. I thought you had no right to tears. She wasn't your child. "How dare you cry?" I thought.

Maybe my own feelings would have been clearer if Sally hadn't taken it so hard. We should have come together and helped each other. But that didn't happen until much later. Sally shut me out of her grief. She nurtured her grief as once she had nurtured Amy. Tears were her only companion. She was a weeping statue. Amy's death summed up our lives. When we were together, Sally and I, we didn't hold each other, we didn't speak. We were two mummies, each of us wrapped up in our personal grief. I never knew exactly what Sally was thinking but I knew she was always thinking of Amy. Sally acted as though Amy was only hers and she was the only one entitled to suffer. Yet she wouldn't speak to me or to you or to her close friends about Amy's death, as though she feared we might catch her grief and weep too.

Sally's selfish grief made me hate her and almost hate Amy too. These feelings of resentment made it harder for me to remember the living Amy, the little girl who had been ours. For a long time, I could only think of Amy in a state of death; the way she died, the way she looked when she was dying, the details of the funeral.

Then, when Sally finally spoke to me, she was cryptic. She kept muttering about the license plate of the limousine that carried Amy's body to the cemetery—Bear II. I would tell her about the muddy ground—the oozing mud sloshing around my shoes, sucking up the coffin, drowning our child's body in the filth. I would mock the minister's pathetic words about the Amy that had nothing to do with my Amy or my grief. When Sally and I began to speak, we spoke only the words that kept us apart. We were no longer mummies, but death and rage and grief were all that we were able to share.

In the past few years almost everyone I know has lost a parent. My parents are still alive. Sally's parents died when Amy was fifteen years old. They were killed in a car accident. Just like Amy. What most people don't realize is that after the first death of someone you love, every death afterward is a reminder of the first. Amy's death kept reminding Sally of her parents' deaths and that made things worse for her. But to me, at least, the order of deaths in Sally's family made some sense. For me, it was the other way around—a cruel trick of fate that my parents were still living and my child was dead.

Amy's death was out of season. My Amy was only nineteen years old when she died. She was just at the beginning of her adult life. She had so many dreams—of being a mother, of one day giving the fuzzy bear that had been her special bear to her own baby, of being a poet or maybe a teacher or a psychologist, of marrying the medical student she had met at college or maybe some other man—maybe a poet. No matter what else she did, or what phases and crazes and crushes she went through, Amy had always found a time and a place for poetry. She must have gotten that from Sally's mother, because neither Sally nor I nor anyone else in our family ever read poetry.

When we got the call from the college dean that Amy was in the hospital, Sally's eyes went blank. I swear I almost stopped breathing. When they said it was a car accident, the shock waves started. It seemed like the shock waves would ripple forever—I thought I would be shaking for the rest of my life. Because of the way Sally's mom and dad had died, I could only think of death. But then I took it all back. I told myself she wasn't dead, that she'd be all right. If I heard the words that Amy might die, I knew that I would die. I didn't want to ask questions. But Sally begged me to ask.

They told me Amy had been badly injured; that the young man who was driving had died instantly. She was in a coma. We got in our car at 10:15 on that moonlit September night and without speaking one word to each other, sped the 250 miles to see our daughter—perhaps for the last time. Perhaps she would wake up, I thought, if only for an instant. I made bargains with God. If only her head had been smashed, then the rest of her beautiful body would be okay and she could still have children. Or maybe her body had been smashed but her wonderful brain with its memories and poetry would survive. I began to pray for small blessings. I prayed that Amy would recognize us and speak to us, that we could hold her in our arms and tell her of our love—before she died.

I realized that I was driving like a maniac. We could have been killed in a car crash too. I think the only thing that kept me steady at the wheel was the thought that Amy needed me, Amy needed me to be okay and take care of her. I sometimes wished that Sally and I had died that night. It's not so crazy, you know—to wish you could die without ever knowing about the worst thing that ever happened to you.

Amy never woke up. It was three days before her life gave out and they unhooked the needles that were feeding her a false life. The doctors said it was a blessing. If Amy had lived she would have been a vegetable. She might have remained alive and plugged into machines for months, maybe years. It was a blessing, they said.

We went back to her dorm. Her roommate had packed up her clothes so that we wouldn't have to look at them. Her books were still on the shelf, her papers on her desk, her bear and her monkey propped up against the pillows on her bed. Our daughter had been writing a poem to her lover, the medicine man who murdered her by smashing her body into a tree. The unfinished poem was on the desk.

After the funeral Sally turned away from me. I wanted to protect *her and I might have felt stronger if she had let me care for her. Maybe that's the only reason that fathers survive the death of a child—they have to be strong to care for the mothers. With no one to protect, I felt like no one at all. I didn't know who to blame, who to hate. God? The dead boy who killed her? The doctors who didn't save her life? Sally was all I had left. I wanted to hold her close and cry along with her. But when she wasn't submerged in tears, she was consumed by rage. It was so unfair. Why had God chosen Amy? Why our Amy, our beautiful, creative, life-loving, generous-hearted Amy? Why not someone else? And then she would look at me—I knew she was thinking, "Why not George?" And in that at least we were together. That was my thought too. "Why not me?"*

And so it went. Sally preserved her sanity by making a museum of Amy's bedroom. She folded her clothes and refolded them. She arranged her closet and rearranged it. She lined up her baby toys first on her bed, then on her linen chest that used to be her toy chest, then in the corner of the bedroom near the window facing out into the street, then on a bookshelf facing into the room, then back on the bed. Amy's room was Sally's sanctuary and no one—except me—was allowed in. But while she allowed me to enter the sacred room, she wouldn't let me into her heart, her thoughts, her memories of Amy. As I would sit in Amy's room looking at her baby things, I remembered how Amy hoarded every toy, every scrap of paper, every broken crayon.

One day—it must have been nearly a year after Amy died—I suddenly understood about the bear. It was the bear, Amy's bear, that saved us from drowning in memories of death. "I understand about Bear II," I said quietly. Sally let me fold her in my arms, while she held Amy's bear in hers. "It was different for me," Sally finally confessed, "because Amy had been my everything." She explained how absorbed she had been in the miracle of her new little baby, twenty years before. "Each day was like waking up to a new love affair, a new Amy." Sally reminded me about Amy's first solid foods, her first words and her first sentence, each small holding-on step, and finally the day she stood up on her own two feet and walked away. She reminded me of that day because when Amy walked away from Sally she toddled right into her big Daddy's arms. Sally recalled the games she played with

Amy, the funny way they talked to each other, a way she had never talked to anyone else and never would again.

Things will never be the same again between Sally and me. What we were together depended so much on Sally being a mother and me being a father to Amy. Sally luxuriated in the passion of Amy's death, the way she had luxuriated in the passion of their love that excluded everyone else. Mothers are that way about personal passion. Or maybe the mothers are there to remind the rest of us of what we are too frightened to feel in ourselves.

You, my wonderful brother, you who Amy trusted and adored, you must understand that I will never be the same. I will never fully recover. I will always wear my mask in public and keep my true life, my life with Amy, private. Even with you, my good listener, and our dearest friend who cared so much for Amy, who I can tell much, I tell only so much. Perhaps, like living a life, living a death comes in small steps. The beginning of my living of Amy's death started with Sally's idea of making Amy's bedroom into a museum. Every time I set foot into that sacred space I would recapture another memory of my baby girl. Only after many months did I realize that Amy could not remain a baby for all eternity. The next step was recognizing everything that Sally had meant about the bear. The bear was not just a baby's toy. Amy had had a life beyond babyhood. The bear had been with Amy since she was two. When she went to nursery school, she took him with her, when she was a teenager he sat propped up on her satin pillows, and then he had gone along with Amy to college, to the place where her life would end. And then there was that other bear, Bear II, the big black car with black windows that carried her to the place where she would be buried in the mud.

It was that raggedy bear that finally gave me back the Amy that had, in fact, lived out an entire life, from beginning to end. Then the memories came, one by one, of Amy's first days at school, her first crush, her love of poetry and the poems she wrote, her sad and frightened eyes when she heard about her grandparents' deaths, the day Sally and I waved good-bye to our little college girl. With these memories I allowed myself back into a life with Sally. I realized that we had collaborated in this business of shutting me out of her grief. I had let her do it and even encouraged her to do it because I couldn't look *in her eyes, or hear the words, or let myself touch her. We both knew that our grief was contagious. If both of us had let go we would have drowned in our tears. I had to remain cold and impervious, so that she could be the one who wailed and shrieked and told the story over and over again. I looked as though I was strong and untouched but I was only playing the part that had been assigned to me. As I allowed Sally to enter my private mourning, she let me into hers. What happened next, as part of this step-by-step reentry into life, was our thought of dedicating an Amy museum to the world. We were almost ready to let Amy live a life in the world as she would have—if only. I started to let her go as I would have—if only. I surrendered my baby to the world.*

Three years after Amy died, Sally and I decided to publish her poetry. She would have been twenty-two and just graduating from college—still every year is marked by how old Amy would have been, where Amy would have been, what she would have been doing. I decided, in fact, to start a small publishing company dedicated to Amy. That was the beginning of my reentry into the land of the living. Sally and I reread Amy's poems, selecting and arranging them for Amy's book, which we entitled Burning Bright. I, who had never written anything except technical reports and postcards, composed a prose introduction that was commensurate with the painful honesty of Amy's poetic vision. Now that Sally and I were holding each other again, I realized that there might be other mothers and fathers whose lost children had been poets, or maybe other mothers and fathers who wanted to write poems or stories about their unborn children, their dead children, and how they lived or didn't live and how they died. It was then, when I started speaking to these other parents of lost children, that I rejoined the human community. Burning Bright was the beginning of Amy's legacy to the world.

You see, if losing a child is losing a piece of your own self, you can still get yourself back, maybe not all of yourself, but just enough to bring back the spirit of your child. Your child cannot live again. Some part of you will never live again. But you can still speak with the spirit of your child that was the spirit of you.

When I began to talk with the parents of those other lost children; when I was helping them find a way to speak for their dead children, I was saving myself. As if for the first time, I realized that the same rain that falls against my window falls on the hills, the flowers, the seas, and on all the living and the dead. I was no longer alone with my private grief. I was no longer an exceptional case, the only father who had ever lost a child. The epigraph to Amy's book tells us:

> the clouds pass
> and the rain does its work
> and all individual beings
> flow into their forms.

CHAPTER EIGHT

✼

WEEPING
MOTHERS

At 7:03 P.M. on December 21, 1988, Pan Am flight 103 exploded. The body of Suse and Peter Lowenstein's twenty-one-year-old son Alexander, a senior at Syracuse University, fell thirty-one thousand feet into a pasture outside Lockerbie, Scotland. Along with Alexander, 257 other passengers and crew members and 11 citizens of Lockerbie were killed. Because of exceptionally high winds that evening, the torn and broken bodies, fragments of the aircraft, and the personal effects of the passengers were cast over an area of 840 square miles.

It was 2:03 P.M. on the east coast of the United States when the plane exploded. Fifteen minutes later, the news was reported on radio and television. Suse Lowenstein was listening to one of her favorite records. Her husband, Peter, was meeting Alexander at Kennedy airport that evening while she stayed at home to prepare her son's favorite dinner—stuffed pork chops with applesauce. Her younger son, Lucas, was finishing up his final exams at Syracuse and would be home in a day or so. By the end of the week, the family would be scuba diving in Hawaii.

At 2:20, one of Alexander's friends called his home in New Jersey. She had been listening to the radio, heard the news, and feared that

Alexander had been on flight 103 with the group of students who were returning from the London-based extension of Syracuse University to join their families for the holidays. But she wasn't sure. After many painful, searching questions, she asked Suse the number of Alexander's flight. When Suse said "103," the young woman had no choice but to report that Alexander's plane had blown up. Half-hoping the phone call was just a cruel joke, Suse shouted into the phone, "Don't you ever play such a nasty trick again!" Suse hung up and immediately reached for the radio dial. All she heard was "last seen in a fireball," and she knew there was no hope. Alexander was dead. Suse doubled over, her head down, both hands clutching her womb.

Three years later, the doubled-over figure of Alexander's mother was frozen in steel, fiberglass, and synthetic stone. Suse Lowenstein, a sculptor, had cast her grief in stone. However, it had taken her nearly two years to reconnect with her initial moment of devastation. The first three stone images she created captured her still trembling in the aftershocks of hate and hopelessness. At that point, Suse could not see beyond her rage. She knew only that she had to save herself from drowning in despair and that as long as she was in her studio working, she was still connected to life and to Alexander. There is a sculpture of Suse in a posture of hesitation and tentative defiance—with her head thrown back, her arms crossed firmly across her chest, her eyes staring straight ahead. Two others, also from this early phase of her grief, are of Suse standing tall, with her her fists clenched as though preparing to destroy all those responsible for the murder of her child.

Within days after the Lockerbie disaster, the Scottish police in cooperation with Scotland Yard and the FBI had established beyond any doubt that a bomb had been planted aboard flight 103. Three years after the bombing, in November 1991, it was further established that the bomb had been planted by two Libyan terrorists, presumably under orders from Colonel Mu'ammar al-Gadhafi, in retaliation for President Reagan's bombing of Tripoli—which was to retaliate for the terrorist bombing of a Berlin discotheque frequented by United States servicemen. The political motive for this Berlin incident, the terrorist act that purportedly set off the chain of retaliations, was alluded to as the "Middle East situation." While the United Nations, the United States, Germany, Lybia, Syria, and Iran were bogged down in juridical priorities and oil, the families of the dead were certain of their priorities. The two Libyan terrorists, Abdel Baset Ali Mohammed al-Magrahi and Al Amin Khalifia Fhimah, were being protected by the Gadhafi government.

The families of the dead could not get their hands on the terrorists, but one suspect was accessible and within the reach of justice—Pan American Airways. They were fairly certain that Pan Am had been negligent in its airport security. If not for the carelessness of Pan Am, the terrorist bomb which had come on board in an unaccompanied piece of luggage would have been discovered. Their loved ones would still be alive.

There had actually been not one but *many* opportunities for the bomb to be found. The luggage containing the bomb had first been boarded on a flight from Malta to Frankfurt. In Frankfurt, the suitcase was transferred to Pan Am flight 103, destination Heathrow, London. At Heathrow, the luggage containing the bomb was transferred to 747 Pan Am 103, destination Kennedy Airport. Furthermore, early in December of 1988, European airports had been put on alert. The American embassies in Europe had warned their employees that sometime during the Christmas holidays an American plane from Frankfurt to New York would very likely be the target of a terrorist attack. And yet despite these crystal clear warnings, Pan Am had not followed the simplest precautionary stipulations of the Federal Aviation Administration. In June of 1992, Pan Am and its security arm, Alert Management Systems, were judged guilty of "willful misconduct." In February of 1993, a federal appeals court in New York upheld the judgment and opened the way for payment of hundreds of millions of dollars in damages to the families.

Then there were the officials of the United States government who, while certainly not responsible for the killings, had behaved with callous indifference toward the civilian families who had lost their loved ones on flight 103. In accordance with standard military procedures, the bodies of the military personnel who had been on Pan Am 103 were returned to their families in metal caskets draped with American flags. Honor guards were assigned to accompany some of these coffins to their local cemeteries, while many others were buried with honor guard salutes at Arlington cemetery.

On the other hand, the grieving parents of the children who had been killed on Pan Am 103 felt that they and the bodies of their loved ones had been "treated like garbage." Of the nineteen civilian bodies that were sent home from Lockerbie to Kennedy on January 3, 1989, seven had to be shipped to other final destinations. The twelve families from the New York metropolitan area were simply telephoned and informed that hearses would pick them up and drive them to Kennedy Airport to fetch their coffins. However, the drivers of the hearses had not been told precisely where to go after arriving at the airport, so after an hour of wandering through a maze of back roads in the outlying areas, the cars finally arrived at their destination—a grim, grayish-white building that announced its business with a sign: QUARANTINE—LIVESTOCK. Neither the State Department nor Pan Am had sent representatives to assist the families who had come to collect the cardboard-wrapped pine coffins containing the remains of their loved ones. Some of the parents would have wanted to hold their children just one more time—even if their bodies were mangled. But the signs on the cardboard wrappers were intimidating: DO NOT OPEN. DO NOT VIEW.

A week or so after Alexander's funeral, Suse and Peter Lowenstein joined with a group of one hundred other families to form an association that would investigate the bombing that had killed their children. This special interest group was called the Victims of Pan-Am 103. One hundred and three days after the explosion and ninety days after they had collected the coffin containing the body of their eldest son, Suse and Peter Lowenstein attended a vigil in Washington, D.C., with more than three hundred families—parents and husbands, wives and grandparents, brothers and sisters and children, each one of whom had lost one or more family members on Pan Am 103. For two years the "Pan-Am 103" group met monthly. They continue to meet bimonthly and also in informal smaller groups.

Largely as a result of the group's publicity campaigns, picketing, and lawsuits, Pan Am is now out of business. The "Pan-Am 103" group also met with State Department officials in an attempt to educate them on the rudiments of ordinary human compassion. The group printed up guidelines on how the State Department should treat civilian victims of terrorist attacks and their families. "Pan-Am 103" is a formidable and persistent organization that continues to pressure the United States government to strengthen and enforce airport security regulations, that continues to pressure the UN Security

Council to keep up its economic sanctions against Libya until the government of Colonel Mu'ammar al-Gadhafi delivers the two terrorists accused of complicity in the bombing of Pan Am 103 for trial. The oil embargo, which the group has also pressured for, has consistently met with a stalemate at the United Nations, as many nations of the UN rely on Libyan oil.

At one of the early monthly meetings, Suse Lowenstein approached Aphrodite Tsairias, a mother who had lost her daughter, Alexia, on Pan Am 103, and asked if she would want to pose for a sculpture commemorating the death of her child. As she was describing her sculpture to Aphrodite, another mother, Shirley Scott, overheard the conversation and asked if she could pose too. Suse Lowenstein might have stopped with three or four figures of herself. She might have kept on duplicating a different aspect of her own grief. But as she became part of a community of other grieving parents, she found her way beyond grief. More certain of her artistic vision, Suse decided on a title for her sculpture, *Dark Elegy*.

Even before Aphrodite and Shirley came to her studio to pose, Suse had already cast two more figures of herself. One figure was crouched over, with both hands clasped over her womb, her head bowed in despair. The other figure was kneeling, leaning forward with both arms outstretched, her strong hands reaching out, her eyes engaging the downcast, weeping eyes of the crouching, helpless Suse. "The first one, the crouching mother, is the me who saw no reason to live and wanted to join my son on the fields of Lockerbie. The other figure, the one that is reaching out, is the sculptor, the Suse who picked me up so that I could be faithful to the proud, independent spirit of Alexander."

Alexander had been a "golden boy"—with blond hair just like his German mother, and a dreamer and idealist like her, too. He was a life-engaging boy whom everybody admired and some adored. While Lucas, the Lowensteins' younger son, also identifies with Suse's adventurous spirit, he tends to be intellectual and practical minded like his Jewish father, Peter. And like his dead brother and both his parents, Lucas is warm, generous, and open-minded. Peter Lowenstein, a lawyer and businessman, is no stranger to trauma. A child survivor of the Holocaust, he and his mother managed to escape from their concentration camp and were somehow miraculously reunited with his father, who had escaped from the camp where he was being held. But

Peter's grandparents, aunts, and uncles perished in the fires of various extermination camps. When Peter was six years old, he came with his parents to New York City, where many years later he met the artistic and adventurous German woman who would become his wife.

Alexander Lowenstein had many characteristics that endeared him to friends, teachers, and neighbors—his captivating good looks, his easygoing, unpretentious charm, his ways of listening compassionately to those who were in need, his nonconformist intellectual style. For Suse, the most outstanding virtue of her son was his heartfelt commitment to independence—his own and everyone else's. When he was a high school senior and visiting colleges, he was immediately sold on Syracuse because of its democratic atmosphere. The antiapartheid demonstration that filled the wide lawns of the college the weekend he visited brought tears to his eyes. He wanted to move right into the shabby wooden tin-roofed shacks that the black students had built and occupied. He wanted to pick up a flag and march with them through the streets of the college town.

Alexander's love of independence was sometimes a great worry to his family, especially when he would go out on his surfboard at four and five o'clock in the morning and not return from the Montauk beaches until long after the sun had set. He was impatient with his cautious parents and on more than one occasion proclaimed, "I need my independence!" And since he never did anything to harm anyone or himself, there was little Suse or Peter could say when he asserted his wish for it.

In late November of 1988, when Alexander was three months into his semester in London, Suse was overcome by an inexplicable urge to visit him. Peter told Suse he thought the idea was foolish. "Why go now, when Alexander will soon be home for Christmas?" Suse, who ordinarily tries to accommodate her husband's more sensible approach to family matters, did not relent on this occasion. She knew she must go. And she did.

Three weeks before Alexander's plane exploded, he and his mother spent a glorious week together, sharing their love of art, talking about old memories, and visiting Germany, where Alexander met Suse's relatives for the first time. During that week, Alexander told his mother he had, at last, discovered his calling and he assured her it had very little to do with surfing. Alexander explained that he would not become a businessman like his father. Nor would he be an artist like his mother. He had realized that he had a knack for helping people. He had begun to recognize that children of all ages, his friends, and even many adults seemed to trust him with their worries. Alexander was going to become a psychologist and perhaps would begin by working with young children.

Now that Alexander is gone, Suse looks back at her runaway week in Europe and wonders what prompted her to do it. As the child of a Hamburg school principal, she had disappointed herself and her family by being a mediocre academic student. Suse's parents were neither sympathetic nor supportive of artistic temperaments, especially not in a girl. Though Suse refused to conform to her parent's image of a good girl, she completed her elementary school education before asserting her artistic ambitions. Instead of taking a job as a floral arranger, which was her father's suggestion as a compromise between duty and art, Suse enrolled in art school. Four years later, after completing her studies in fine arts, Suse also completed her rebellion. Instead of returning to Hamburg after visiting her parents' new home in South America, she exchanged the return ticket her father had given her and ran away to New York City, where she later met Peter Lowenstein. Although Peter was a practical, down-to-earth man with a good head for business, he was not exactly the kind of man her Lutheran parents would have chosen for Suse.

Perhaps, Suse wondered, it was her rebellious nature and the courage of her artistic vision that had given Alexander his love of independence. Yet she realized that as he became a young adult, he had given that love of independence back to her. It seemed that all their unpredictable reunions—at the shores of Montauk, on the streets of London, with their visit to her family in Germany, had been about independence.

In Montauk, at the entrance to the beach where Alexander loved to surf, Alexander's surfer friends joined with the mayor of East Hampton township to create a town park called "Lowenstein Court." In Lockerbie, Suse has built a cairn over the spot in the field where his body fell. This memorial of rocks from the field is crowned by a sundial and a cave with shells and sand from Montauk.

The cairn in Lockerbie is for Alexander; but *Dark Elegy* is not only for him but for all the children who were lost, and for the mothers, daughters, grandmothers, and wives who lost loved ones. "When I work," Suse has said, "I think of all the children who were lost. Their photographs hang on the wall at the entrance to my studio. Alexander is there, too, on the other wall. I speak to him every day. I think about him all the time, even when I am thinking about something else. Funny, I think about him more now than I ever did when he was alive. His spirit is somewhere, maybe right here, in this room, right now, listening to us talk about *Dark Elegy*. Alexander wants me to hold up and carry on. Perhaps he is the spirit inside the Other Suse, the one that picks me up every time I am feeling like I can't go on."

Dark Elegy began with six figures of Suse. Soon there were eight figures, six of Suse, one of Aphrodite, one of Shirley. Then there were fifteen. Then twenty. Mothers, mostly, volunteered to be included, then widows came forward to join the mothers. Then grandmothers. The fathers and the husbands and the grandfathers, however, did not come. "They know they're welcome," says Suse, "but it has to do with the difference between men and women. The mothers weep. The men don't feel comfortable showing their grief."

As each of the women recreates her posture of shocked grief, Suse Lowenstein takes several photographs of her. Later, using the photographs as her inspiration, Suse molds a small model in plaster. She then prepares the heavy steel armature that will hold up the larger-than-life-size figures of the mothers. Near the center of each armature, in the space that will become the heart of the mother, Suse places a treasured memento of the lost loved one—a poem, a necklace, an earring, a shoelace, a photograph. After the armature is ready, Suse encloses the steel foundation with transparent chicken wire that she forms into the essential shape of the posture assumed by the women. Fiberglass strips, which are cured in a liquid synthetic stone that can withstand the elements, are dyed in the primal earth colors of terra cotta, burnt sienna, umber, yellow ochre, and bronze ochre. The sculpture takes on its final shape gradually as Suse Lowenstein molds the fiberglass strips around the chicken wire frame, forming them into muscle, shoulder, thigh, belly, breasts, hair, eyes, nose, ears, cheeks, and mouth.

When it is complete, *Dark Elegy* will include 125 figures. The earth-colored stone mothers, wives, and grandmothers—with their mouths open, screaming, eyes weeping, fists raised in anger and despair, fingers covering the mouth, hands clutching the head, arms reaching to heaven, bodies kneeling in prayer, crouching in terror, and stretched out in longing—are naked in their grief.

From 1969 until 1976, the citizens of Argentina were caught in the cross fire between Maria Estela (Isabelita) Martinez de Perón's right-wing terrorist Peronists, for whom torture and execution were a daily routine, and the left-wing terrorist guerrillas of the People's Revolutionary Army, who rioted and bombed and slaughtered. These seven years of terrorism and counterterrorism primarily involving "military" men and "military" targets were a prelude to the "Dirty War," a violent reign of terror that would be waged against the civilian men, women, and children of Argentina.

In March of 1976, shortly after the exile of Isabelita, the military junta led by Jorge Rafael Videla instituted the *Proceso,* the Process of National Reorganization, which promised to restore law and order to Argentina. The primary functions of the *Proceso* were to destroy the leftist guerrilla movement and to ensure that the menace was permanently eradicated, to wipe out every trace of left-wing thought. The *Proceso* was empowered to abolish all previously existing civil and human rights in order to achieve their goals without opposition. The day after Videla came to power, every judge who was not committed to the *Proceso* was deposed. From then on, only Videla's hand-picked judges were allowed to preside over an Argentinian courtroom. Any lawyer who dared to defend the rights of a person arrested for leftist "propensities" could expect that he or she would soon be arrested for exhibiting left-wing sympathies. The guiding principle of the *Proceso,* as stated by the governor of the province of Buenos Aires, was "First we will kill the subversives and then their collaborators; then their sympathizers; then those who are indifferent to us, and finally those who show any fear."

After the Dirty War was over, what everyone had suspected was confirmed. The *Proceso* was responsible for the imprisonment, torture, and murder of thousands of young men and women, pregnant women, infants, and young children. Babies born to mothers in captivity were killed or sold or adopted by military families. But during the reign of terror, very little was known about the fate of the children.

They had simply vanished. There were rumors that the children were being tortured, but since there was no proof of death, their parents could not mourn. On the other hand, to keep believing in the existence of a child who had vanished meant that the parents would be haunted by images of the child's helplessness and by fantasies of the tortures the child was experiencing. In some families, the psychological torment of arrested mourning produced psychosomatic illnesses, a disintegration of relationships with other family members, and a profound sense of alienation from the human community.

Since the parents and grandparents of the missing children did not know where they had been taken or what was happening to them, or whether, in fact, they were still alive, they began to refer to their lost children as the "*desaparecidos*"—those who have disappeared. People began to say, "He is a disappeared" or "She was disappeared," or "My disappeared grandchild." Videla's torturers would tell their captives, "Since we disappeared you, you're nothing."

By 1980, approximately twenty to thirty thousand young men, women, and children had been "disappeared"; that is, they had been grabbed from the streets, from their apartments, from their classrooms, and never seen again. High school students who had signed petitions for better classrooms, union leaders who had organized strikes and the union members who had participated in them, intellectuals who questioned the state's actions, entire families whose names were found in the address book of someone suspected of subversion were "disappeared." Children were tortured in front of parents suspected of subversion. Grandparents and parents were tortured in front of children suspected of subversion. And after the torture was over, those who had been tortured were generally disappeared. A few were released as examples of what would happen to anyone who dared to oppose the *Proceso*. The terror nearly succeeded in suppressing and rooting out all opposition of any kind. But there was one force the *Proceso* had overlooked.

The military government had underestimated the power of the bond between parents and children. On April 13, 1977, a year after the disappearances began, a group of fourteen women gathered at the Plaza de Mayo in Buenos Aires. They were mothers who had previously tried every "legal" means to locate their missing children. The mothers were hoping that if they presented themselves as a united group and stood in a place that was visible to the offices of justice, the government would pay attention to their plight.

It was a Saturday, a convenient day for the mothers, free of their jobs and household tasks, but also a day when the government offices were closed. Not yet organized in their purpose, the mothers merely walked into the plaza and stood silently in the shadow of the white obelisk monument, erected to celebrate the beginnings of the first Argentine Republic on May 25, 1810. Since they looked like an ordinary group of women out for a stroll on the Plaza de Mayo, nobody paid any attention to them. The mothers soon realized that they would never accomplish their purpose unless they met on a business day.

It was illegal to demonstrate, especially in the Plaza de Mayo, where a gathering of protestors was considered a public affront to the authority of the state. Still unsure of the extent of their courage, the mothers chose Friday at 5:00 P.M. for their next meeting, "forgetting" that most of the government officials would have already left for their weekend holidays. Of course, no one was there to notice them, but they persisted in their Friday vigils, and finally on the fourth Friday, police vans arrived, the officers took names and ordered the women to leave.

Once they had been noticed, the mothers sought more attention. Their courage was growing. They decided to meet the following week on Thursday at 3:30, when more people would be passing by. After a few months, as the police gradually realized that the women were mothers of disappeared children, they gave the group a name—*Las Madres de la Plaza* (the Mothers of the Plaza)—the very name the mothers had secretly chosen for themselves. It was not until mid-September that *Las Madres* found an emblem that demonstrated the full emotional meaning of their purpose and their name.

In the five months between April and September, *Las Madres* had grown from a small group of fourteen to nearly fifty. When the mothers who lived in the La Plata districts south and west of Buenos Aires heard about the Mothers of the Plaza, they wanted to join them, and their chance came when the Catholic community from Buenos Aires planned a march to the Lujon Cathedral to say rosaries for the peace of Argentina. A group of nearly four dozen mothers, from Digue, Haedo, Moreno, Castelar, and all over La Plata, agreed to participate in the religious procession, hoping that the presence of so many mothers of disappeared children would make a dramatic impact on the other marchers. But how would they be noticed, they wondered, if they all came from different directions, if they were simply faces in the crowd? One of the women suggested they wear something white on their heads—a mantilla or a handkerchief. "Or better yet," another woman added, "one of our children's muslin diapers; it looks like a handkerchief, but it will make us feel closer to our kids." Each of the mothers from La Plata had saved at least one of these mementos from her child's babyhood. It was agreed that they would wear the precious white cloths on their heads when they went to Lujon.

The day arrived and the whiteness of the diapers the mothers proudly wore shone in the sun. Of the sea of people that gathered in front of the Lujon Cathedral, the faces of the white-scarved women stood out, their lips moving as they huddled together in a circle saying rosaries for their missing children. The word *desaparecidos* was whispered at first, and then repeated louder, then shouted defiantly. Other women emerged from the crowd to ask for help in finding their own *desaparecidos*. A week after the march, everyone in the town of Lujon was talking about *Las Madres*, the women with "the white handkerchiefs." The *madre* who had organized the women from La Plata was Hebe de Bonafini.

Two years after Videla's reign of terror was over, Hebe de Bonafini recalled how she had been transformed by her two sons: "After so many years, my sons were actually nurturing me, they were teaching me." As they were growing into manhood, Jorge and Raúl de Bonafini, like most adolescents, began to challenge the authority of their parents. They rebelled against everything their mother and father had taken for granted. They expressed dismay with the world they knew and spoke of their dreams and hopes for the rights of all human beings. Their father, Humberto, a factory worker who had asked no more of life than a decent wage that would enable him to support his wife and three children with pride and dignity, had allowed himself only one hope, one dream—and when his sons were able to go to the university, Humberto's dream came true. As for Alejandrita, his youngest child, it was quite enough that she was virtuous, steady minded and good-natured like her mother.

Jorge and Raúl were smart, curious boys who frequently shared what they learned with their father. They would lecture to him about the masquerade democracy of the Peróns and the insidious terrorism of Isabelita, but Humberto at first did not know what they were talking about. Eventually, he began listening to what his sons were saying. He vowed that he would try to read more and think more seriously about politics even though he was usually too tired after a day at the factory to do much more than turn on the official radio and TV stations. He began listening to the empty, conventional words of the government, however, with a questioning mind—something he had never done before. However, in the end, it was not Humberto but Hebe whom the sons recreated in their own image. Hebe realized that a miracle had taken place: "It was like being born all over again, almost as though my sons had brought me into the world."

Before Hebe had been reborn, the universe had extended no further than the walls of her home. Her days and nights were filled with the routines of homemaking and child-rearing. There were no surprises in her life. She was calm and satisfied. Then, when her boys began to speak up for what they believed in, all at once there was drama and excitement in the house. There were arguments and discussions every night. Poor little Alejandrita didn't understand what was going on, what with her brothers shouting strange words and pounding on the table and upsetting her mother and father. The sons brought home books, newspapers, and pamphlets. They sat around thinking and brooding. They questioned everything and would never simply accept something because it was a "given." So the mother began to read, to question and to speak her mind. Without her realizing it, her powerful love for her sons was slowly but certainly being transformed into a new kind of love. What she began to feel for her sons—and they for her—was respect, a strange, tender admiration and mutual pride. As a result of her sons' tutelage, Hebe de Bonafini's clever mind, which had lain dormant for many years, burst into life. Her sons taught her not to fear; they gave her moral vision, they gave her the strength to speak the truth. She comprehended the rightness in their rebellion: "We must have left them a world with some dark regions, some obscure feelings of shame." Once Hebe had been transformed into a mother who let her sons nurture her, she was able to voice the mysteries of parenthood. She truly understood what it meant to be a parent and even what a parent meant to a child. "In our own way, we, their parents, were their history, and they our mirror that reflected our mistakes and virtues."

Jorge graduated and became a physicist who sometimes taught at the university. In the midafternoon of February 8, 1977, a group of secret police drove up in their unlicensed, unmarked cars and forcibly entered the home of Jorge Bonafini. Jorge was at the university when the men arrived, and when he came home and saw his smashed-in door, he knew the men were waiting for him and he knew he was about to be disappeared. But he also knew it was futile to try to escape. A few hours later, when Hebe came by to visit, she saw that Jorge's entire house had been ransacked and looted. She saw the blood and water on the bathroom floor. The terrified neighbors, who had watched from behind their curtained windows, told her how the men had waited for Jorge—some in the house, some in the cars. They told her that Jorge had decided not to run away, that the men had tortured him and then thrown his body into the trunk of one of the cars. Jorge was never seen or heard from again.

A few weeks after Jorge disappeared, one of his friends advised Hebe to get a writ of habeas corpus. Hebe did not know what a habeas corpus was, but soon she found out where and how to obtain one. Carrying this precious document that was the key to her son's life, she began to make the rounds, asking questions about her lost son. She visited police stations, army bases, prisons, and the offices of Interior Minister Albano Harguindeguy.

She had already been to the Ministry of Justice twice before. She knew she would have to stand on line for hours until it was her turn to speak to the female police officer who would smile sweetly and lie to all the mothers who were seeking information about their lost children. The cop would promise to intercede personally. "Oh, poor thing," she'd coo. "Your story is special. Just give me your name and your address and I will try to do everything possible." Hebe wanted to believe the officer's promise, but she knew better. The pretty cop with the honeyed voice would write down every word and turn over the information to the secret police. Hebe looked around at the other women; everyone was suspicious, yet everyone was desperate. *Everyone* had a special case and everyone knew the officer's promise was a lie. Hebe began recognizing the same women she had seen week after week.

One evening, on her way home to Digue in La Plata, one of the women she had seen at the army base and in the corridors of the Ministry of Justice spoke to her. The gray-haired woman with sunken eyes told her that she was looking for her twenty-four-year-old daughter. She had been looking for five months, ever since the men had come to take her away. Her daughter was pregnant. This thought was so inconceivable, so grotesque, so impossible for Hebe to comprehend. She realized the situation was far worse, far more sinister than she had allowed herself to believe. "There are more of us," the woman said. "We are meeting. We are starting to work." A group of mothers was working to get interviews with influential people. They were going to meet the following Friday at the Plaza de Mayo to sign a petition.

Hebe had been nervous about meeting publicly in the Plaza de Mayo, but by the time she left the plaza that afternoon she shared a feeling of solidarity with the twenty other mothers present. The leader of the group, Azucena, explained about the letter they had written asking Videla to tell them what had happened to their children. Hebe signed in a large, firm signature that informed Videla she was not ashamed of her son's name. She was now one of the Mothers of the Plaza.

Hebe's trips to Buenos Aires from Digue took four hours. She had to wake up at 6:00 A.M. to prepare that evening's dinner. She would wax the floors at midnight when she returned after another frustrating day at the ministry. Humberto, who had just been promoted in his job and had many people working under him, left the search for Jorge up to Hebe. Like many other husbands of a *Madre,* Humberto had to learn how to take care of things at home. Humberto had to be a mother to Alejandrita and to watch over Raúl as a mother would. Hebe realized she was "being more of a mother for the child that wasn't there than for the ones still with me."

Each week more women met, and not just mothers, but grandmothers, wives, sisters, daughters, even women whose entire families were still safe at home took the risk of supporting the cause of *Las Madres.* Six months after their first tentative gathering in April, and two weeks after the march to the Lujon Cathedral, the Mothers of the Plaza felt unstoppable. An army of mothers, grandmothers, wives, and sisters gathered every Thursday at 3:30 at the Plaza de Mayo, in the heart of the city's European quarter, the Calle Florida, with its swanky shops, wine bars, and *confiterías.* The women walked in a silent circle, sixty yards wide. The names of their children and grandchildren and the dates of their disappearances were embroidered on the backs of the white kerchiefs that had been adopted as the symbol for peace and mother-child unity. Hanging from their necks and across their chests were photographs of the lost young men and women, little children, and babies.

Las Madres now numbered in the hundreds, so they dared to demand information on the whereabouts of the disappeared. Videla had just returned from a visit to the United States where he promised that "nobody who tells the truth will suffer reprisals." On October 5, 1977, the Mothers placed an advertisement in the popular daily newspaper, *La Prensa,* and under the headline WE ASK ONLY FOR THE TRUTH was a list of the names of 237 *desaparecidos,* followed by each mother's signature. Ten days later, several hundred women gathered in the plaza, while 150 more delivered a petition with 24,000 signatures to the Congress offices in the Casa Rosada, the pink palace at the far end of the plaza. The petition demanded that the disappeared reappear alive: "They took them away alive, we want them back alive." Two hundred people were arrested, not only many of the mothers who had delivered the petitions, but also Argentine and foreign journalists working for CBS, NBC, UPI, and *The Wall Street Journal.*

Las Madres had become a visible force. And then the reprisals began. The mothers had sustained their courage by believing that even a government that tortured and murdered would not attempt to smash an organization of mothers whose only demand was information about their children. In December, the leader of *Las Madres,* Mrs. Azucena De Vicenti, was captured along with nine other mothers and two French nuns. They were never heard from again. The women had been turned in by a young man, Gustavo Niño, alias Captain Alfredo Astiz of the secret police, who under the pretext of searching for his disappeared brother had volunteered to help the *Madres* with their cause. At first this devastating incident threatened to destroy the group. The week before Azucena was captured, three hundred women marched bravely through the plaza. The week after, only forty women showed up. It looked as though the mothers had been defeated.

Each day more children and grandchildren disappeared. In April of

1978, Jorge's wife Elena was arrested while having tea at the home of a friend. She disappeared. A few months later, while Raúl was attending a meeting of trade unionists, several carloads of armed men surrounded the meeting hall. Everyone who attended that meeting disappeared.

Despite the threat of torture and death, *Las Madres* managed to defy Videla throughout 1978. Led by Hebe de Bonafini, a small group of women continued to gather every Thursday at 3:30 and walk silently around the obelisk in the center of the Plaza de Mayo.

And then the reprisals became deadly earnest. No one was spared. The women were gassed and beaten with police riot batons. Many were arrested. Some were disappeared. By February of 1979 the women were reduced to gathering on the side streets around the plaza. Soon the extreme violence of the police made even such timid gestures of opposition impossible, and the women took to meeting in churches where they could count on the priests not to talk. They would pretend to pray, sitting with their heads bowed low. Hebe de Bonafini worried that the crouched position of the women would give Videla's men the impression that the *Madres* had weakened. They were crouching, yes, but like a tiger waiting to pounce at the right moment. *Las Madres* would not let Videla triumph—*nunca más,* never again.

In May of 1979, Hebe de Bonafini was appointed as the first president of *Las Madres de la Plaza.* Three months later, *Las Madres* announced that they were an officially registered organization. They opened a bank account in the name of the organization and gave money to help care for the children whose parents had been disappeared. In the last days of 1979, the worst year of reprisals, Hebe de Bonafini decided to lead the mothers back to the Plaza de Mayo on the first Thursday of the New Year. Las Madres vowed never again to yield their space to the military even if threatened with death.

On January 3, 1980, when *Las Madres* suddenly reappeared in the plaza, the police were taken by surprise. The next Thursday, Videla's men were waiting for the "enemy" to appear. Police, soldiers, and plainclothes security men were everywhere, milling around the plaza and standing on the balconies of the Casa Rosada. But strangely, as though they knew the world was watching, the police did not insist that the mothers leave. Videla had imagined that the presence of so many armed men would scare the mothers away. But the mothers persisted. Finally, Videla's men built an enclosure with railings in the middle of the plaza for the mothers to stand. To enter the space, the mothers had to show their white cloths. With this ridiculous gesture of authority, Videla surrendered the Plaza de Mayo to the Mothers.

Videla had miscalculated. He had assumed that absolute terror would bring absolute silence. He had assumed that parents who disagreed with their childrens' radical views would not object if these children were silenced. In fact, his reign of terror succeeded in radicalizing men and women who would never have demonstrated in the streets—not for any issue, not for any type of government reform. He had not counted on the strength and will of mothers who would defend the lives of their children—to the death, if necessary.

In 1981, Videla's regime was overthrown by another military junta, which was replaced by still another junta in 1982. However, the real power remained in the hands of the *Proceso,* who continued to control the legal system, the police, and the army itself. The *Proceso* certainly did not expect the Mothers of the Plaza to be among the fearless warriors who inspired the middle-class rallies that would sweep Raúl Alfonsín's radical party into power.

On October 29, 1983 the state of siege ended. When President Raúl Alfonsín took office in December, he set up a national commission to investigate the fate of those who had disappeared. Stories were told by those who had survived their tortures. The identities of 8,960 of the disappeared were established. The unmarked graves were opened, and some of the bones were identified and named.

Alfonsín knew that with the exception of the Netherlands and the Scandinavian nations, every one of the "civilized" world powers had either turned their backs on the disappearances or actively condoned them. He was well aware that President Ronald Reagan regarded his democratic government with suspicion. He knew that if his party, the so-called Radical Party, was to survive, he must not linger over the memories of the junta. A few of the high government officials who condoned the disappearances were imprisoned. And while he did not accede to the junta's demand for a general amnesty, Alfonsín sought a form of justice that could be administered quickly and efficiently. He put a statute of limitations on the trials and granted amnesty to those who had merely followed orders.

Consequently, most of the terrorists, the men who had driven around in unlicensed cars scooping children off the streets, the men who had tortured the children and disposed of their broken bodies in mass graves or dumped them from military transport planes into the Rio Plata, were neither brought to trial nor punished for their crimes against humanity. And although Alfonsín's investigations had revealed the fates of thousands of the disappeared children and grandchildren, the whereabouts of approximately two hundred kidnapped babies, the children of parents who had disappeared, were still unknown. It was common knowledge that many of these babies had been adopted by the families of the military men who had tortured and murdered their mothers and fathers. The Grandmothers of the Plaza, a special group that branched off from *Las Madres* during Videla's reign of terror, continued to search for their missing grandchildren.

The siege was over. But the criminals were still at large. The Mothers of the Plaza were among the forces that had brought the Alfonsín government to power. Now that the terror was over, *Las Madres* would continue their Thursday vigil in the Plaza de Mayo until every torturer was brought to justice, including those who had merely followed orders. No government would be permitted to censor the memory of what had happened to their children and grandchildren. All children would learn what had happened to the disappeared, so that no child would ever disappear that way again.

Alfonsín's cautious amnesty policies did not succeed in appeasing the military. In 1988, Alfonsín's democratic government, which had lasted much longer than any other civilian government in the past forty years of Argentinian history, was overthrown by the military-backed Peronist government, headed by Carlos Saul Menem. President Menem wasted little time trying to undo many of Alfonsín's democratic reforms and soon began to institute his own disappearances. In 1990, human rights workers, journalists, judges, and in short, many critics of Menem's regime had become targets of death threats. In January of 1991, Hebe de Bonafini drafted and published a strongly worded attack on President Menem's decision to pardon members of the former military government for the crimes they had committed during the Dirty War. In retaliation, President Menem denounced Bonafini and other members of the *Las Madres* organization as "traitors to the motherland."

These traitors to the motherland are the weeping mothers who dared to counter a culture of terror with a mother's outspoken language of grief. In a nation under a siege of terror, only a few had dared to speak out, among them the Permanent Assembly for Human Rights, the Service of Peace and Justice, and the Mothers. The nation had been paralyzed with fear. Two million had fled the country. The solution for the remaining Argentinians was to retreat to private life and not do anything that might call attention to their children. The frightened citizens had to find a way to rationalize their failure to speak out against the juntas. *Las Madres* became the mark of the nation's shame. They were called "*Las Locas de la Plaza.*" Some said that the children of *Las Madres* must have been subversives; that they must done *something* to have been disappeared. A group of feminist psychoanalysts from Buenos Aires, feminists in fact, claimed that the mothers were an embarrassment to the women's movement and an advertisement of a demeaning female stereotype. They said that the use of the *mater dolorosa*, the mourning mother, legitimized the nation's negative patriarchal image.

The weeping mothers became the conscience of a sickened nation that had lost all reason and conscience. A few Argentinian psychoanalysts who worked alongside *Las Madres* discovered that when the reign of terror ended, the so-called Crazy Mothers of the Plaza seemed much saner than the Argentinians who had complied with the rule of silence. Whereas the Mothers maintained their psychological integrity, the parents of disappeared children who were terrorized into silence are now afflicted with numerous psychological disorders. Not only did these parents suffer an endless and unbearable grief, not only did the uncertain fate of their children prevent them from mourning, but to defend themselves against a full realization of what was actually happening to their children they had to deny reality itself. Many still have difficulty distinguishing reality from fantasy. Others suffer from learning disabilities and memory disorders, as well as extreme dissociative reactions, which make them uncertain of who they are. The Mothers, however, despite their catastrophic losses, were able to retain a sense of reality, to reaffirm their identities and to strengthen their emotional connections with their disappeared children.

Nancy Hollander, a historian from the United States, interviewed the Argentinian analysts who worked with *Las Madres* and summarized their conclusions: "This experience [of speaking out for truth] is healing precisely because the individual who has known traumatic loss is no longer cut off from the group. Her loss is no longer individualized, detached from its historical context and from the collective process, but is now part of the political struggle which produced it and can now potentiate its reparation."

Las Madres were first mothers and grandmothers who simply wanted their children back. But soon after they took their personal crusade to the streets, they realized they were fighting for human causes that transcended their personal tragedies. For a parent to recreate in herself the possibilities and hopes that her child embodied requires a special transformation of narcissism. The Mothers found their way out of grief by finding a way to reflect back to the world the ideals that their disappeared children had represented. Many of these women who might have spent their entire lives hiding within the walls of their orderly households were forced out into the world by the tragic fate of their children. They found in themselves the courage, intellectual fervor, and moral vision that would have made their children proud.

By emulating the hopes, wishes, dreams, and ideals of her sons, Hebe de Bonafini welcomed her children back into herself. By fighting for the causes they had believed in, she regained a sense of her power to generate life, to nurture life and to protect it. Jorge and Raúl de Bonafini were among the lost ones who were never heard from again. But their mother vowed that as long as she lived she would continue to honor the memory of her sons by speaking out for the truths they had taught her. "I have had to recapture them with honesty and return to them, if nothing else, a piece of their lives. I feel them present in my banners, in my unending fatigue, in my mind and body, in everything I do. I think that their absence has left me pregnant forever."

CHAPTER NINE

✻

NECROPOLIS

"What a necropolis the human heart is."

—Gustave Flaubert

When Amy Gordon, Alexander Lowenstein, Jorge de Bonafini, and Raúl de Bonafini died, their parents found a way out of grief by transforming their personal mourning into a form of communal sorrow. They scaled the wall of solitude and discovered an extended human community filled with values and ideals that enabled them to feel human again. What otherwise might have remained a closed, personal family matter, an endgame of eternal grief, became instead a source of regeneration.

In earlier centuries, the rites of passage that accompanied the significant transitions of human life—birth, puberty, marriage, and death—imparted to each individual a sense that his or her personal life was embedded in some larger human community. The socially ritualized process of mourning offers consolation to the bereaved by interpreting death as the natural expression of a grand cosmic order that nurtures and holds. In the modern age, the diffuse rhythms of communal mourning have been transposed into the passionate elegies of melancholia.

In today's modern societies, where individuality, self-interest, and self-fulfillment are the reigning ideals, the personal melancholia that has always been an unconscious aspect of mourning is simply *more conscious and emotionally accessible*. However, these same ideals often deprive individuals of a sense of belonging to a larger human community. The privatization of mourning also corresponded to the growing insularity of the nuclear family. The more the family isolated itself from the larger community, the more parents began to value and cherish their children. Thus today, when a child dies his or her parents are even more susceptible to the torments of a never-ending grief.

In the nineteenth century, the emotional bond between parent and child, which had existed since the beginnings of human time, deepened and intensified. The intimacy and passion of the parent-child dialogues, particularly the child's capacity to mirror all that the parent wished to be, was supposed to compensate for the harsh indifference of the world outside the family cocoon. Like the artist, the hero, the virtuoso, the mystic, all those idealized figures who stood apart from society on the basis of their personal uniqueness, the child became another symbol of the spiritual qualities that would enable the individual to withstand and survive the dehumanizing, materialistic values of the machine age.

During the Romantic period, the child represented nature, imagination, innocence; in short, everything that was antimachine. The Victorians sentimentalized childhood, viewing it with nostalgia as the time of "heavenly pastures" and "daisied fields," the "golden gate" of goodness and perfection. They also saw the child as the symbol of escape from the prison house of social existence. Peter Pan, the boy who lived eternally in his never-never land of childhood, was the cult hero of the day.

Upper-class and intellectual women dedicated poems to the child and composed political tracts about the importance of childhood. For a decade or two, under the sway of Rousseau's teachings, these same women freed their infants from their swaddling bands and fired their wet nurses. But the fad of motherly devotion did not survive long. Most upper-class women went on praising the glories of motherhood but did not bother much with motherwork. They returned their infants and young children to wet nurses and nannies and maids. They sent their six-year-old sons off to boarding schools and their pubescent daughters to convents and private girls' schools. When the children were at home, teatime and bedtime were often the only moments of intimate contact they had with their parents.

However, in the typical bourgeois family, there was a conscious and deliberate attempt to develop a bond of intimacy between parent and child. While the father tended to be more impersonal in his defined role as the transmitter of duty and authority, the mother's role was to impart the personal values of tenderness and love. It was the mother who was in charge of the family haven. It was the mother who was responsible for the well-being and happiness of its inhabitants. For the mother, the full-time occupation of rearing her children was a profoundly personal matter that affected her belief in her own self and in the value of life itself.

While the medical care available to middle- and upper-class children had improved considerably by the middle of the nineteenth century, the infant and child mortality rate was still around 50 percent. Typically, the time a woman spent in child rearing was matched by the time spent in child burying and grieving. Even the happiest, most robust household was periodically haunted by the shadow of a dead child and the tears of grieving parents.

How might a nineteenth-century, middle-class mother have responded to the death of a child? Gustave Flaubert's mother, Anne-Justine-Caroline, whose own mother had died in childbirth, eventually lost four of her six children. I have imagined what Madame Flaubert might have thought as she looked back on her long life of bearing children, rearing children, and burying children.

Anne-Justine-Caroline Fleuriot was born September 6, 1793. She married Achille Cleophas Flaubert on February 13, 1813. She died April 6, 1872.

From the late summer of 1870 until the early spring of 1871, during the last months of the Franco-Prussian War (1870–1871), the Flaubert country estate, Croisset, was commandeered by the Prussians. Madame Flaubert and her son took refuge in her Rouen apartment, and until she returned to Croisset, Madame Flaubert was preoccupied with images of soldiers sleeping in her beds, spitting on her floors and ruining her furniture, and horses trampling on the magnificent Croisset gardens, where her son, Gustave, had buried his manuscripts to save them from the invaders. From the middle of February until late April of 1871, Madame Flaubert was cared for by her granddaughter, Caroline Commanville, in her house in Neuville. Then, suddenly, the war was over.

It is July 1871. Gustave's manuscripts have been retrieved from the gardens. Madame Flaubert has returned to Croisset. I have portrayed her absorbed in an inner dialogue as though she were conversing with an old friend who would comprehend her rambling journey through the history of her life. She sits propped up in her bed, awaiting a visit from her granddaughter.

I am waiting for Caroline. I wrote to her last week telling her how much I miss her. I know she has to travel from Neuville, where she lives with her husband, but it's hard for me to wait. I feel so lonely and helpless. Gustave is off in Paris and he'll be gone for at least a few weeks. The maid, Julie, is here. She's been with us since Gustave was three years old. In a few minutes Julie will come upstairs to plump up the pillows, and change my shirt and wash me and feed me some good, hot broth. But it's my granddaughter, Caroline, I want. Doesn't she realize how much I need her? Why isn't she here?

Sometimes I think that Caroline never forgave me for making her marry Commanville. What were we to do? Her mother was dead. Her father was mad. Gustave and I were her only family. We worried about her. She was a romantic girl of seventeen and all dreamy eyed about Johanny, her drawing teacher, and we certainly didn't want her to run off with him. And then there was that nice Dr. Grout, who seemed entranced with Caroline. But he hated medicine and was training to be a psychiatrist; his financial prospects were not too good. Gustave told Caroline that a boring but rich lumber merchant (like Commanville) was worth a hundred exciting but poor artists who were always suffering and eventually went mad. How different that was from his customary lectures to her about "the trap" of respectability. When it came to his niece's marriage Gustave wanted her to be safe, so he supported my plans to marry her off to Commanville.

Caroline has spent eight years with a man who thinks only about buying and selling and accumulating money—and sometimes I think that I know more about managing money than he does. For a few years while she was married, Caroline was passionately in love with

Baron Leroy, a distinguished, intelligent, and artistic man, who appreciated her sensitive intelligence and beauty and flattered her with the attentions that a young girl craves. But she gave him up out of her sense of family duty.

Caroline is the last of my babies. I always think of her as my baby. I sometimes have trouble remembering yesterday or last week but I can still recall, as though it happened this morning, the day that Caroline was born. Ah that terrible day—that day of promise in the midst of my worst nightmare. My granddaughter came into her life a week after my husband died, in the same bed where he took his last breath. Achille Cleophas, my husband for thirty-five years, died twenty-six years ago last January. My daughter, Caroline's mother, died two months later. Before I knew what was happening, God had taken from me the two most precious things in my life, my husband and my daughter.

Baby Caroline's mother—her name was Caroline too, Caroline Eugenie Flaubert Hamard—had come to Rouen to have her child. She wanted to be in a familiar place, near her loved ones. She arrived just as her father's fevers were getting worse. Without thinking of her own condition, she tried to help me to care for her poor, sick father, my brilliant Achille Cleophas, my life and joy, my husband, the famous surgeon. How tender she was, clasping her father's hand, pressing the gentle warmth of her life into his icy body. A pregnant woman should not have been touching the hands of a sick person with gangrene climbing up his leg and into his heart. Her brother, Achille, is a doctor too. It was he who botched the operation on his father's thigh. He should have saved his father, but he killed him. He should have protected his sister, as I should have. We are all to blame. Ah, why did I let her come into the sickroom?

When my granddaughter was born, joy returned to our shrouded house for a brief moment. And then—Oh! Each time I remember, I weep again. Each time I tell the story, it's like it happened today.

All this illness and death and dying happened only two years after Gustave had his first fainting fit. He kept fainting and having his "flashes" and "absences" and almost died ten times from his attacks. After my husband died, I had to take care of Gustave. He was too sick to keep up with his law studies. He had only gone to law school to please his father and said that the law was "the most poisonous invention of all creation." Gustave knew he would have been a terrible lawyer. After he knew he was safe from law school, his attacks grew milder and he began to regard his illness as a blessing that had liberated him to do what he really wanted. Now, he is a great writer, a celebrity wherever he goes.

My other son, Achille, the one who is a doctor—I think he felt guilty about killing his father. After his father died, he succeeded him as the resident director of the Rouen Hospital, the most respected medical position in Normandy. He lost himself in work and became more like his father every day. What little time my son Achille had left over from his patients, he spent with his wife, Julie, and his daughter, Juliette. To this day, I never go to his house unless I am invited, and I never had a great feeling in my heart for my granddaughter, Juliette. Twice, though, I felt a deep compassion for her; when her husband committed suicide and then again a few years later when her three-year-old daughter died of the measles. Caroline, my granddaughter, is my consolation for all that God has taken from me. And of course, so is my Gustave.

Gustave adored his sister, Caroline, "his good little rat." To this day, he tells his friends that she was the only woman who ever made him completely happy. After baby Caroline was born, we three, my beautiful daughter, my poor sick son, and I, tried to be like a new little family. We wept for their father and cared for the baby. Caroline decided to stay on in Rouen with us instead of going back to her own home in Paris. Even with my husband gone, even with the house shrouded in black, every once in a while we could pretend we were a complete family again. I began to believe that it might be possible to live again. I began to believe I would have my children near me forever. I forgot that my daughter had a husband. When Caroline and Gustave and I were together it was as though Emile Hamard had never happened. Oh, why did she marry that fool, a drunkard who didn't have a brain in his head? I can still remember Gustave's words, "She has married mediocrity incarnate."

Within a few weeks after the baby was born, the color seemed to come back to my Caroline's cheeks. We expected that soon she would return to Paris. And then the worst event of my life happened. Caroline got very sick and seven weeks later she was dead. It was as though the first death, Achille's death, hadn't really happened until the second death came. I thought I would die of grief when Achille died, but the world had not lost its value for me. I had looked to my daughter, her belly full of new life, for hope. The child was coming. Caroline embraced so much that I had loved in my husband, so many memories. When she died, she dragged what was left of her father into the grave with her. That is why my granddaughter means so much to me. She is my life; she and Gustave. They are all I have. My daughter's death reminded me that I have spent my entire life in the company of death. Ever since Caroline died, I have been watching out for death— keeping an eye on every movement, listening for every sound.

Three of my children died when they were only babies. When people tell me how lucky I am to have two such marvelous sons, I always wonder if they understand anything at all about how a mother feels about the children she has lost. A mother never forgets her dead babies. Never. Until the day she dies, she remembers how they died and when they died. Each year when their birthdays roll around her heart fills with sadness. As their death-days approach and for a week afterward the mother walks under a dark cloud. Six months of every year I am reminded of death.

Achille, my first child, was for Achille Cleophas. The first son belongs to the father. My second child, a little girl, my very first little Caroline, died when she was twenty months old. She was in that stage when children love to run all over the place. She was saying big words and talking in sentences. She had dark brown eyes just like mine. She was already playing mama with her dolls and draping my scarves around her, pretending to be a big lady. Caroline was mine. I was already dreaming of the day when my Caroline would be old enough for me to teach her to read. From the day that I married Achille, I decided that I would be the one to teach all my children to read. Achille was his father's child, but it was me, his mother, who taught him to read. Even as a child, he was quick to learn. We knew he would be a doctor just like his father and my father.

I could tell from the way that Caroline cooed and imitated sounds and learned new words that she would be as smart as her brother. All my dreams and my hopes were with her. Her death came just like that. No warning, just a cough and a fever and it was over.

For some reason, I'm still not sure why, and I still wonder about it, Caroline's death was much worse for me than the death of little

Emile-Cleophas, who joined his sister in heaven when he was eight months old. Funny what I remember about Emile. I still see his big eyes and his thin little arms and legs that could never grow any fat on them. He seldom smiled, and when he did, his smile was as frail and thin as his body. When he died, I cried for weeks. I kept wondering what I had done wrong. Maybe he died because I kept thinking about Caroline. Every time he looked in my eyes he must have seen the deadness and longing. Maybe that's why he couldn't smile fully. A frail child needs an energetic, determined mother to bring him into life and make him live, and after my little Caroline died, I was dead inside.

My husband Achille didn't seem to understand how important it was for a mother to have a girl. So after Caroline died, I didn't trouble him much with my memories or tears. My insomnia and migraines got worse, but I kept my grief to myself and pretended that our son Achille was all that mattered. But the truth is, I didn't recover from the loss of my second baby, my first little Caroline, until my next daughter was born, until God gave me another girl child some years later.

Poor Gustave, no wonder he was such a dreamy, out-of-this-world boy. He was born only a year after my fourth baby, his brother Jules Alfred, the one that was supposed to take the place of little Emile. After Jules, I certainly didn't want another boy. By then I was desperate to have another Caroline. How could quiet, sad-eyed little Gustave know it wasn't his fault that he wasn't the girl I longed for? I tried to hide my disappointment. But children know, even little newborn babies whose eyes are shut most of the time know. Gustave must have felt left out of my thoughts and feelings right from the beginning. With Jules it was different. Jules was sick like Emile, but he was a fighter and he made so much noise and fuss that I never had a moment to get lost in my grief over Caroline. He yelled and yelled until he got my attention. Poor Gustave just sucked his fingers, twirled his hair, and dreamed about having a mama.

Then when Jules, my sick, naughty, noisy little Jules was two and one half years old, he died too. What I remember about Jules was this boy who fought and fought while he shivered and coughed and vomited bile. Once again I was burying a child. And poor little Gustave, he missed his brother and kept looking around for him and kept asking when it would be his turn to die.

Each time another baby died my mind went back to the death of

Caroline. *As I stood by the little graves, it was always the image of my baby girl that tugged at my heart. It was always the memories of my years on the rue du Petit Salut, my first home, with my dear husband and our first babies, Achille and Caroline, that kept coming back to me as the time of dreams—the time of the lost dreams.*

For those few years, I almost forgot that I am an orphan. My twenty-year-old mother, Camille, died the day after I was born. My father never got over it—they had just married the year before. My father was a doctor so he tried to forget his sorrow by keeping himself busy with his patients. Though he didn't know much about caring for children, he did his best to be both father and mother to me. To this day tears come to my eyes when I remember how he used to tuck me into bed and kiss me good-night. But then, when I was ten years old, my father finally died of loneliness and grief.

From the time I was born I was moved from here to there, from a wet nurse to a gloomy house where I lived with a father who could never quite forgive me for killing his wife, to a boarding school, to the home of my godfather and back again to boarding school until Achille took me in his arms and carried me off to the little house on the rue du Petit Salut. It was my first home, the only home that was truly mine. Even now that I have Croisset with its draped windows overlooking the Seine and the acres of gardens and trees, I still long for my first little house with its tiny windowpanes and the winding outside staircase that led up to our cozy apartment. It was a warm, friendly nest and just right for an orphan girl like me.

Two years after Caroline died, we moved to the gray, cold walls of the Hôtel Dieu, the hospital apartment overlooking the courtyard where the sick and the dying kept going in and the amputated and the dead kept coming out. Every time I looked out the window I was reminded of death. I thought of my mother, my father and my dead Caroline. And then Emile was born and he died, and then Jules. Maybe the move to Hôtel Dieu is what stilled my hopes? Maybe that was why my migraines got worse and I couldn't sleep at night? I kept wondering. Would I ever have another baby girl? And would I ever have another real home?

By the time Jules died, in June of 1822, Achille was a full surgeon and the chief of the hospital at Rouen. He bought a large family plot at Cimetière Monumental and had a grave made ready for Gustave, who was as frail as his brothers had been and born under a bad omen—between the death of Emile and the death of Jules.

After thirteen years of marriage and six years at the Hôtel Dieu, I gave birth to a baby girl. Of course, I named her Caroline. She was sickly just like Emile and Jules. I could barely stand up sometimes with my migraines and lack of sleep. But I was determined that she would live. When Caroline was six months old, Julie, the maid, came to live with us. With Julie there to help me, I was able to muster my strength. Julie also took over the care of Gustave, leaving me free to give all my attention to Caroline. I was there night and day, to hold her and rock her and make sure she lived. This time I would defeat death.

Caroline was always sick with one thing or another and there were a few times when I was sure she would die. But I gave her my soul and coaxed her into life. She learned to read at once and was an obedient child who did everything I asked of her. If it had been up to me, Caroline would have been afraid of everything, afraid to move. With the help of her brother Gustave, she got into plenty of mischief. How my heart would pound as I watched them climbing up the trellis of the hospital walls to peek at their father's surgery. But I knew that a little naughtiness was necessary—even for a girl.

When Gustave was seven years old and began to invite his friends over to the house, he would insist that little Caroline be allowed to join in with their games. I let the children play in the billiard room. The billiard table became a stage; the skulls, bones, and skeletons that Gustave borrowed from the hospital laboratories were the props, and my discarded scarves and dresses became glorious costumes. Little Caroline was the costume designer, prop girl, and audience, while her brother and his friends acted out the murder and mayhem. When Gustave went off to Rouen, I missed the bloodcurdling screams and the naughty words—and so did Caroline.

Caroline and Gustave were a perfect pair. She gave Gustave the adoration I could not give him. He gave her the spirit of fun and mischief that I was unable to give her. Gustave wrote plays for her. She liked to perform and he liked to direct. She made him feel important by following his directions and doing everything he told her to do. He confided his dreams and his writing projects to her. He acted the buffoon for her, and made up jokes, and entertained her with funny faces.

She laughed and asked for more. I gave her an English governess and music lessons with a friend of Chopin. When she outgrew my teachings, Gustave guided her reading and made sure she acquired good study habits. By the time Caroline was seventeen, she was an accomplished pianist and spoke perfect English. She was pretty. She was talented. She was good-natured and affectionate. Gustave and I had done well.

After she became a woman, she had migraine headaches and insomnia—just like me. Her father and I were always worried about her health. So when she went on her honeymoon with Emile Hamard, we went with them. Not one to be left out of a family vacation, Gustave came along too. Hamard did not like us very much and he knew we looked down on him. But he was too much of a weakling to protest the family honeymoon. And Caroline was too good a girl to stand up for herself, especially with Gustave on my side. Before we even got to Genoa, Caroline was feeling sick, even less well than usual. I knew her every gesture, her every thought, and I knew that Hamard had won. She was pregnant. She was his. And he got his proper revenge. After promising to live in Rouen so that Caroline could be near her family, he took her off to an apartment in Paris.

Mothers never like to say it, but I think we all have a favorite child. Caroline, my last child, was the sweetest and most clever of them all. Upstairs, in Gustave's studio, there in the window overlooking the garden, on a pedestal, is the marble bust that Gustave commissioned after she died. You can see how beautiful she was. She was only twenty-one years old and just in the bloom of life when God took her from me. First, the chills came. Then her temperature rose. It was puerperal fever. She could barely raise herself up to nurse her baby, then she'd fall limply back on her pillows.

It took her father two months of agony to die. It took Caroline seven weeks. For me and Gustave, life consisted of waiting for death and watching helplessly. The real nightmare was watching the life go out of my daughter and hearing her screams. Through it all, she kept her baby at her side. I am deaf now but I can still hear my daughter's agony. Whenever Caroline screamed out in pain the baby would wake up and scream along with her. Though her ideas were confused, my daughter's mind was still working. She still remembered me and still remembered to tell me how much she loved me.

The burial was a continuation of the nightmare. My daughter's grave was too narrow for the coffin. The gravediggers had to hack away at the dried earth and they were so rough that the coffin almost turned over. Finally, one of the gravediggers leaped up onto the coffin. He stamped his big filthy boots just above my daughter's head, stamping and stamping until he forced the coffin into the earth. Gustave was shivering. I wondered, as I had since the day he was born, if he would be next to be buried.

Two weeks after my daughter's burial, we baptized the baby and named her Caroline. Once more a child had come into the world and murdered her mother. Once more a father could not forgive the child. Hamard moved into a little cottage down the road so he could be near his daughter. But he was so grief-stricken and bewildered about the death of his wife that he simply handed his child over to me. I would give her a proper home, and I would never let her out of my sight. I had lost my husband and my precious daughter, nearly all the world that really mattered—except for Gustave. But I had my little orphan grandchild, my new little Caroline. She became my hope and salvation.

Julie, the servant who takes care of me now and helped me to care for my daughter and Gustave when they were children, was there to help me with my granddaughter. What would I have done without Julie? Mothering my little orphan, my baby, my new little Caroline saved my mind. For the first months, I could not cry for my daughter. I kept myself so busy that there was no time for tears. And when at last the tears came, my son said I was a weeping statue. Every time I looked at my granddaughter, Caroline, I was reminded of my beloved Achille, my beloved Caroline. At night, after the baby was asleep, and Gustave and I would sit down at the dinner table, I would take one look at the empty places and burst into tears.

My perpetual sadness must have brought Gustave back to his childhood. Even then I was the mother who was never his. As I moved about the house in my black dress draped with a long black shawl, I cast the shadows of sorrow on the walls. I could not speak to Gustave or console him for the loss of his father and his sister. My voice, when the words did come, was flat and monotonous. I was even more alert to danger and death than I had been before. My body was always tense, waiting for a new disaster to strike. If the baby whimpered, if

Gustave mentioned a headache, if a pot dropped in the kitchen, if any sound roused me from my melancholy, I would wail, my voice rising to a shrill peak of panic.

Gustave went to his studio but he could not write. Of course, men have all kinds of ways of recovering from grief. Gustave found relief by reading passages from the poets. He couldn't cry over Caroline's death, but poetry about death brought copious tears. Three months after his beloved sister died, Gustave found another way to triumph over his grief.

He thought his affair with Louise Colet was a secret. She even tried to blackmail him into staying with her by threatening to tell me all. But I saw everything, the constant letters back and forth, which he left lying about on his desk, the lies he told me when he suddenly went off to Rouen and Paris. A few months after they met he wrote to her, "Since my father and sister died, I have had no ambition left. They carried off my vanity in their shrouds and they keep it." Colet did a pretty good job of restoring his vanity. Only she began to act as though she owned him. She became quite the pest.

Whatever happens to a man, whatever calamity may befall him, a man, at least, is free; he can explore the whole range of the passions, go wherever he likes, overcome obstacles, savor the most exotic pleasures. All a woman has is her children. I had my granddaughter. And I had Gustave. Colet drove my son crazy with her constant demands for love, but I knew that Gustave was mine. I knew what he would do with her after his vanity returned—he would use his love for me as an excuse to get away from her. And I was right. He told her, "My mother needs me. She is distressed by my slightest absence. Her sorrow imposes a thousand unimaginable tyrannies upon me . . . I don't know how to say no to someone who implores me with a grief-stricken face and tears in her eyes." He kept telling everyone it would be a cruelty to leave me. But leave me he did; first by taking a walking tour through Brittany with a friend.

He was going to be gone an entire summer. Anything could happen. I was convinced he would die if I did not keep watch over him. I hired a large coach, packed it with everything a six-month-old child might need, and with Caroline in my arms I followed Gustave, meeting up with him and his friend at prearranged stops. In Brest we all clapped hands as Caroline took her first steps.

When we got back to Croisset, Gustave stayed around long enough to protect me from Hamard, who had gone completely mad and was threatening to take back his daughter. Fortunately Hamard's own family had him declared mentally incompetent, so he could not make his claims on my baby. A year later, tragedy struck again. Alfred Le-Poittevin, Gustave's dearest friend, a man he claimed to love more than anyone else (including me or his sister Caroline) died.

Then Gustave went where I could not follow him. Of course, then neither could Colet. He escaped from us and from the messy business of caring for a little child by going off on a two-year trip to Egypt. The doctor convinced me that travel would be good for his health, or I never would have let him go. You understand? I was convinced that my children might die if I could not watch over them. And yet I wanted so much for Gustave to get better and lead a normal life—maybe even marry a proper, normal woman. I gave him 25,000 francs to pay for the trip.

He wrote to me at least once every month, and whenever I didn't have a migraine, I responded right away. As he was nearing the end of his trip, while he was in Constantinople, I wrote to him, asking if he planned to get married when he got back home. He answered immediately, telling me that writers are not fit to be husbands. And then he promised that I would never have a rival and that he would never love anyone as much as he loved me. I read his beautiful words over and over, and can still remember them. "There is no desire or passing infatuation that could replace something which lies hidden in my Holiest of Holies. Some may reach the gates of the temple, but none will ever enter in."

When he returned, Caroline was five years old. The baby nonsense was over and done with. We went off to London, the three of us, to find a governess. The first one did not work out. She was devout but extremely severe. At every opportunity Caroline would flee from her governess and take refuge with Julie in the kitchen. Caroline's free spirit was an affront to the governess's pride. When Caroline did not listen, the governess would slap her face. Gustave and I could not tolerate her maltreatment of our poor child. We dismissed the governess and soon afterward found exactly the right person.

By the time Gustave had returned, I had already taught Caroline to read and write. Now that we finally had a good governess to teach

Caroline English and English manners, Gustave could take over her intellectual development. History was taught in his study, he lying back in an armchair reciting the accounts of the ancient heroes and their conquests while his little niece lay spread out on his bearskin rug taking in every word. It was the way it used to be with his sister—the mastermind and the adoring student. He taught her geography in the garden, by modeling the mountains, islands, bays, and gulfs of the Earth out of the earth of Croisset. He expected Caroline to memorize the lessons and report back the next day. He would correct her until she got things right. Soon my granddaughter knew the entire history of the Greek states, and by the time she was ten Gustave expected more discipline. He insisted that she take notes on his lessons and he would not allow her to drop a book halfway through no matter how much it bored her. He would lecture to me and to Caroline that he would not allow a niece of his to acquire the unsystematic mentality that was, as he put it, "the customary attribute of persons of her sex." He was determined that his niece would have the intellectual qualities of "a true man."

Gustave and I were content. With him to supervise her intellectual qualities and the new governness to teach her manners, she would have the education of a man and the manners of a proper young lady. During those five years when Gustave was writing Bovary and teaching Caroline history and geography, everything was peaceful in our home. Since Caroline was in good hands, I was free to turn all my attention to Gustave. He was safe at home at last and totally occupied with his writing. I could keep an eye on him, feed him the right foods, devote myself entirely to arranging his daily life. Every now and then he would invite me into his studio and read a new Bovary passage to me.

One day after listening to the part where Emma Bovary visits her baby's wet nurse, I remembered that I had read a similar scene in Balzac's Un Médecin du Campagne. I took the Balzac out of the bookcase and showed Gustave how everything was the same; the way the cottage looked, the effects on the mother, everything. He was quite amazed by my discovery and pleased to have his observations confirmed by a writer who cared as much about detail as he did. I was pleased too, and proud that I could do more for my son than just worry about him. I know my Gustave respects me for being a careful, thoughtful reader; he knows that he got his love of books from me.

When I was growing up, books were my only companions. I was a lonely, unhappy child, but the stories I read and the characters I encountered introduced me to a whole marvelous world that existed beyond the gloomy walls of my home and boarding school. After my father died, I had no one at all to care for me or love me, but I dreamed and prayed that someday someone would come along and rescue me. And sure enough, Achille Cleophas came for me. And he was a doctor, just like my father.

The day we were married, I promised myself that when we had children, I would be the one to teach them to read. My first son, Achille, learned to read easily and quickly, but no matter how hard I tried, Gustave couldn't even learn the letters of the alphabet, much less read a word. I began to worry that he might be the family idiot. Then, shortly before his sixth birthday, just like that—as though he had taught himself overnight—he started reading. From then on, he would read all day, and sometimes into the night. And even when he wasn't reading, he carried a book wherever he went. By the time he was nine years old he was writing stories and plays. To celebrate my thirty-eighth birthday, Gustave wrote an entire history of the reign of Louis XIII and dedicated it to me. I could never have been a writer; to be a writer you have to take chances. I was always too frightened of losing myself, of straying from home, of doing anything out of the ordinary. But despite my own fears, I gave Gustave the courage to be and to do what I could not do myself.

During the Bovary years, the household ran on the schedule of Gustave's writing habits. Nobody, not even little Caroline, was permitted to make a sound until 10 A.M. Gustave worked late into the night and he needed his sleep. In the mornings, after Gustave had looked over his mail, he would knock on the wall to summon me. I would dash up the stairs at once and sit quietly by his bed until he was fully awake. Except for our arranged morning signal, if Gustave rang the service bell at any other time during the day or night, my heart would pound with the terror that he was having another attack. I had no life. My life belonged to Gustave.

I did everything I could to make sure he would stay with us. But these days Gustave and I are always arguing about money. Gustave has extravagant tastes. And I, by nature, have always been prudent. During the five years that he was writing Madame Bovary, our money disputes were minor. My son had few visitors and rarely left Croisset, except in the winter months when he preferred a rented apartment in Paris. The serious troubles began after he became a social celebrity. Gustave was earning good sums of money from his writing, and combined with the inheritance from his father, he should have had enough to support himself. But his showy tastes gobbled up every penny. In order to bail Gustave out, I was forced to sell one of the farms my husband left me. Now that I feel my own death approaching, I worry constantly about my Gustave. If he was not able to live on seven thousand francs while spending most of the year here, with me, in Croisset, where he pays nothing, how will he manage later? What will happen to Gustave after I die? Who will watch over him? Will my children take care of each other after I am gone? I will speak to Caroline when she comes. She must promise to be kind to her uncle, to watch over him the way I have, to make sure he is well taken care of.

Two weeks after Anne-Justine-Caroline died, her son Gustave realized "My poor dear old mother was the person I loved the most. It's as if part of my entrails have been torn out." Madame Flaubert left Croisset to her granddaughter, Caroline Commanville, with the stipulation that Gustave should have the use of his studio and bedroom until the day he died. Two years after Madame Flaubert's death, the financial ruin of Ernest Commanville threatened to turn Gustave into a homeless pauper. When the Commanvilles decided that they had to sell Croisset or become paupers themselves, Gustave begged his niece not to throw him out of his studio. Caroline held her husband off as long as possible, and Gustave was allowed to stay at Croisset on a day-to-day basis. A year before his death in 1880, Gustave Flaubert was reduced to accepting a state pension arranged for him by his friends.

Gustave Flaubert died without having children. His childless niece, Caroline, was widowed in 1890. The only surviving grandchild of Achille Flaubert did not have children. Caroline, who inherited her uncle's unpublished letters and manuscripts, as well as his library, furniture, pipes, clothing, and Egyptian artifacts, turned her villa at Antibes into a Flaubert museum. She named it Villa Tanit, after the goddess in her uncle's flamboyant historical novel, *Salammbô*. When she was fifty-four years old, after nearly a decade of devoting herself to her uncle's memory, Caroline married Dr. Franklin Grout, the man who had loved her before she married Commanville and the brother of her best friend, Frankline, wife of Auguste Sabatier. Until Franklin died in 1921, they shared an exciting and creative life at Villa Tanit.

When Caroline died in 1931, the closest descendents of the Fleuriot-Flaubert families would be the children and grandchildren of Frankline née Grout and Auguste Sabatier. Anne-Justine-Caroline Fleuriot-Flaubert is a major character in Lucy Chevalley-Sabatier's account of her "Aunt" Caroline's life. Caroline's recollections reveal that although Madame Flaubert was not the best of all possible mothers, she was not as hopelessly dismal as many of her son's biographers portray her.

Even though Madame Flaubert herself was rigid, grim, tense, stingy, and cautiously conventional, she subtly encouraged a sense of generosity and rebellion in her children. Beneath her distant, glacial manner, she was a profoundly sympathetic and devoted mother. To convey the extent of the attunement between her uncle and her grandmother, Caroline explained, "His mother transmitted to him an emotional susceptibility and feminine tenderness; at the sight of a child, his generous heart would be touched to the core and tears would well up in his eyes."

Madame Flaubert's extreme possessiveness was a burden to all her children but especially to Gustave, who, except for his occasional "escapes," lived under his mother's roof his entire adult life. He is buried in the Cimetière Monumental in the tiny child's grave that his father built for him in 1822, and his small, unassuming tombstone is shouldered up against his mother's imposing monument. He had many love affairs with many women, but his guilty attachment to his mother prevented him from committing himself to any of them. And no matter how brilliant his writing or famous his name, in his heart he would always be a dreamy boy, searching for a mama he could call his own.

Nevertheless, Madame Flaubert actively supported her son's wish to be a writer, and in fact it seems her mournful preoccupations might have served as an unconscious source of inspiration to him. When Gustave was a young child, he could do little to animate his mother. As he grew older, though, he began to notice that his mother enjoyed it when he, Caroline, and his friends acted out rowdy tragedies. By the time he was ten years old, Gustave realized that his mother came to life when he told her about the stories, essays, and plays he was writing. Not so with his father, who promptly fell asleep whenever Gustave tried to interest him in his writings. Though his mysterious "attacks" nearly killed him, they turned out to be the blessing that released him from his obligations to his father. By becoming a writer, Gustave fulfilled the dreams and hopes of his mother, who had transmitted to him her love of the written word.

Inscribed on the pages of *Madame Bovary,* Flaubert's most popular novel, are the sorrows that haunted his mother's life—and his own. *Madame Bovary* describes the death and silencing of the Roualt-Bovary families. When Emma Roualt-Bovary committed suicide and Charles Bovary died a year later, they left a child. The orphan's name was Berthe.

CHAPTER TEN

✳

BERTHE'S
DEAD MOTHER

At 6:00 A.M. on Sunday, September 26, 1841, just as the orange sun rose over the russet plains of Yonville, a baby was born. Charles Bovary, the district's health officer, was the joyous father. "It's a girl!" he shouted for all of Yonville to hear.

Emma, the mother, fainted. A girl was the confirmation of her helplessness. Again she had that awful feeling of being a crippled bird that could never soar above the conditions of her existence. She was, and always would be, the wife of a mediocre country doctor, who could not afford real lace for their baby's caps or the boat-shaped cradle that she had seen in Rouen. A boy would have been her salvation, a revenge for all her deprivations. A boy—she had already named him George—would have fulfilled her own frustrated ambitions. George could have traveled the world, embarked on adventures, climbed mountains, tasted exotic pleasures, discovered the secrets of nature, perhaps become a famous surgeon—a real doctor.

Emma lay as if dead. Félicité, the sixteen-year-old orphan who served as Emma's maid, had wrapped the baby tight as a mummy. She cradled the tiny package in her arms and wondered if God had sent another orphan into the world. The pharmacist's wife, who had the reputation in Yonville of being the best mother in all of Normandy, had rushed across the road to see the new baby. She urged Emma to wake up, to hold her baby, to look at her sweet face. Félicité said nothing. For nearly three years now, she had witnessed her mistress's emotional storms, her mysterious fevers, her heart palpitations, her loss of appetite. Félicité had learned the power of Emma's sufferings, which, when they lived in Tostes, had persisted and gotten worse until poor Dr. Bovary was at his wits' end. The doctor adored his wife and had done everything in his power to soothe away her sorrows. When at last he recognized the futility of his efforts, he gave up his comfortable practice in Tostes and moved to Yonville, a livelier town where he hoped his wife might find happiness. The moment he told her of his decision, Madame's spirits improved. By the time they arrived in Yonville, she was pregnant. Félicité respected her mistress's moods. She knew that Emma would not look at her baby until her fog lifted.

Emma kept her head turned away. She bit her lips. Only by steeling herself from feeling any tenderness could she manage to hold back her tears. She concentrated on her agonies: the soreness of her back, her belly, her vagina, her limbs; she thought about her wretched life, the money she did not have, her cramped house, her peasant of a husband, the George she had lost.

The new baby entered the world in a glow of sunshine. Her father's joyous greeting was his promise of eternal love and protection. But Félicité was right. Emma's despair was an implacable force. In the next four years, the ball of light that had crimsoned the sky on the morning of the baby's birth would be clouded over and slowly eclipsed.

Several days after the baby was born, Emma regained her spirit. She would try to turn defeat into triumph, as she had so many times before. She did not have a boy, but she could, at least, find an inspiring name for the little girl.

First she considered romantic names; Italian ones ending in *a* or perhaps Yseult or Leocadie. She went through the calendar of saints' names. And then, as so often before, Charles did something to make a mockery of her hopes. He suggested the girl be named for his mother. Emma had to press her nails into her palms to keep from screaming.

Charles would never understand her. Nothing would ever change. The bitter tears she had been holding back since the baby was born streamed forth. She was inconsolable. She wept the entire afternoon.

Her tears brought Emma back to 1835 and her last year at the convent. A letter had arrived from her father, explaining that her mother had died. Emma cried for three days. She had consoled herself with thoughts of heavenly harps on a heavenly lake, of virgins rising up to heaven and meandering along paths of roses. Now, as she recalled those days, she thought about the memorial picture framed with her mother's hair and the flowers she had picked for her mother's grave on the first Friday of each month. Her father had almost recovered from the pain of her mother's death, when her brother, who was only twenty-seven, died of cholera. After that her father's sadness never left him. Except on feast days when he would get drunk and dance, all he valued were his meals and his comforts. He brooded about the deaths of his wife and son, worried about paying his debts, and wondered where he might find a husband who wouldn't quibble over Emma's meager dowry.

As she compared the expansive dreams of her childhood with the narrowness of her current existence, Emma wondered if *her* terrible sadness would ever leave. She knew her father had been relieved to be rid of her. She had hoped that the birth of his grandchild would rouse him from his sorrows. But he claimed to be too busy with the final harvesting to attend the christening. Perhaps if the baby had been George? Emma felt like an orphan, alone and forgotten, surrounded by strange, unfriendly faces. She recalled her wish to be buried beside her mother and then wondered if she should memorialize her mother by naming the girl Marie. No! Such a plain name would not do. Besides, the image of the cancer eating away at her mother's breast made Emma shudder. How wise she had been to resist the pharmacist's citations from Rousseau, his accolades to motherhood, his exhortations on the joys of breast-feeding. She could take solace in one thing at least. The baby was in the arms of the best wet nurse in Yonville, Madame Rollet.

A handsome young clerk, Léon Dupuis, who took lodgings with the pharmacist and had spent many a lonely hour in his tiny bedroom imagining Emma's hair unwinding from its tidy knot and spreading out across his pillow, mentioned to the pharmacist that Magdalene would be a perfect name for the Bovary child. When Charles Bovary's mother learned of the young man's suggestion, she was furious. She had had quite enough reminders of depraved women from her philandering husband and her flighty daughter-in-law who read novels by George Sand. She could have put up with Clara, Louisa, Atala. But Magdalene, never.

Ten days after her daughter's birth, Emma finally found the inspiration she had been searching for. It was a Wednesday, the Yonville market day. The festive commotion in the marketplace jogged her mind into a vision of the one extraordinary event of her marriage to Charles. Two years earlier, while they were in Tostes, she and Charles had received an invitation from the Marquis d'Andervilliers to attend a ball at his chateau, Vaubyessard. At Vaubyessard she had waltzed with a viscount, eaten a maraschino ice from a silver-gilt shell and listened to talk of roses in Genoa and the Colosseum in the moonlight. The marquis had called to a lovely young woman whose hairdo was crowned with clusters of pomegranate blossoms, "Berthe."

A few weeks after Berthe's naming ceremony, Emma had the urge to hold her baby in her arms. She set off, down the main road of Yonville toward the countryside, for a visit to the cottage of Madame Rollet, the wet nurse.

Usually, when an infant was boarded out to a wet nurse, she might only see her parents if and when they came by to drop off some fresh clothing or linens. Many children would not see their parents again until they were six months old, maybe a year, maybe two years, maybe older. Seventy percent of the infants who were boarded out did not survive their first year. Foundlings and infants whose parents never visited fared the worst. Even in the best of circumstances, with a trustworthy wet nurse, with parents who visited frequently, an infant had a 40 percent chance of dying in the first year of life. If their parents were shopkeepers or workers, those infants who managed to survive their first year with a wet nurse would become permanent boarders until they were old enough to contribute to the family income.

Berthe was a healthy, sturdy baby, and her wet nurse lived just a mile or so down the road from her parents' house. She could easily be taken home for a visit, and her parents could come to see her whenever they wished.

It was noontime when Emma set out on her little journey. The sun's glare off the slate roofs against the blue sky burst into silvery sparks of light. Even though Emma carried a parasol, the bright light hurt her eyes. The pebbles on the road made it difficult to walk. Within a few minutes she was exhausted. She was considering going back when suddenly Léon Dupuis appeared. He offered Emma his arm. At the end of the street, the handsome young couple turned left onto a narrow path lined with privet. But not before all the ladies of Yonville, including the mayor's wife, had had a chance to peek through their shutters and observe that Madame Bovary was leaning against Monsieur Dupuis.

The privets, the veronica, the dog roses, the nettles were all in bloom. On each side of the road were the hovels of the poor. In the meadow were pigs on manure heaps and cows rubbing their horns on trees. Flies were buzzing about everywhere.

Madame Rollet's hovel could be distinguished from the others by the presence of an old nut tree that cast its benevolent shadow over the tiled roof. Even inside, the Rollet cottage had niceties that placed it a cut above the rest. Monsieur Rollet was a carpenter. The customary bare earthen floor was partially covered with wood planks, and the little cottage had three small windows instead of the usual one. For a bed, most of the neighbors had only a boxlike structure filled with a bale of oats. Monsieur Rollet had built a proper wooden bed. They also had a cotton mattress stuffed with wool. They were too poor to afford a bedcover, but Madame Rollet always managed a few touches of elegance throughout the house. She had patched a broken pane with a blue paper star. She had cut out from a perfume advertisement a painting of the goddess Fame blowing her trumpets and had fixed it to the wall next to the mantelpiece with six of her husband's shoe nails.

Monsieur Rollet had few carpentry jobs during this year of economic depression. Madame Rollet's wet nursing and child care business enabled them to survive. Madame Rollet was a shrewd bargainer. She knew how to take full advantage of her position and how to wheedle extras like soap, coffee, and brandy from the parents of her little charges.

And here came Madame Bovary in a beautiful silk dress, holding onto the arm of Monsieur Dupuis. The moment she saw the young couple walking past her lettuce patch, Madame Rollet instructed the four-year-old boy from Rouen, who had been left in her charge since he was an infant, to straighten his shirt, wipe his nose, and stop whining. As the gate swung open, she came to the door of her cottage, holding a suckling infant in one arm and pulling the Rouen child along with the other. Madame Bovary took one look at the scabs covering the little boy's face and was overcome with nausea and dizziness. Had it not been for Léon's presence, she might have fainted.

Emma saw Berthe's wicker cradle on the floor of the Rollet's only bedroom. Against the back wall was a large, uncurtained bed. On the other side was a small window with a patch of blue paper.

Emma picked Berthe up from her cradle. She rocked her baby in her arms and sang softly. Léon was struck by the contrast of Berthe's filthy surroundings and Emma's lovely nankeen dress. Berthe, who had been nodding off and drowsing after her feeding, was frightened by the sudden swooping motion. She didn't recognize the smell that held her, or the black eyes that stared down at her. She spit up a bit of milk on the collar of the funny-smelling dress. Emma stopped singing and put Berthe back in her cradle. Madame Rollet ran over to wipe off Emma's dress.

"She's always doing that to me. I am always washing her. If you tell the grocer to let me have soap whenever I need it, your baby will always stay clean."

Emma's only wish was to get home as soon as she could. But Madame Rollet ran after her, reciting the litany of her sleepless nights, asking for a pound of coffee that would last her a month of breakfasts. Emma said yes to everything, including some extra coffee and a jug of brandy for her husband. Madame Rollet promised to rub Berthe's tender feet with the brandy. But Emma wasn't listening; she wanted to escape from the misery of the dirty water trickling through the grass, the clothes thrown on the ground drying in the sun, the worn sheet lying across the hedge, the smell of sour milk, the sight of the little boy's scabs, the sound of Berthe's cries.

Berthe, who had been upset by this break in her routine, looked around for the patch of sunlight and the moving shadows that entranced her. She couldn't find them. She wanted back the blue eyes and the smell of Madame Rollet's familiar, earthy, milky, fuzzy dress.

Emma and Léon returned to Yonville by a pleasant road along the river. Except for the rustling of Emma's nankeen skirts, all was silent. They spoke for a few minutes about the latest shows in the Rouen theater. Then, as they had nothing else serious to say, they spoke commonplaces. By the time the couple arrived back in Yonville, their mutual enchantment had transformed the murmur of their banal words into a sweet intoxication. They had fallen in love.

Four months later, when Emma could no longer bear the torments of her unfulfilled passion for Léon, she summoned Berthe home from the wet nurse. Berthe was crucial to Emma's plan to distract herself from thoughts of Léon by becoming a virtuous housewife. She had already begun going to church. She had taken her household in hand. Emma's virtue was no blessing to Félicité. Her chores increased. She had to arrange Monsieur Bovary's nightcaps in even piles, to sew buttons on his shirts, and make sure his slippers were warming by the fire when he came home from visiting his patients. Now Emma was thrifty and counted every lump of sugar. She gave to the poor, not only food and firewood but also the skirts and petticoats she used to hand down to Félicité. The baby who had been summoned home to assure Madame's salvation would mean preparing *bouillie,* washing bottles, changing the baby's diapers and clothes, and not having a moment to rest.

The first week she was home, Berthe missed Madame Rollet and cried for her. She missed the little boy who used to push her down when she tried to sit up. She didn't understand why Madame Rollet didn't appear when she started to cry and she constantly spit up the strange taste of the *bouillie* which Félicité fed her from a glass bottle. But Berthe had an easygoing temperament and recognized a good thing when she felt it, so she soon made the best of the strange new life that had come to her. She especially liked the warmth, the glow of the fireplace, and the freedom to crawl around on a soft rug. Instead of pushing Félicité away and spitting out her feedings as she had done at first, Berthe began to recognize Félicité's smiling face and the games that made her laugh. Find the finger and peekaboo were Berthe's favorites.

Then there was her big soft Papa, who had been visiting her once a week while she was at Madame Rollet's. He kept telling her she was home to stay and she got the sense of his words. He showed her the garden and promised her flowers when the springtime came. He carried her on his shoulders to visit the pharmacist's children, who all made a big fuss over her. He carried her upstairs and downstairs, showing her the cradle draped with lace, her toys, and the shiny gilt candlesticks on the mantelpiece in the parlor.

And then, every morning and every evening, there was the strange, pretty, black-eyed lady, with long black hair and jingly bracelets, who hugged and kissed Berthe. She was told to call this lady Mama.

For nearly a month, Berthe enjoyed the great honeymoon of her life. When company came, Félicité would dress her up and bring her down to the parlor. Mama would undress her to show off her pretty legs to the ladies sitting in the parlor. Mama would look into her eyes and sing the joys of motherhood. The ladies of Yonville raised their eyebrows and looked knowingly at one another from behind their veils. But Berthe felt the truth in her mother's songs of love. Every inch of Berthe's little body warmed with happiness when her Mama sang her praises. The look in her mother's eyes told her that she was the most wonderful, beautiful, exciting creature in the entire world.

Berthe would crawl about on the carpet while her parents ate dinner before the fireplace. She would gurgle when Mama leaned over Papa's chair to kiss him on the forehead. She wanted to be enclosed in this circle of warmth. She would hold out her arms. Her Papa held her on his knees. Her Mama leaned over and kissed her on the forehead.

Then the honeymoon ended. Berthe sensed the bad news coming. And so had Félicité. Emma's attempt at virtue was not working. Her heart pounded with envy and hatred. Every time she looked around, her eyes fell on a new sign of her deprivation and discontent. She whimpered and complained all day long; there was always a dish that was prepared incorrectly, a shabby curtain, a chair that wasn't velvet, Berthe's dirty fingers. At night, she turned away from her husband. Sometimes she could not sleep. Since she was feigning happiness and virtue to her husband, and feeling only contempt toward his every gesture, she became even more desperate to throw herself into Léon's arms. When Charles was visiting patients, Emma would stretch out across her bed, gasping and sobbing, tears running down her cheeks.

Berthe spent most of the time feeling frightened. One evening in April, a terrible thing happened to her. It so frightened and humiliated her that she awoke the next day with no memory of what had happened. But the event was memorialized in other ways. From that day on, even when her mother made a fuss over her, Berthe could detect her mother's falsity. From that day on, Berthe began to question the validity of her own self.

Berthe had been playing with Félicité in her mother's room. She had been practicing standing up. And each time she succeeded, Félicité would clap. And Berthe would try again. Soon, however, her enthusiasm diminished and she began to look around as though someone was missing. Félicité understood Berthe's low-keyed mood. "Mama went to church. She'll be home soon." Berthe didn't know what church meant but she got the idea that her Mama had not disappeared forever.

The moment Emma arrived back home, she sent Félicité down to prepare dinner and sank mournfully into her armchair. Her visit to church had only increased her despair. Caught up in self-pity, she did not notice Berthe, who was holding on to a table and standing up, trying to get her mother's attention. Berthe wanted two things, and she was determined to get them. First, she wanted to show off her latest accomplishment. But more than that, she wanted to just get as close as she could to her mother, the object of her desire. She tottered over to her mother's armchair, holding on to the furniture that separated them. When she arrived at her destination, she pulled on the strings of her mother's apron.

"Leave me alone," said Emma, who wanted only to immerse herself in her sorrows. She shoved Berthe away. Berthe waited a moment and then made her way back, this time leaning on her mother's lap and raising her blue eyes to gaze at her mother's beautiful face. In her openmouthed adoration Berthe dribbled a little rivulet of saliva onto her mother's silky apron.

Now Emma was furious. "Will you leave me alone!" Her mother's loud voice and twisted face terrified Berthe. Berthe cried. But instead of picking her up and comforting her, Emma used the full force of her elbow to push Berthe away, screaming "Go away! Go away!"

Berthe fell against the brass hook on the washstand and cut her cheek. There was blood. Berthe was howling. Emma ran to her. Emma called for Félicité at the top of her lungs. Charles appeared in the doorway. Berthe could not see him through her tears, but she heard her mother's false words. "Look darling," she said to Charles, "our dear baby was playing and cut her cheek." Charles reassured Emma, ran across the path to get some plaster from the pharmacy, and covered the cut on Berthe's cheek.

Berthe could not be consoled. She eventually passed out from exhaustion. Emma did not go down to the parlor for dinner. She hovered over her baby's cradle musing bitterly on her wasted virtue. She studied the tears that had dried at the corner of her baby's eyelids, the pale blue eyes that peeked out from beneath the lashes, the cheek that had been pulled to one side by the plaster.

"What an ugly child," thought Emma.

But Emma did not give up on Berthe. And Berthe, who wanted so much to share her tricks and games and excitements with her mother, did everything she could to bring a flicker of joy into her mother's eyes. The next morning when Berthe stood up, Emma clapped her hands and told her what a wonderful baby she was. Berthe was elated. She stood up, again and again. Emma resolved that she would never again harm Berthe and she never did. And she never again told her to go away. Not in so many words, that is. Whenever Berthe saw her mother slumped in her armchair, staring off into nowhere, she knew that her antics and feats, her very presence would be an intrusion. Berthe still longed for the fragrant embrace of her mother, but she had learned to keep her distance.

In August of 1842, Félicité took Berthe to the Agricultural Fair. Berthe had been sad and cranky most of the summer and Félicité thought the fair would cheer her up. She was right. Berthe was excited by the tricolor flags, the sounds of the band, the crowds, the fancy dresses, the dancing, and the colored lanterns. That night, Berthe and Félicité watched from the window as the fireworks shot into the air. Berthe fell asleep hopeful. The next morning, when Félicité brought her up to her mother's room, Emma gave Berthe a big hug and a smile. The color had come back into her mother's face. Félicité knew that the sudden change in her mistress's mood was due to her afternoon at the fair, where she had been accompanied by the elegant and handsome

Monsieur Boulanger. Poor Berthe thought it was she who was the exciting, desirable one—the one who had brought her mother happiness. She became more hopeful.

About seven weeks after the fair, Emma came into the parlor one day to show off her new riding costume to Berthe and Félicité. Berthe clapped her hands. Charles, who was thrilled to find Emma in a good mood, insisted that she accept Monsieur Boulanger's invitation to go riding with him. Later that afternoon, when Félicité saw Emma returning from her ride, she brought Berthe to the window so the child could watch her Mama teaching the horse to trot and prance.

Winter and spring came and went. Emma paid little attention to Berthe, but she had lots of new clothes and her face glowed with a strange new light. Then slowly, the light seemed to fade from her eyes. Now Berthe gave up hope. Would her mother ever come back to her? Had her Mama disappeared forever?

One sunny spring afternoon in 1843, a basket arrived from Grandpa Roualt. In the basket was a turkey and some fruit, and a letter with a special message just for Berthe. Although Berthe had never met this Grandpa, her mother and father had told her all about him and about how every year just before Easter he sent a turkey in memory of the time her Papa had set Grandpa's broken leg. If it hadn't been for Grandpa Roualt's broken leg, Mama and Papa might never have met.

The day that the basket came, Berthe was romping on the lawn while the grass was being raked. She was lying facedown in the haystack, playing a catch-me game with the gardener's rake, while Félicité held on to her skirt so that she didn't get too carried away. Suddenly Emma burst out of the house. "Bring her here," she called out to Félicité. "Bring her over to me."

Berthe's mother picked her up and kissed her. "I love you so much, my darling child. So much!"

She brought Berthe into the parlor and held her on her lap. She read Berthe the message from her grandfather:

"I am very sad that I don't know little Berthe Bovary yet. I have planted a plum tree for her in the garden under your old window. No one may touch it except to make jam for Berthe. I will put the jam in the cupboard until she comes to visit. I kiss you daughter, and son-in-law, and the little one on both cheeks." Whereupon Emma kissed Berthe on both cheeks and noticed the spots of dirt in her ears.

Emma took off all of Berthe's clothes. She washed her from head to toe with the warm water that Félicité had heated up. She changed her underwear and her shoes and her stockings. "How are you my dear baby? Have you been well? Your mamma has missed you. Have you learned any new games? Have you been crying? Have you been sick?" Emma spoke to Berthe as though Berthe had been away on a long trip and had only just returned. But of course it was Emma who had retreated into one of her black moods and had just come back. By now Berthe didn't trust her mother's attentions and love. She felt the falseness of her mother's words, but she yielded to her anyway and fell in love all over again. Emma would stay close to Berthe just long enough to win Berthe over again, and then she'd disappear again.

Soon, there was a great excitement in Yonville. Félicité told Berthe that her Papa was going to do a great, important thing—a miracle; he was going to straighten out a stableboy's clubfoot and make it perfect. Her mother started kissing her father again and making a big fuss over him. The circle of warmth between them returned, and they drew Berthe into it.

Then, just as suddenly, all the gloom returned to Berthe's house, and this time her Papa was sad too. Félicité explained to Berthe that everyone was sad because poor Hippolyte, the boy with the clubfoot, got sick from the operation and died. Her father sat all day, slumped over in his chair. Her mother had a mean, angry look in her eyes. A few minutes later, Berthe saw her Papa look over at her Mama with a sad face. He held out his arms to her, "Kiss me, darling."

Then Berthe heard the terrible words again. "Leave me alone! Go away!" Her mother's face was red with fury. "What's wrong?" asked Berthe's father. "You know I love you. Please calm down. Come to me. I love you."

"Enough!" screamed her mother. She ran from the room, slamming the door behind her so hard that the barometer fell to the floor with a crash and broke into pieces.

Berthe's father continued to look mournful. He didn't even bother to visit his patients. However, within the week, Berthe's mother's eyes were shining with joy. The house was full of bustle. Emma kissed Charles and tried to cheer him up. Félicité knew that her mistress was in love again and was again meeting with Monsieur Boulanger—each day and sometimes at night after Charles was asleep. Berthe had lost her mother yet again. She finally gave up hope.

Berthe was the daughter of a severely depressed mother who came to life only when she was "in love." Every now and again Emma would look at her little girl and rouse herself into an imitation of devoted motherhood. Whenever Emma fooled herself into believing that the virtuous love of motherhood might be a substitute for the forbidden passions of "having a lover," her voice rang false to Berthe. Berthe began to dread the false notes even more than her mother's absences.

On April 3, 1846, when Berthe Bovary was four and a half, her mother swallowed a fistful of the arsenic powder that she had stolen from the pharmacist's shelves. As Emma lay dying, she asked to see Berthe. Félicité woke Berthe up and carried her into the bedroom. Berthe was still half asleep and thought it was one of those special mornings when her mother would give her presents and sweets. She looked around for her presents and then noticed her mother. "How big your eyes are, Mama. You're so white. I'm afraid." She was too frightened to let her mother kiss her.

Berthe was sent to stay with Madame Rollet until after the funeral. When she returned, she immediately asked for her mother. Charles told her that her mother was away on a trip and would be bringing back a bundle of toys for Berthe. Berthe mentioned her mother several times again but then in a few weeks forgot all about her. She was cheerful. Or so it seemed.

The next year, near the end of August, Berthe went to the garden to summon her father to dinner. He was slumped over on a bench in the arbor, clutching a lock of her mother's hair. Berthe thought he was teasing her by pretending to be asleep. She poked him. When he fell over and refused to wake up, Berthe still thought he was playing. She called to him again, shook him and shook him again, unable to take in the fact that he was dead.

The deaths of Berthe's parents bring into focus the death motifs that pervade *Madame Bovary*. Actual scenes and intimations of illness, bodily mutilation, loss, depression, bereavement, and death, even the seasonal flowering and decay of plants and foliage, are far more prevalent than the fleeting moments of romance and sex granted to Emma. The glowing romantic excitements were Emma Bovary's desperate attempts to hold at bay the black depressions that would otherwise have overwhelmed her. To the other middle-class wives in Yonville, the doctor's wife was an outrageous show-off, a rebel who threatened the very structures of their social order. However, Félicité, who was privy to her mistress's sorrows, had been aware of the mournful preoccupations that lay beneath Emma's outward frivolity. Though Félicité would spend many hours ironing Emma's petticoats, polishing her boots and delivering messages to her lovers, countless more hours, days, and months would be spent attending to Emma's depressions.

Artistic creation serves many functions for the artist, among them a possibility for carrying out the work of mourning. The form, themes, contents, and style of the work of art will often reflect different facets and stages in the mourning process. Gustave Flaubert, the creator of Emma Bovary, was on intimate terms with death. His ongoing experiences with loss, the fact that he was born between the deaths of two of his siblings and therefore suffered indirectly from his mother's depressive reactions to those deaths, influenced the construction of his way of life and of all his writings, but particularly *Madame Bovary*. The novel is permeated by the deaths of family members—not only Berthe's immediate family, but Emma's mother and brother, Charles's first wife, Charles's father, Rodolphe's mother. When he wrote *Madame Bovary* between 1851 and 1857, Flaubert was unaware of how much his first "realist" novel embodied the personal losses he himself had suffered in the preceding decade.

The novel spans the years of 1841 through 1848. The critical date when Rodolphe abandoned Emma is September 2, 1843, at which time Emma collapsed. First, Charles thought she had brain fever. Then he thought she had cancer. Emma did not begin to recover from this depression until the following spring when she finally fulfilled her passion for Léon Dupuis. A year later, soon after Léon deserted her, Emma committed suicide, and the next year Charles died of grief.

In early January of 1844, Flaubert barely survived two attacks of a serious illness, thought to be epilepsy. In 1846 he suffered the deaths of his father and his beloved twenty-one-year-old sister, Caroline. His brother Achille's surgical procedures on his father's thigh led to the gangrene infection that killed him. This incident appears in *Madame Bovary* as the botched miracle operation that kills the stableboy, Hippolyte. Caroline's nightmarish burial, with the gravediggers stamping on her coffin, would become the model for for Flaubert's description of Emma Bovary's burial.

The reader of Flaubert's novel, like the narrow-minded ladies of Yonville, is generally caught up in Emma Bovary's pursuit of romantic love. This theme assumes the center stage, distracting the reader from the themes of depression and death that hover in the background. Nevertheless, they insinuate themselves onto the margins of consciousness. When considering this novel from the point of view of the lost and abandoned child, Berthe Bovary, these marginal themes of depression and death push their way to the front and center.

Two months after Berthe's mother committed suicide, Félicité, the maid who had been Berthe's primary caregiver during the first four years of her life, stole her mistress's clothes and ran off with a servant who worked next door. Charles tried to be both mother and father to Berthe, but he was too distracted by his longings for Emma to pay much attention to her. Even after Félicité left, and Berthe had no one to take care of her, it did not occur to Charles that his motherless child might want to visit with Madame Rollet, the woman who had been her wet nurse for six months and also her foster mother during Emma's severest depressions. Berthe never saw Madame Rollet again. To Berthe it seemed that she had simply disappeared. The pharmacist's wife, who had wanted to advance her standing in Yonville by befriending the doctor's wife, now protected her children from the sin of Emma's suicide and Berthe's shabby poverty by forbidding them to play with Berthe. After her father's funeral, there was just enough money to pay for Berthe's trip to her grandmother's house. The grandmother died during the same year, leaving Berthe in the care of an aunt, "who is poor and has sent the child to work in a cotton mill."

Between the ages of four and six, Berthe Bovary lost a mother, her two substitute mothers, her playmates, a father, a grandmother, and also her maternal grandfather, who in his grief over the suicide of his daughter became paralyzed. To compound Berthe's plight, she was abruptly reduced from the status of a relatively well-cared-for middle-class child to a child laborer, the equivalent of a slave. At the end of the novel, seven-year-old Berthe Bovary exits from the social class of her birth to enter the social class of Félicité and Madame Rollet.

Very likely, Berthe Bovary would have died soon after her poverty-stricken aunt sent her off to work in a cotton mill. In addition to dying of the typical diseases of childhood like typhoid, scrofula, and cholera, factory children died of amputated limbs, tuberculosis, and newly labeled diseases such as "cotton phthisis" and "cotton pneumonia." By announcing in the last paragraphs of *Madame Bovary* that Berthe would be sent to a cotton mill, Flaubert was announcing the end of the Roualt-Bovary families and the beginning of the Age of Progress. For Flaubert, who despised progress and the Industrial Revolution, Berthe was not an actual child, but merely a symbol of the death of bourgeois innocence.

Within the realm of her fictional reality, Berthe was abandoned by her family, cast aside by her creator, and virtually abandoned by most readers of the novel in which she appears. It is surprising that so little notice has been paid to Berthe, whose presence and eventual fate are crucial to an appreciation of Flaubert's novel. Still it is not surprising that Berthe's experience as a fictional child echoes the lament of an actual child who loses her family: "Nobody notices how lost I am. No one can find me."

While Berthe's father lived, he had noticed her. For Charles Bovary, Berthe had been a source of light and hope. Until the day he died, Charles doted on his little Berthe, seeing in her a miniature incarnation of all he adored in Emma. As his mother had done with him, Charles cajoled Berthe with baby talk, made her cardboard dolls, read to her, gave her jams and candies, and said "no" only when he absolutely had to. When she was three years old, he began teaching her how to read.

For her mother, Berthe had been a shadowy presence that came into focus only during those rare moments when she was summoned forth to banish the blackness of her mother's melancholic moods. These moments of vitality, rare as they were, had been just salient enough for Emma to become "Mama" for Berthe. However, before she was a year old, Berthe already sensed that her presence would never be quite enough to animate her mother. She knew she could not rival the flurries of excitement preceding her mother's trips to Rouen.

Even her sparkling Algerian silk shawl was more exciting to Emma than Berthe. And Berthe knew that.

Psychologically, the mother Berthe lost forever when she was four and a half had always been a "dead mother." A psychologically dead mother is a physically alive mother so entirely possessed by bereavement that she cannot value her living child. The child gazes into her mother's eyes in search of love and admiration and finds in this mirror the blank nothingness of despair. Upon seeing an absence and emptiness where the child expects an animated dialogue, the child becomes confused and frightened. This glimpse of deadness inside her living mother is a perplexity that will continue to haunt the child. To survive the profound rejection of the blank mirror, the child begins to transform her living mother, who is sometimes, but never predictably, a source of vitality, into a distant, inanimate object. Thus, the psychological experience of a dead mother is partially a creation of the child. A "dead mother" does not awaken an expectation of dialogue. If the appetite for dialogue ceases to be aroused there can be no letdown of an unconsummated dialogue.

Every child, every adult, female or male, harbors a dead mother along with all the other mothering images she or he has constructed out of experiences with an actual mother. Every now and then, every mother has responded to her child's gaze of love with the blank mirror of some deadness inside her. Somewhere in every woman's (or man's) experience is a bereavement for some precious aspect of her being that got lost. This eternally lost aspect of the self may be a child or a parent who has died; it may be a belief or ideal like freedom or justice; it may be the sense of oneself as a vital and powerful person. This lost someone or something forms a pocket of deadness in every soul.

Though her sorrows permeate the pages of *Madame Bovary,* Flaubert's mother, unlike Emma Bovary, was not an emotionally "dead mother." Anne-Justine-Caroline Fleuriot never had a mother, and her father died of grief when she was ten years old. She was a lost and lonely child who sought solace in reading about the lives and loves of fictional characters. For a brief period after she married Achille Cleophas and they moved to the rue du Petit Salut, she actually knew the meaning of true happiness. But then, from the day that she lost her first little Caroline and for the rest of her life, Madame Flaubert was prone to depressions, which were only temporarily alleviated by her anxious concern for the welfare of her surviving children. Madame Flaubert's mournful preoccupations with the children she lost often interfered with her relations with her living children. But her passionate desire to go on living despite the losses she suffered also conveyed an indefatigability and sense of vitality to her children. Gustave was enveloped by his mother's depressive moods and always painfully aware that she was lost in thoughts about her unfulfilled dreams and hopes. Still, he sensed how much she valued him.

By the time her baby was born, Emma Bovary had lost everything that had once been precious to her: her childhood family, her childhood dreams and illusions. The very condition of womanhood was to Emma a constant reminder of her lost childhood dreams. It is unlikely that the birth of a son, the George that Emma had been longing for, would have made much difference in the long run. There was a deadness in Emma's soul that a burst of excitement might momentarily dispel. However, no child or lover could banish that deadness entirely. The wish and longing to be buried beside her mother was more powerful than Emma's passion for living.

Berthe's involvement with bereavement began long before her mother committed suicide. The same "Mama" who occasionally mirrored the love and admiration that Berthe anticipated and longed for more often offered her only blank unresponsiveness. Such a partial and unpredictable deprivation of dialogue can sometimes lead to a permanent confusion between animate and inanimate, between the real and the unreal. *What makes this uncanny experience terrifying is the child's own rage, which can only be expressed when the child deanimates and "murders" her mother, again and over again.*

René Spitz's early studies on the deprivation of reciprocal dialogue demonstrated that no human child can survive without dialogue for very long. His later writings are more concerned with the differing psychological responses to partial deprivations of dialogue. Of course, when René Spitz was writing about the importance of reciprocal dialogue he was not thinking about Berthe Bovary. Nevertheless, much that he said inadvertently refers to Berthe's experience with her dead mother, as well as to the effects of the father's personality death on Judge Daniel Paul Schreber, and Flaubert's attunement to his mother's depressions. Though these cases differ, they all illustrate the effects of a partial deprivation of dialogue and an element of the uncanny.

Spitz's writings on the distinctions between animate and inanimate and the uncanny effects that accompany a deterioration of dialogue are also particularly relevant to René Magritte's experience of his dead mother Régina. The emotional effects of Régina Magritte's deadness can actually be seen in her son's paintings and will be explored in the next chapter.

In 1961, Spitz was invited to speak at a meeting honoring his contributions to psychoanalysis. After some thought, Spitz decided that an informal narrative, depicting his beginnings as an analyst and showing the steps leading up to his current theories on the human dialogue, would be in keeping with the personal spirit of the occasion. However, in June, a few months after Spitz received the invitation, his wife, Ella, died. When René Spitz lost Ella, he lost his heart for celebration. He knew he would be unable to speak about his life's work in the absence of the person who had shared that life with him for fifty-three years. He wrote a sober, technical paper entitled "Life and the Dialogue."

"Life as we know it is achieved through the dialogue." This was to have been the concluding sentence of Spitz's scientific presentation. But as he approached those written words, Spitz became aware of the unconscious significance of his subject. Instead of finishing, he looked up from his prepared paper and confessed to his audience that his talk had been more personal than he had intended. Ella, he explained, the one whose loss made it impossible for him to recite a narrative about himself alone, had inspired the subject matter of his talk. "Life and the Dialogue" was a memorialization of the fifty-three years of a life with Ella, the person who had made his life a life worth living.

Like many psychologists who were intrigued by the enigma of the uncanny and wanted to solve it, Spitz was also drawn to a contemplation of mechanical dolls and waxworks. Spitz opened his presentation with a description of the figures in Madame Tussaud's waxworks: illustrious men and women in postures appropriate to their fame, infamous murderers, weapons in hand, mutilating and slaughtering their victims. While all the wax figures were designed to look lifelike, some were equipped with mechanical devices that enabled every muscle of their waxen bodies—including their eyes and eyelids—to move. These puppet figures looked so real that many of the visitors half-expected them to speak. And a few of them did. Of course, everyone knew the figures were wax. The whole business was just for fun, and part of the fun was pretending to believe in the illusion. Without the pretense on the part of the audience, the wax figures would have fooled no one. Each day, there was always one practical joker who would be inspired to pose like a waxwork and then suddenly come to life and scare the daylights out of a few "innocent" spectators. Said Spitz, "There is a strange fascination about the idea of the inanimate creating the illusion of life, and also about the living posing as inanimate. This fascination permeates a great deal more of our thinking than we are usually aware."

In the course of his presentation, Spitz refers to his earlier critiques of Harlow's experiments on the nature of love. In their emotional effects, Harlow's terry cloth mothers, who had glowing eyes, cuddly bodies, and sometimes even movement and warmth, were very much like the moving figures in Madame Tussaud's waxworks. The infant rhesus could be fooled. The audience at Madame Tussaud's is only pretending to believe; they "know" the real truth. The audience senses that something is missing from the wax puppets. Even the ones that speak are incapable of reciprocal dialogue. The effect is uncanny, but not at all terrifying. The bewilderment is playful, and except for the playful aggression on the part of a few practical jokers, there is no rage to complicate the bewilderment.

Spitz's lecture went on to demonstrate how the reciprocal dialogue with a living partner endows an infant with the psychological means to distinguish animate from inanimate. Furthermore, Spitz emphasized, in the absence of dialogue, the infant's libido withers and his aggression remains crude and untamed. The child's ego, his experience of self, his character and his personality are stunted and distorted. In short, a human being who is totally deprived of dialogue becomes "an empty, asocial husk." And life in the human sense must be a social life.

The partial deprivation in a derailment of dialogue does not prevent a person from participating in a social life. Sometimes, in fact, the confusions between animate and inanimate, the bewilderment, and even the rage, become inspirations for works of art.

All artists are somewhat like the practical joker in Madame Tussaud's waxworks. They count on having an "innocent" collaborator who will fall for the trick. Whether he is a crass practical joker or a sublime poet, the creator of illusions always needs an audience that is willing to pretend to believe in the illusion. Some artists, however, are possessed by a fascination with the idea "of the inanimate creating the illusion of life, and also about the living posing as inanimate." Their creations are repetitive experiments that flirt with the uncertain borders between animate and inanimate. The repetition arouses our suspicions that some personal trauma might have inspired and motivated the artist's fascination. The poems, the paintings, the statues, the novels, the songs suggest the poignancy of a derailed dialogue. And yet, these works of art have the vital something—the dialogue—that is missing in the artifice of Harlow's mothers and Tussaud's waxworks.

René Magritte, an inveterate practical joker, was also a consummate artist who, in his paintings and sculpture, could deanimate and murder his dead mother over and over again. Yet with each gesture of bewilderment and rage, Magritte also brings his dead mother, Régina, back to life.

CHAPTER ELEVEN

*

PORTRAITS OF A
DEAD MOTHER

On November 21, 1898, as the hooded moon cast a pale light over the rooftops of the provincial town of Lessines, Belgium, Régina Bertinchamps Magritte gave birth to her first child. It was a boy! Régina and her husband Léopold named him René. A few months before their son was born, the young couple had moved from Gilly, the village where Régina had been born and raised. Régina felt better about the move when her husband agreed that her widowed mother, Emilie, could come to live with them in Lessines. Léopold, a traveling salesman, was an optimistic, outgoing young man who fully expected to prosper in business and be a good provider for his family. But every once in a while, he worried that something might be wrong with his wife. Her face was often shrouded in gloom. Her eyes were dull and lifeless. She stared out at the world as though she were looking at nothing. Whether the cause was her delayed reaction to her father's death or the move away from her childhood home, Léopold did not know. At any rate, he was pleased that his mother-in-law was there to support Régina and to help her care for little René.

On May 10, 1900, when René was one and a half years old, Léopold moved his family back to Gilly. A month after the move, a second son,

Raymond, was born, and two and a half years later came Paul. Then, in 1904, when Léopold became a merchant of edible oils, he moved his family again, this time to Chatelet. Régina's mother, who was probably weary from all the moving around, remained in her home-town of Gilly. First Léopold rented a house previously occupied by Régina's brother. Five years later, the Magrittes moved to a much larger house that had been built and decorated according to Régina's specifications. Léopold hoped that this new grand house would make his wife happy. But Régina's sadness could not be dispelled by alter-ations in her environment. Having her mother with her and having a new baby every year or two had helped Régina to feel better—but only for a while. The new house didn't help at all and seemed to make Régina even more depressed.

Régina attempted suicide several times, and once nearly succeeded in drowning herself in the basement water tank. Léopold was desper-ate. He told the servants to keep on eye on her during the day. He locked her in her bedroom at night.

At 4:30 in the morning on February 24, 1912, when René Magritte was thirteen years old, his mother managed to find the key to her room. She escaped and drowned herself in the Sambre, a narrow river that ran along the backyards of Chatelet.

After two decades of silence about his mother's tragic death, René finally confided the story of Régina's last and decisive suicide attempt to his closest friend, the artist Louis Scutenaire, who some years af-terward included the story in his 1942 monograph on the by then fa-mous surrealist painter René Magritte. This is how the story went:

When Paul, the youngest son, was nine years old and still sleeping in the same bedroom as his mother, he awoke in the middle of the night to find his mother's bed empty. He roused the rest of the family. The father and the three boys searched the house, but Régina was nowhere to be found. Then someone noticed footprints on the path leading from the house. The family followed the footprints to a bridge that crossed over the Sambre. There, at the rail of the stone bridge, the footprints stopped.

When the corpse was found, Régina's nightgown was wrapped about her face. "What did this mean?" everyone wondered. "Had Régina veiled her face in order to shield her eyes from the death that was about to overcome her? Or had the swirling waters of the river shifted the gown up over her eyes?"

The Scutenaire account of Régina's suicide was repeated verbatim in every succeeding biographical account of René Magritte. Now that the family secret had been exposed, it seemed the hidden meanings of Magritte's paintings became clear. To anyone who fancied himself au courant with Freudian theory, it was obvious that the repetitive visual images produced by the adult surrealist painter were the outcomes of the "castration" trauma experienced by the young boy who discovered his mother's suicide and her exposed genital organs at the same instant. After all, the hidden faces and shrouded heads, the blank eyes that reflected nothing, the distorted, dislocated, and mutilated torsos, the flesh of living bodies fusing into leather or cloth or wood, and especially *The Rape,* that weird and hilarious face shaped like a torso, with nipples for eyes and pubic hair for a mouth and a navel for a nose that looked as if it had been eaten away by syphilis—these images must symbolize the trauma of "witnessing" the genitalia of his mother's faceless corpse.

The fact is the tale that René Magritte told Scutenaire was not entirely true.

The police records and newspapers of 1912 reveal that the body of Magritte's mother was not recovered until the second week of March, seventeen days after her suicide. It had been carried one kilometer beyond the bridge. Furthermore, when the body was found, the immediate family was not present. The corpse was kept in the home of a friend until it was identified by Régina's brother, Alfred Bertinchamps. Therefore, Magritte never did see the naked torso and shrouded face that figure so prominently in his paintings. This more accurate depiction of the events surrounding Régina's suicide, discovered by Magritte's most recent biographer, David Sylvester, has cast doubt on previous psychoanalytic interpretations of Magritte's art, which all made much ado of the adolescent boy's sighting of his mother's half-nude corpse.

Upon hearing the "true" story, the scoffers of psychoanalysis had a good laugh. All along they had been contending that Magritte did not need the concrete visual image of his mother's corpse to animate his paintings. Magritte had been influenced by the surrealist painters of his day, many of whom painted headless torsos and mutilated female bodies. Magritte had simply appropriated the artistic motifs of his time.

It is true that René Magritte was something of an imitator; in his youth, he copied other surrealists, and in his middle age he duplicated many of his own paintings. He was also an inveterate practical joker. One of his favorite sports was spoofing psychoanalysis, and it was never certain if he was mocking Freud, or tweaking his surrealist colleagues who credited Freud's theory of dreams as a major inspiration for their artistic credo. He would produce paintings that would trick his psychoanalytic acquaintances into making their favorite sexual interpretations. As Magritte explained to an art critic who had fallen for the Freudian obvious, "Apropos the Freudian interpretation of objects . . . If in dreams a necktie, for instance, means a sexual organ, if dreams are a transposition of waking life, *waking life is equally a transposition of dreams.*"

The real facts of Régina Magritte's suicide did not put an end to interpretation. The stark discrepancy between what had actually happened to Régina's body and the story Magritte told his friend inspired considerable speculation concerning Magritte's psychological motives for claiming to witness his mother's exposed corpse. Since Magritte so enjoyed tricking his interpreters, possibly the story he told Scutenaire was another of his macabre practical jokes? Was Scutenaire, himself a great practical joker, in on the scheme? Scutenaire, who only heard the story once, insisted that he had reported it exactly as Magritte had told it. Magritte had given him the impression of a series of events occurring within the time frame of one night. Perhaps, Scutenaire conjectured, his friend had simply taken the two separate sets of events—those occurring on the night of the suicide and those occuring seventeen days later, when the body was recovered—and condensed them into a single narrative. David Sylvester suggested that Magritte's fantasy of seeing his mother's corpse was based on his "obsession with hidden faces," which he then "imposed on the tragic event of which there was no clear picture and which was therefore a blank waiting to be filled in."

Devious or genuine, Magritte's false recollection of the events surrounding his mother's suicide exposes something crucial about his inner experience. The events we misremember and the stories we make up about ourselves reveal as much, if not more, about our "true self" as any actual events. Biographical truth is always an ambiguous truth where the borders between truth and falsehood are more to the point than any supposed "real" truth. Modern biographers listen intently to the words of a false witness, who very often tells a more exquisite truth than the so-called honest or unbiased witness. A false story is always a symptomatic reflection of a true story, which can never be known anyway.

The significant question is *not* whether Magritte actually *saw* his mother's corpse the night she was fished out of the river. René Magritte did not have to see his mother's dead body or her head wrapped in a nightgown to be affected by the image. The image had been conveyed to him in words that must have been just as terrifying and impressive to a thirteen-year-old boy as any concrete visual image would be. René had heard the story of the discovery of his mother's corpse not just once but several times, from Jeanne Verdeyan, the governess who took over the care of Léopold's three sons after his wife's death and soon afterward became his common-law wife.

Indeed, in terms of unconscious psychological motives, the differences between calculated lies, practical jokes, or honest misrecollections are often less significant than their similarities. The desire to put one over on the experts and try to persuade them to believe that *something untrue is true* is a sure sign that something else even more dreadful is, in fact, true—that the truth is something *the joker would prefer to regard as untrue*. An honest misrecollection has a similar psychological motive. The unconscious strategy in either case is to highlight a frightening detail in order to conceal a truth that would be even more painful if it were acknowledged.

The image of Régina's corpse with its exposed genitalia—vivid, dramatic, grotesque, terrifying, even exciting in its own perverse way— would have been an ingenious cover-up for a more frightening and confusing aspect of Magritte's mother. The shrouded heads, the detached faces, the blank eyes, the mirrors that reflect nothingness, the flesh transformed into cold stone and dead wood are the crux of Magritte's childhood trauma. Régina's suicide was the lucid finale in the life of a severely depressed woman. When she was alive, her face was often shrouded in sorrow, her eyes were often a blank mirror. She was, like Berthe Bovary's mother, "a dead mother."

Régina seemed to have sought relief from her depressions in pregnancy and child rearing. But as her sons, one by one, outgrew childhood, Régina gave up trying to mask her sadness. The lurid eroticism of the naked torso conceals the bewilderment of a child who could never be certain of who or what he might find when he gazed into his mother's eyes. The uncertain borders between real and not real, animate and inanimate, living and not living would be a terrifying enigma to any child whose daily life is darkened by the knowledge that almost nothing he does or says has the power to animate his mother.

Such a child, of course, would feel humiliated and impotent—perhaps even emotionally "castrated." He would also be enraged with the mother who repeatedly aroused his appetites for dialogue, only to turn away from him into the world of nothingness, only to become pregnant with another child who, for a time at least, seemed to succeed where he had failed so miserably. The psychologically dead mother not only confuses the distinctions between inanimate and animate, she also incites rage and unconscious fantasies of retaliation in the mind of the child she repeatedly rejects and humiliates.

Magritte was right to scorn the simplistic interpretations that reduced complex human emotions to an obvious one-to-one visual correspondence between exposed genitalia and castration anxiety. Furthermore, it did not help at all to account for the aesthetic power of his work. In those days, psychoanalysts and their followers in the art world had a simple explanation for the meaning of the term "castration." They attributed the male child's castration anxiety to his accidental but inevitable sighting of the female's "castrated" genital organs. Castration, however, is not an actual or real physical attribute of the female genitals; it is a fantasy created in the mind of an injured party who wants to hurt the one who has hurt or insulted him.

In the course of growing up, every little boy and girl must eventually suffer the humiliation of knowing that no matter how lovable, adorable, and delightful they are, they are not big enough or powerful enough to satisfy all of their mother's desires. The body of the motherly mother, the Madonna who thinks only of her child, is a familiar place, cozy and homey. The body of the sexual mother, the woman who desires the father, is unfamiliar and unfriendly, an affront to the child's omnipotence, a devastation to his belief that he is all his mother needs. And every child, at one point or another, feels enraged with the sexual mother whose adult body reminds him of his intrinsic impotence. It is the humiliated child, in a fit of retaliatory rage, who makes the mother pay for her rejection by fantasizing a mutilation of her offending bodily parts—the eyes that turned away, the arms that embrace another, and especially that unknowable, mysterious place inside her where she makes babies.

All of this is usually unconscious. All that the humiliated, rejected child experiences consciously is his uncontrollable urge to mutilate and destroy—to shriek, to bite, to tear, to pinch, to kick. When his tantrum is over, the familiar world of home is restored and the violence is forgotten.

For the child of a "dead mother," however, the violence is not so easily repressed. The child of a dead mother is repeatedly reminded that he is inadequate in fulfilling his mother's needs and consequently must also cope with the rage that his mother's rejection inevitably invites. The mutilation fantasies that are unconscious in the ordinary child threaten to become a reality to the child of a "dead mother," and this possibility is terrifying to the child who, of course, needs and loves his mother and wants to protect her from any harm. For the child of a "dead mother" the blurring of distinctions between animate and inanimate, real and not real, spills over to affect the child's perceptions of rage and body mutilation.

Magritte's paintings fascinate and move us because they achieve a remarkable visual synthesis of bewilderment and violence. Magritte is something like the practical joker at Madame Tussaud's wax museum, who expresses his aggression by creating a confusion between animate and inanimate. If the images in a Magritte painting were to present themselves in real life, we would be terrified. However, viewers of Magritte's work are not scared by what they see. They are puzzled by the images. They experience a vague anxiety verging on excitement. But they also know that the disturbing juxtaposition of seemingly incongruous images are deliberate illusions.

Psychoanalysis should not be employed to interpret the hidden symbolic meanings in Magritte's paintings. Rather, his art should be employed to enlarge psychoanalytic appreciations of the human plight. To grasp the full significance of Magritte's artistic illusions, his paintings should be looked "at," not "into." Magritte's art and the way he patterned his artistic career can provide psychologists with insights into the mind of an adult whose childhood was haunted by the perplexities and ambiguities of living a life with a psychologically dead mother.

Fortunately for her children, before she drowned, Régina had been alive enough often enough and powerfully enough to provide them with the animated dialogue that infuses a child with emotional vitality. Her sons were not entirely deprived of dialogue and therefore did not become violent, asocial husks. René, Raymond, and Paul were also fortunate to have a father like Léopold Magritte who, while unable to cure his wife of her depressions, did give his sons the courage and the wit to survive their mother's abandonment. He had a lively disposition and enjoyed children and childhood games. He apparently didn't reprimand little René when he frightened the servants by dressing up like a priest, lighting incense, and mumbling a macabre version of the mass for the dead. And when his preadolescent sons became known as the neighborhood terrors, he was tolerant. Léopold Magritte was a typical, respectable, bowler-hatted bourgeois. He was not an artist, but he had a keen eye for each son's special talent and did whatever he could to support him in his ambitions.

All three of Régina's sons found moments of salvation by writing surrealist poems. Eventually, the middle child, Raymond, resolved his childhood dilemmas by becoming a respectable businessman, just like his father. Paul became a professional pianist who went by the name of Bill Buddie. Like his brother, René, he continued to write in the surrealist tradition. René, of course, became a famous surrealist painter.

Fortunately for René Magritte, his talents flourished in an artistic climate that sanctioned the violation and sabotage of conventional images. The crisis of the real object that preoccupied the surrealist painters and poets corresponded to the personal dilemmas of real and not real, animate and inanimate that preoccupied Magritte.

During World War I many young European artists, on both sides of the trenches, became disillusioned with every aspect of their culture and society that was in any way associated with military violence. They founded their own art movement, which was as much a social and political program as it was a school of art. It was, in fact, an entire state of mind. In 1924 this state of mind was given the name surrealism by its titular founder, the poet André Breton. Breton credited Freud's *Interpretation of Dreams* with the discovery of the amoral, irrational, uncontrolled region of the mind that inspired the surrealist vision. Freud was flattered but protested that he could not recognize himself in the surrealist manifestos that glorified him as a heroic underminer of conscience and reality.

Magritte could not cry when his mother died, but when he discovered surrealism he found a home for his tears—and for his rage. The surrealist credo of sabotage and dislocation appealed to Magritte's sense of personal trauma. Maldoror, the fictional hero of the surrealists, was "a phenomenology of aggression." As Suzi Gablik, one of Magritte's early biographers, explains, Maldoror "inflicts gratuitous suffering without suffering himself; he contradicts all laws, both human and divine." Maldoror was "something bleak, evasive, menacing, the darkness of the human mind." Antonin Artaud, the French actor and surrealist theorist, proposed a Theatre of Cruelty, proclaiming, "It is cruelty that cements matter together, cruelty that molds the features of the world." In his early surrealist manifestos, André Breton proclaimed that "the simplest surrealist act consists of dashing into the street, pistol in hand and firing blindly, as fast as one can pull the trigger, into the crowd."

For Magritte, the son of a "dead mother," the surrealist state of mind was made to order. He would become a Maldoror in the guise of a respectable bourgeois. With the mantle of surrealism about his shoulders and a bowler hat planted firmly on his head, he had permission to paint whatever came to his mind and to say whatever he wished to say. He said he wanted "to make the most familiar objects howl."

In his autobiographical sketch *La Ligne de Vie* (Lifeline), Magritte describes how he discovered his artistic calling while playing in a cemetery. From the time he was ten years old until he was twelve, he spent his school vacations with his paternal grandmother and aunt in the rural town of Soignies. In the nearby woods was a cemetery, so ancient and deteriorating that it had long since been abandoned by the living. There, among the crumbling tombstones and monuments, he and a little girl played their graveyard games and explored the vaults beneath the monuments. "We used to lift up the iron gates and go down into the underground passageways," recalled Magritte. One autumn afternoon, just as he and his playmate emerged from one of the dark, gloomy vaults into the bright sunlight, René saw, standing among some broken columns and fallen leaves, "a painter who had come from the capital and who seemed to me to be performing magic." René had never seen an artist before.

When he was twelve years old, Magritte produced his first paintings. Then, in 1915, the year he began taking classes at the Académie Royal des Beaux Arts in Brussels, Magritte remembered that magical sunlit moment and related it to the emergence of his artistic calling.

This memory of playing in the cemetery makes it clear that Magritte was already preoccupied with death for at least two years preceding his mother's suicide. However, the most vivid details of the memory were probably invented after his mother's suicide, as most childhood memories are what psychoanalysts refer to as screen memories—the more vivid a memory image, the more likely it is an invention designed to screen out other images that would be frightening if remembered. For example, Magritte's recollection of his mother's suicide, whether misremembered or falsely remembered, is a screen memory. The vivid detail of witnessing her naked corpse screened out the more frightening experience of her emotional deadness when she was alive.

Since Magritte spent countless afternoons playing in the cemetery, that aspect of his screen memory is doubtless accurate. However, the magical sunlit moment, the glow of revelation is more likely a construction that came after Régina's death. In René's actual life, a dark tragedy had clouded over the light of childhood. In the cemetery memory, the light of day replaces the nighttime darkness of the tomb. The seventeen-year-old art student remembers himself as a child finding his life rather than as a child who lost his mother. In the half-truth of this memory, Magritte was also half right. Art would become the solution to working through the emotional perplexities surrounding his "dead mother." An artist could violate reality by painting sunlit landscapes against the background of cloudy nighttime skies—or the other way around, if he wished. An artist could be a detached observer of death. An artist might even resurrect a dead mother in his paintings—over and over again. And an artist had permission to express his rage by distorting and mutilating as many bodies as he wished.

Magritte could recall almost nothing about how he felt at the time of his mother's death, except for a "great pride at the thought of being the pitiful center of a tragedy." This tendency to transform a dark and fearful event into a moment of triumphant light was an obsessive striving of René's character. The pity and tragedy of losing his mother are given expression. But the emotional effect of the tragedy is reversed. The orphaned boy is not abandoned or lost; he is the center of the world's attention.

The repeated loss of his mother in childhood would be reenacted in Magritte's adult life as he repeatedly lost and refound his wife. Two years after his mother's suicide, René fell in love. Just before the outbreak of World War I, the fifteen-year-old René Magritte met the bright-eyed, lovely thirteen-year-old Georgette Berger at a country fair, as they were riding on the brightly painted horses of a carousel. It was love at first sight. But as he later explained, somehow or other, he "lost" sight of Georgette until several years later, when once again they "found" each other quite by chance. Between the two chance findings of Georgette, Magritte studied painting, edited a magazine, and served two years in the Belgian army. He happened upon Georgette in 1920, when she was working behind the counter at an artist's supply store.

When two years later René married Georgette, he promised himself and her that he would never lose her again. However, he nearly did lose Georgette again in 1923, shortly after their marriage, and then once again in 1936 when Magritte actively provoked the recurrence of loss.

In 1923 the "losing" was precipitated by an unfortunate act of fate. Magritte's response, however, transformed this fortuitous occurrence into a replication of the loss of his mother. Georgette was pregnant, had a miscarriage, and then lingered for many months in a severe postpartum illness. She gradually recovered from this illness, which may have been accompanied by depression. However, Magritte reacted as though he had lost his wife forever. He was overcome with anxiety and underwent a profound loss of his sense of reality. He spoke of looking at a familiar landscape "as if it were only a curtain placed before my eyes. I became uncertain of the depth of the countryside, unconvinced of the remoteness of the horizon."

As so often happens when a childhood loss has been denied, a loss or near loss in adulthood evokes the emotions and fantasies that belonged with the earlier event. This return of the repressed emotions infiltrates and exacerbates the adult's responses to the later loss. Georgette's lingering postpartum illness must have called to mind Magritte's mother's lingering and incurable depressions. He made up his mind that he would never again be threatened with the loss of his wife—or the loss of a child. Magritte renounced fatherhood.

The crisis of almost losing Georgette also precipitated a crisis of artistic vision. Magritte explained that his return to reality began when a friend showed him a page from an art magazine containing a photograph of Giorgio de Chirico's surrealist painting *Song of Love.* He wept.

Song of Love depicts a surgeon's red rubber glove nailed to a gray stone wall, alongside an antique stone head of a Grecian hero, with a large, pale green stitched canvas ball in the foreground. It was the "unexpected combination" in de Chirico's painting that touched Magritte's soul. Here, at last, was a form of painting that could convey the shock and bewilderment that resonated with his inner experience, "that pictorial experience which puts the real world on trial."

Real flesh-and-blood humans might tempt a direct expression of rage. However, the unexpected combinations, the shocking disjunctures between incongruously juxtaposed nonhuman, nonliving objects did *violence* to the banal realities of the ordinary rational world. The disorienting visual perspectives and the violent visual disjunctures that Magritte painted were ingenious mental compromises that contained his rage in the context of animate and inanimate, real and not real.

The rage was regulated and disguised but its menacing presence was never too far from the surface. In later years, as Magritte described his discovery of *Song of Love,* he recalled de Chirico's surgeon's glove as a boxing glove. The graceful de Chirico head had "seeing" eyes and long, lifelike flowing locks. But in *The Memory,* Magritte's 1942 imitation of the painting that made him weep, the statue is a woman, her eyes a stony blank, her lifeless, tightly plaited hair locked in place. The left side of her stone face, from the temple down to the chin, is covered with a patch of plastic-like blood that seems to be flowing from a fresh wound. In the left foreground, near the neck of the stone head, is the enigmatic iron ball that the biographer David Sylvester refers to as the "Magritte trademark." Is it simply an innocent imitation of de Chirico's cloth ball? Or is it the weapon that inflicted the wound? Or is it a child's toy—a ball that has rolled away from the garden lawn where it belongs?

The enigmatic ball, with its suggestive slit across the middle, is called a grelot. Grelots are, in reality, small iron bells, the jingle bells attached to the harness that encircles the neck of a horse. But what does Magritte's grelot signify? Why does this image recur so frequently in Magritte's paintings—attached to curtains, on the cushions of wicker chairs, on the ground, in the sky, in forests, as inner structures of the human head, as the blossoms of flowering plants, but never around the neck of a horse, where it belongs?

The grelot is one of Magritte's most subtle renditions of his unconscious experience of his depressed, psychologically dead mother, Régina. By placing the familiar, charmingly innocent grelots in unfamiliar contexts, Magritte transformed a commonplace object, something familiar and homey, into something mystifying and menacing. In the passage from *La Ligne de Vie* where Magritte describes his subversive propensities for "showing objects situated where we never find them," he employs the grelot to illustrate his artistic motives. "I caused the iron bells hanging from the necks of our magnificent horses to sprout like the treacherous plants at the edge of the mountain precipice."

Magritte wanted "to make the most familiar objects howl." The most familiar object, the image that represents a child's first home, is the mother's body. What happens when that intimately familiar and friendly object is transformed into something unfamiliar and mystifying? When Magritte compared the innocent grelots to treacherous flowering plants, he was unconsciously alluding to the deeper treachery of a dead mother who is still alive. Just as the merry tinkling of the grelots urges the horses on, and the seemingly innocent flowers lure an unknowing observer toward the abyss, so too does the innocent good mother lure the child toward her, inciting him to sweet desire and then rejecting him cruelly.

Like Magritte's mysteriously displaced grelots, a psychologically dead mother is an unpredictable combination of the charmingly familiar and the menacingly unfamiliar. By arousing the appetites and desires of her child and then frustrating the anticipated consummation, a "dead mother" is bewildering, disorienting, anxiety provoking and enraging. The child of a dead mother is frightened by the extent and power of his rage even if he is not entirely conscious of how that rage governs his life. The vague anxiety, perplexity, and confusion evoked by Magritte's displaced grelots give the viewer an immediate emotional experience of the uncanny effects produced by a "dead mother." As for the rage, all that remains is an eerie sense that the reality of a familiar object has somehow been violated.

Images of grelots are one version of Magritte's dead mother. Images of birds are another, and Magritte's rage is often symbolized by these images. The violence is blunt and specific. In 1925, the year that Magritte regained his sense of reality by deciding to put the real world on trial, he painted his first surrealist image. A black-curtained window opens onto a familiar, peaceful country landscape. Outside the window is a huge white arm reaching toward a tiny bird that eludes capture. From that fluttering, elusive, red-breasted bird, Magritte went on to paint a bird pecking at the eyes of a dislocated head, deformed birds assembled on piles of decomposing rocks, four birds with bleeding breasts and necks falling out of a "murderous" sky, a woman whose shadow appears in the shape of a bird. In *The Pleasure,* a woman surrounded by grotesque birds is lustily devouring the flesh of a bird; the blood from the bird's breast is splattering over her starched lace collar.

In 1930, after three years in Paris trying to earn his seat at the surrealist café tables and secure his reputation in the Parisian art world, Magritte returned to Brussels. He settled into a seven-room ground-floor apartment with a small garden. He began a daily routine of walking the dog, playing chess, eating dinner at home alone with Georgette or with some neighborhood friends.

Most of Magritte's post-1930 images are bewildering but instead of provoking violent dislocations, they evoke a sense of tranquillity and unity. It seemed that Magritte had decided to finally make himself at home in the world. In 1936, a mental image came to Magritte that confirmed his new artistic vision. Once again the image of a bird, or in this instance a "not-yet-bird," is assigned the role of muse.

One night in 1936, I awoke in a room in which a cage and the bird sleeping in it had been placed. A magnificent error caused me to see an egg in the cage instead of the bird. I then grasped a new and astonishing poetic secret, because the shock I experienced had been provoked precisely by the affinity of two objects, the cage and the egg, *whereas previously I used to provoke this shock by causing the encounter of unrelated objects.*

Elective Affinities, his 1933 painting of a huge egg nearly bursting out of a wire cage set in a frame of wooden table legs, had already expressed his poetic revelation of 1936. Afterward, (supposedly in 1936), Magritte painted *Clairvoyance,* a self-portrait of the artist studying an egg but painting on his canvas a bird in a cage. This peculiar dating of the two egg-bird paintings, which seems to reverse what the titles declare, may have been another of Magritte's practical jokes. Biographer David Sylvester attributes the misdatings of *Clairvoyance* and *Affinities* to an honest misrecollection on the part of the artist. Either way, the eggs and the birds, even their reversals in space and time, are essential aspects of Magritte's unconscious "dead mother" story.

Nineteen thirty-six, the date of Magritte's purported discovery of his "elective affinities," is the same year that he lost Georgette for the third time. Magritte was commuting to London, preparing an exhibition of his paintings. There, he was smitten with a stylishly gorgeous British model, a Mrs. Sheila Legg, who often posed for surrealist installations. Since he wanted to enjoy his fling with Mrs. Legg and did not want to hurt Georgette or arouse her suspicions, Magritte arranged for his friend, Paul Colinet, to distract his wife with an affair of her own. He composed an explicitly detailed letter to Colinet describing how best to pleasure Georgette and hold her interest. Georgette, much to everyone's astonishment, pursued her affair with determination and zest. She asked Magritte for a divorce. When the Germans occupied Belgium in 1940, Georgette stayed on in Brussels with Colinet while Magritte took refuge with the Scutenaires in the south of France.

The year or so of Magritte's separation from Georgette corresponds to the German occupation of Belgium and France. Magritte's personal dislocation also marked a bewildering mutation in his artistic style, which he referred to as his "Sunlight" period. Whereas earlier he had imitated surrealists, he now appropriated the flamboyant colors, swirling brushstrokes, and iridescent landscapes of the French impressionists. Whereas earlier Magritte had countered the bright optimism of bourgeois society with his dark, almost violent, anxious paintings, he now employed lighthearted charm as a weapon against the horrors of Nazism. As he had once transformed the darkest periods of his childhood into moments of sunlit revelation, now as a middle-aged artist, Magritte tried to reverse the blackest years in European history by aligning himself with the forces of light. Magritte argued, "Against the general pessimisms I uphold the quest for joy and pleasure."

In this seemingly perverse turnabout, however, Magritte was also unconsciously reaffirming his fundamental artistic creed. And once again he was unconsciously evoking an image of his dead mother. Magritte would insist that the unexpected combination of charm and menace was more forceful in its effects than obvious depictions of violence. Magritte's counteroffensive of charm and brightness in a time of despair was provocative and scandalous. The most generous, most forgiving interpretations of Magritte's sunlit period were that the whole business was some monstrous practical joke on the part of an artist temporarily deranged by the traumatic times.

The French surrealists were appalled by Magritte's reactionary optimism. André Breton, in his catalogue essay for the 1947 International Exhibition of Surrealism, chastised Magritte, referring to him as "a backward child who thinks he can guarantee a fine day for a promised treat by fixing the barometer needle at 'set fair.' "

It seemed to Magritte that the French had turned their backs on him because of his Belgian origins. Breton's remarks were seen as the culmination of a subtle rejection that had been going on since Magritte's early years in Paris, where he and Georgette were never quite radical enough to be admitted to the surrealist "inner circle." And then there was the popular French joke: "What is the difference between a potato and a Belgian?" "The potato is cultivated." Magritte was determined to show the French. As the rejected Belgian painter prepared to strike back, he decided to forget about charm.

The exhibition in 1948 of his *fauve* (wild beast) or *vache* (Belgian cow) paintings was accompanied by an outrageous catalogue, *Putting One's Foot in It*, written with scatalogical flair by his old friend and first biographer, Louis Scutenaire. David Sylvester, the eminent British art historian and dedicated Magritte biographer, whose usual tone is respectful and cautiously measured, entitles this chapter of his hero's life "Up Yours."

Magritte's counterattack on the French was a series of paintings that amounted to a vandalism of all of modern art. In six weeks Magritte dashed off thirty-nine works, dating some of them back to 1947 so that his impudent haste would not be detected. Magritte was in a state of agitated elation as he instructed Scutenaire "to fling it in their faces with a preface dipped in vitriol." Was this new aberration yet another symptom of some incipient madness in the respectable bourgeois Magritte or merely another of his macabre practical jokes?

Magritte confessed to Scutenaire that he had wanted to continue with the *vache* approach. "It's my natural propensity—slow suicide." However, he was still trying to make amends to Georgette, and she preferred his "well-made paintings of Yore." "In the future I shall exhibit of Yore. I'll find a way of slipping in some good hefty joke from time to time." Magritte won Georgette back and they were never separated again until his death on August 15, 1967. He gave up on open warfare and slipped back into his disguise. The master of the camouflage and tricks of nature set up his easel in a brightly lit corner of his bourgeois parlor with its overstuffed furniture, chiming clocks, china birds, draped curtains, and sunflower wallpaper where he once again attempted to disguise himself as a respectable, bowler-hatted man.

René Magritte, the camouflaged Maldodor, was an outspoken admirer of Edgar Allan Poe. Poe, with his quasi-philosophical theories, fantasy landscapes, themes of mutilation and perversion, insanity, intoxication, and crime was an out-and-out Maldodor, credited with being the nineteenth-century forebear of surrealism. Poe was also a favorite of Baudelaire's, who then relayed Poe's fondness for the bewildering effects of the uncanny to the surrealist painters. When the Museum of Modern Art in 1965 gave a large-scale exhibition of Magritte's work, they treated the visiting artist to the spectacular and lavish receptions that New York City museums are famous for. As for Magritte, the high point of this first and last American visit was his pilgrimage to the Poe house in the Bronx. When Magritte entered Poe's bedroom and saw his narrow bed, he wept.

Merely from the bare outlines of Poe's childhood we can understand why the Belgian painter might have been drawn to the American writer. A year after Poe's alcoholic actor father, David Poe, deserted the family, his beautiful and talented actress mother, Eliza, died a lingering death in the presence of her three young children. The orphaned three-year-old Edgar was then separated from what remained of his family—his sister and brother—and taken in by a childless couple, John and Fanny Allan. Fanny, his foster mother, was an affectionate woman with a capacity for gaiety. However, there were long periods of time when she was bedridden and emotionally remote. And no sooner did little Edgar imagine that he had at last found a safe haven than Fanny and John moved to England, where they shipped their foster child off to one of the grimmest British boarding schools. Fanny died when Edgar was twenty years old. When John Allan remarried and his new wife bore him a real son, he severed all connections with his provocative adopted son, who drank himself into stupors, gambled away his school money, and was perpetually in debt.

Both artists had lost a mother in childhood and been a "witness" to those deaths. Both artists suffered repetitions of their childhood loss through accidental and self-provoked incidents of losing and being lost. However, Magritte's attraction to Poe was not based simply on these similarities. It was Poe's artistic response to childhood loss that spoke to Magritte, rather than any overt correspondences in their life circumstances. Both Poe and Magritte were emotionally implicated in the same human dilemmas: the uncertain borders between animate and inanimate, living and nonliving, the antipathies between nature and art. Both were attracted to themes depicting the mutilation, fragmentation, and displacement of bodies. The undertones of death, deaths on the verge of happening, after-death experiences, stories featuring coffins, and dialogues across the frontiers of life and death in Poe's tales would a century later find their visual counterparts in Magritte's paintings.

For all their resemblances and resonances, however, the differences between Poe's artistic solutions and Magritte's are even more telling. It was as though each artist had set out to illuminate and express what remained unconscious in the other. Whereas the writer was always flagrantly and flamboyantly, even perversely, displaying the mutilated female bodies that haunted his mind, the painter, except for his "uncharacteristic" escapades of visual violence, became increasingly objective, restrained, and emotionally detached. The writer's ink flowed out of the studio and into the streets, covering the earth he walked on.

The painter marked out the corners of his living room and dining room for his easel. His palette was clean; the thinly painted surfaces of his paintings reveal nothing of the painter or the process of painting. Poe intentionally creates the shivering thrill of fear, the desolate moods of horror and death, while Magritte typically achieves his uncanny effects only indirectly and dispassionately.

Magritte's *Le Démon de la Perversion* and his several versions of *Le Domaine d' Arnheim* bear the titles of Poe's tales but bear no overt resemblance whatsoever to Poe's narratives. However, for all their manifest differences, the paintings and the tales are vivid images of a dead mother.

Poe's Arnheim tale is closer to Magritte's screen memories of childhood, where a menacing darkness and gloom is gradually transposed into a moment of sunbright revelation. The tale plays out the dark-light reversals that Magritte plays with in many of his paintings. Briefly, Poe's story reverses the tragedy of his own life by taking the protagonist, the voyager-artist named Ellison, through darkened mountain gorges, from one closed-in, deadened landscape to another until finally the artist arrives at the glowing landscape of his visionary garden of Eden. The last of the gorges suddenly opens up onto the light, animated, flourishing fairyland where flowers sparkle and radiate like jewels. The lost voyager has been restored to the welcoming embrace of a kinder and gentler Nature.

There is no embrace of love in Magritte's Arnheim paintings. The centerpiece of each is a huge stone mountain in the shape of an eagle. In all but the last of this series, the eagle-mountains are covered with snow and ice. The unrelieved whiteness is assaultive in its intensity— almost blinding. In the 1949 version, the violence implicit in the icy whiteness is made explicit. The glass window that shelters the viewer from the distant icy eagle-mountain has been "somehow" shattered. On each fragment of glass, Magritte has painted one part of the shattered, mutilated body of the icy eagle. The outdoor eagle remains intact in its icy remoteness. The visual effect is uncanny, especially since it calls to mind the curtained window overlooking the familiar green landscape with the hand reaching to capture the elusive red-breasted bird—Magritte's first surrealist painting, his first surreal image of his elusive dead mother.

In the last of Magritte's Arnheims, dated 1962, the effect is less dramatically uncanny but no less graphic in its depiction of the dead mother. Here an icy azure-blue eagle-mountain is set against a narrow strip of pale blue daylight sky on which sits a crescent sliver of nighttime moon. Below, in the foreground, perched precariously at the edge of a stone wall that separates the viewer from the viewed, is a prickly twigged nest containing three fragile unhatched eggs. The stony mother eagle that wraps her wings around the edges of the painting is the entire environment surrounding her still-unborn babies. The viewer wonders, are the three little eggs part of the living world, or will they be claimed by the inanimate world of the stone eagle? The edge of a stone wall distances the viewer from the tragedy. What will happen to the three little babies who emerge from these eggs? One could never bond with such a mother. This lack of connection between mother and child is emphasized by the separation of the nest from its natural environment. In this cold, forbidding landscape there is no vision of grace, there is no longing; there is no desire; there is no hope of a return to mother. On the other hand, of course, there is no awakening of appetite, no possibility of disappointment or hurt, in the blank eyes of this monstrous stone eagle.

Recall that a dead mother is partly a construction of the child, who must somehow transform the mother into a deanimated, toneless object in order to avoid the hurt and humiliation of looking into a blank mirror. The eye may be blank and reflect nothing, but the one who is looked at is still alive. By removing the fleshy life from a body and transforming it into dead stone, we deprive it of its power to excite. If there is no expectation of an animated response, there will be no disappointment or hurt when no life exists.

Magritte's icy landscape visions sabotage Poe's utopian dream of resurrection and renewal. Instead of a glowing fairyland of hope, where the lost child is restored to the gentle body of Mother Nature, Magritte confronts the viewer with a landscape of frozen remoteness and stony petrification.

However, the petrified stone eagle gives birth to the little eggs that will generate new life. For all that their "dead mothers" could not give them, apparently Régina Magritte and Eliza Poe also inspired a passion in their sons for unveiling the naked truths of life and death. The two sons of the two dead mothers renounced fatherhood but went on to create living works of art. In an attempt to resurrect and animate their dead mothers, Magritte and Poe convey the uncanny effects of a dialogue that blurs the boundaries between living and nonliving matter, a dialogue that incites rage and violence. Nevertheless, as the dead mother comes to life in Magritte's paintings and Poe's tales, she engages us in a dialogue of Life. We see her. We hear her. Her ghostly presence is palpable. Artists, even as they testify to death or the uncanny presences of death in life, are always testifying to the tenacity of human dialogue.

CHAPTER TWELVE

❧

IMAGES OF ABSENCE,
VOICES OF SILENCE

Within reach, close and not lost, there remained, in the midst of the losses, this one thing: language. This, the language, was not lost but remained, yet in spite of everything. But it had to pass through its own answerlessness, pass through a frightful falling mute, pass through the thousand darknesses of death bringing speech. It passed through and yielded no words for what was happening—but it went through those happenings. Went through, and could come into the light of day again, "enriched" by all that.

—PAUL CELAN, 1958

After the Holocaust, philosophers argued that silence would be the only humane response to what happened. Only silence can honor the dead. To write lyric poetry after Auschwitz would be barbaric. Poetry, music, and songs are celebrations that transfigure an unthinkable fate into something meaningful. How does the artist, who is nothing if he does not speak, resist the verdict of silence? He creates a dialogue of degeneration, a language of broken words and incomplete phrases, representations of nonimages and blank canvases, symphonies of silence that invite the listener into a shattered, shelterless world.

Paul Ancel, who after the war renamed himself Celan, was born in 1920 in Romania, to German-Jewish parents. In 1942 his mother and father were deported to concentration camps and murdered. Celan himself escaped death by crossing over a selection line dividing those who were being sent to a forced labor camp and those destined for a death camp. After the war, Celan translated from French, English, and Russian into German and wrote essays and poetry in German. In his famous poem "Death Fugue," he tortures and fractures the language of those who murdered his parents and in the process resurrects his mother and creates his true "mother tongue." In 1970, Celan drowned himself in the Seine.

Celan resisted the verdict of silence by creating a language that defied traditional structures. As he said, language had to pass "through a frightful falling mute." Similarly, history had to pass through a Silence before anyone could bear to listen. Massive trauma can only be articulated belatedly. While the traumatic event is happening, the victim must be blind and deaf and mute. He must blank out what he would normally see and hear and tune out what he would normally feel and think. Otherwise, he would not survive.

In 1986, the Holocaust survivor Primo Levi described this barely human survival strategy and explained that the inhuman conditions of a Lager [concentration camp] prevented the prisoners from "acquiring an overall vision of their universe."

> The prisoner felt overwhelmed by a massive edifice of violence and menace but could not form for himself a representation of it because his eyes were fixed to the ground by every single minute's needs. . . . At a distance of years one can today definitely affirm that the history of the Lagers has been written almost exclusively by those who, like myself, never fathomed them to the bottom. Those who did so did not return, or their capacity for observation was paralyzed by suffering or incomprehension.

In some fundamental sense, almost by definition, *massive* trauma is unwitnessable. In order to be a witness or to bear witness to an event one must be consciously and psychologically present when the event is occurring. But in a concentration camp, to be present means to become aware of an apocalyptic reality and, consequently, to become conscious of one's own unimaginable suffering. To be present requires a person to do more than merely see or hear; to be present means to be able to feel and experience what is happening. This level of awareness would either overwhelm a person's nervous system with terror and kill him immediately or so weaken his mind and body that he would be marked for extermination. Consequently, those who actually did witness the atrocities of the Holocaust are either dead or suffered too much to ever know what actually happened to them. Only the survivors can testify, and since (in order to survive) they could not be fully present during their own massive traumatization, even they cannot truly bear witness.

Remarkably, the survivors who could, at best, register fragments of what was happening to them, somehow decades later communicated the feelings and thoughts about what had happened to them to their children. It was their children who would testify as to what happened to their parents.

Most survivors of the Holocaust could not remember or speak of what they had experienced, but their psychological absences and tortured silences transmitted to their children events these survivors had been unable to witness. In "Psychoanalytic Contributions to Holocaust Studies," Milton Jucovy reported that in general, resistance fighters and those who actively opposed the Nazi terror were more likely to tell their children about their Holocaust experiences than those who were survivors of concentration and death camps. One of the defining features of massive trauma is the factor of silence, especially having to silence terror, rage, and grief as one witnesses the torture and extermination of family members. Children of extermination camp survivors, who *typically* were more severely traumatized than other survivors, tend to be more tormented by the traumas of their parents' Holocaust past than other children of survivors.

But wherever and however the parent survived, the child of a survivor becomes an unconscious witness to the deliberate and systematic extermination of millions of human beings by other human beings. By remaining silent, the survivor hopes to preserve whatever shreds of sanity remain. She hopes to grow back into a whole human being. When a Holocaust survivor brings a child into the world, she is looking to the child for a second chance at life. She is hoping to shelter her child from the atrocities she suffered. However, in most cases, the shelter of silence becomes a Holocaust monument that casts its shadows over the life of her child. When the child of a survivor is finally able to weep for her survivor parent or parents, she will weep for all the victims of the Holocaust. However, that ability to weep is usually a long time coming. At first the child knows only that one or both parents are hiding some terrible secret. And the child wonders, "What is the meaning of the absence, the silence? What is this truth that must never be spoken?"

In an extermination camp, each dawn brought a new selection, where virtually by chance one might be selected to live while a beloved relative or friend was selected to die. When the parent was in the camp, the human dialogue—the very thing that makes life a life worth living—became irrelevant and even dangerous. Crucial to the Nazis' extermination technique was a systematic terrorism calculated to dehumanize concentration camp inmates. If the prisoners no longer resembled human beings, they could be treated like vermin who deserved to be exterminated. Any sign of emotion could incite the rage of the commandants and capos who were in charge of the selection process. Therefore, if a prisoner chose to survive, he had to conceal his humanness. To choose life became a matter of merely not-dying. To want or desire more than bread or a blanket would bring certain death. Therefore, the complex network of needs, wants, desires, and passions that had defined one's humanity up until then had to be reduced to simple need. Shame or guilt, or any feeling that displayed an attachment to or concern for others marked the person for the gas chambers. The terror and panic that are appropriate responses to an apocalyptic reality would have led directly to extermination. Fear of any kind could not be shown. Anxiety, however, was essential to survival; without anxiety, one couldn't evaluate the dangers. The balance was exquisitely delicate; one had to experience just enough anxiety to be alert and effective, but not enough to be overwhelmed by the horror of what was actually happening. The usual defenses of the ego with its infinite subtleties and ingenious compromises were now superfluous and a threat to survival.

To not-die one had to build up a shell, armor the ego, and deform the self into a nonthinking, nonfeeling machine. Armoring the self is not the same as preserving it. Self-preservation entails having a sense of self and experiencing oneself as an animated, thinking and feeling person. But when a person chooses merely to not-die, he must blunt all sensations and perceptions, shut out the abysmal realities, and close off all animation or vitality. Then, after achieving this robotization, after succeeding in adapting to a bizarre, impossible reality, after choosing to not-die, one *might* live; that is, if one was not *selected*.

The daily assault on our dignity and self-esteem, our sense of power and control, our bodily integrity—the entirety of a human being's narcissism—would eventually undermine the will to not-die. For some prisoners, the loss of all power or control over their destiny brought them to an extreme state of robotization where the self was reduced to sheer reflex existence. Thus the "closing off" defense that began in an effort to armor the self could result in a total depletion of a person's narcissistic reserves, a psychological equivalent of death that increased one's susceptibility to disease and eventually resulted in one's actual physical death.

When night descended denial was easier for the concentration camp prisoners. One could relax his armor. A prisoner might recall the earlier days of milk and honey and imagine relaxing into the sweet, comforting arms of family and loved ones. He might fantasize about the better and more noble world that was coming. At night, the prisoner might close her eyes and dream of returning home. A common dream recalled by many survivors was that "they had returned home and with passion and relief were describing their past sufferings to a loved one, and were not believed, indeed were not even listened to."

After World War II was over and life gradually resumed some semblance of normalcy, the survivors were plagued by the guilt and shame of having survived when others did not. The survivors had simply chosen to not-die—and they had not been selected. They might have been proud of their exceptional strength of will, of their ability to defeat those who would have reduced them to excrement. Instead, the survivors felt that they should atone for not having died, for having witnessed the slaughter of their loved ones, for having submitted to the humiliations and degradations, for having abandoned all the values and ideals of virtue that make life a life worth living.

It is understandable that the survivors would have remained silent.

But how do we account for the silence of the rest of the world? After the war, a massive psychological resistance, not unlike the numbing and "blanking out" of the survivors, preserved the sanity of the world. It took three decades for the world to begin to absorb what had happened at Auschwitz, Bergen-Belsen, Buchenwald, Dachau, Treblinka. What had happened was "death, total, absolute death—of man and of all people, of language and imagination, of time and of the spirit." So spoke the Holocaust survivor, Elie Wiesel, in 1975.

Even now, a half century after the extermination of six million European Jews and six million other "impure" races—a total of over fifty million if one figures in the Polish, the Russians, the Hungarians, the civilians and soldiers of the not-so-impure races who were also slaughtered by the Nazis—there are still some who would rather believe that it could not have happened, that it did not happen. Or, even if *the* Holocaust did happen, they reason, it was no worse than the other holocausts: Hiroshima, Vietnam, Cambodia; no worse than what the Israelis do to the Palestinian Arabs or the Iraqis do to the Kurds, or the Turks did to the Armenians, or the Serbs to the Muslims and Croats, or what the Croats once did to the Jews and now do to the Serbs, or what the Nigerians have done to the Ibo, or what the whites of all Western nations have done and still do to colored peoples all over the world, or what "Americans" have done and still do to Native Americans.

Finding the truth of the Holocaust so devastating to their ideals of human virtue, few people wanted to hear that the persecutions suffered by mothers and fathers could actually create nightmares in their children, even in their children's children. What might this reveal about the other holocausts?

Much has been learned from *the* Holocaust survivors, their children and their grandchildren, and can be applied to every survivor of massive trauma. The human dialogue resists its own extermination. The unwitnessable, unspeakable horror of massive trauma is transmitted belatedly, long after the event is over and then, at first, only through images of absence and voices of silence. After the unimaginable atrocities they suffered, the survivors managed to make homes in new lands, learn new languages, earn money, raise new families to replace those they had lost, carry on the human dialogue. A generation later, the children of Holocaust survivors testify to the effects of their parents' massive traumas on their own lives.

Until the Holocaust secrets became bearable enough for the rest of the world to articulate, the children of survivors had no way of knowing that their current emotional plights were indirect outcomes of the atrocities suffered by their parents. If the child of a survivor sought professional help, she often faced a silence in the consulting room that mirrored the silence in her home—and in the world. Therapists, even those who had treated other children of severely traumatized parents and should have known better, did not want to believe that the nightmares of the Holocaust survivors could go on to become the nightmares of their children. The children of survivors made it easy for us to maintain our self-deception, for they had come to us for the relief of symptoms that might have afflicted any person. Yet something was oddly and crucially different about these patients, and we all suspected it.

Not until the late 1970s, when therapists who were treating children of survivors began to share their experiences, did we begin to grasp the meaning of the events that transpired in our consulting rooms. The most common symptom among the children and adults we encountered were phobias—school phobias in the children and agoraphobia, a terror of leaving the house or walking in the streets, in the adults. Out of the blue, the child of a survivor would be overcome by bouts of inexplicable sadness, spells of uncontrollable weeping. A few were self-mutilators. Some sought relief from psychosomatic illnesses, such as colitis. All were plagued by dreams and fantasies of body mutilation. All were beset by fears of bodily damage and illness. All complained of an eating disorder. In these ways, the children of survivors were not unlike many of our other patients or, in fact, not unlike the vast numbers of people who never enter a therapist's office.

What made our experiences with children of survivors distinctly different was our own uncanny sensations of speaking with the dead. Our consulting rooms were filled with voices and gestures of the dead. The terrors in our patients' fantasies and dreams were only partially theirs. The children of survivors were living out and dreaming out their parents' nightmares. The children were enacting experiences and relating fantasies that could only come from a person who had actually been in a ghetto or extermination camp and actually observed the slaughters and deaths of her loved ones, her friends and neighbors, the strangers who became her cell mates—the murder of her own soul. Since the survivor parent had been unable to witness the horror, she could not remember it. And if she did remember, she remembered only fragments, and even these were rarely, if ever, put into words. The child of the survivor had been sheltered from the truth. But the child was living the nightmare.

What term could describe and encompass this uncanny experience? When psychologists begin to get anxious about the dialogues transpiring in their consulting rooms, they very often come up with a jargonish phrase to contain and absorb their anxieties. For example, in the early post-Holocaust years, therapists who were treating survivors latched onto the labels "survivor's guilt" and "identification with the aggressor." But these terms, which were comfortably familiar to psychoanalysts and other psychologists, turned out to be a new form of persecution for the survivors, whose awesome experience was trivialized by this sort of jargon. However, sometimes strange new words and phrases are necessary to describe strange and bewildering experiences. And if the word that is created is the right word, it not only helps to provide answers to troubling questions but also helps to convey psychological meanings commensurate with previously unimaginable human experiences.

Early in the 1970s, the psychoanalyst Judith Kestenberg, a survivor of anti-Semitism who had left Vienna in 1938 just prior to the Austrian capitulation to the Nazis, gave the name *"transposition"* to the psychological process of unconscious cross-generational transmission of massive trauma. At first Kestenberg's term was as bewildering to therapists as the experiences we were trying to comprehend and absorb. But once we grasped the profound implications of Kestenberg's new word, we discovered some answers to the question, "If the parent cannot remember and will not speak, how does the child know?" Moreover, through our understandings of transposition, we also discovered within ourselves emotions that enabled us to empathize with the complicated inner life of the survivor's child. Transposition corresponds to something vital and enduring in the human dialogue. Transposition, which technically refers only to the transmission of *massive trauma*, can in fact be used to describe the reciprocal dialogue between every child and his parent.

Transposition describes the uncanny experience where the past reality of the parent intrudes into the present psychological reality of the child. Transposition is an anomalous version of the ordinary psychological process whereby the wishes, desires, fantasies, ideals, and experiences of a parent are unconsciously transmitted to a child. Transposition is generational transmission run amok. Transposition turns the ordinary dimensions of space and time inside out.

What makes transposition so much more awesome than ordinary generational transmission is the *amount of psychological space* the parent's past occupies in the child's ongoing existence. Transposition also refers to *reversals of ordinary time,* whereby the temporal positions of parent and child are exchanged. Since the parent's past occupies the psychological space that would ordinarily belong to the current life of the child, the child must give up her right to exist in her own present. What makes transposition so monstrous and preternatural is that it entails the transmission of *massive* trauma.

Whereas any parent will consciously encourage a child to imitate and identify with her courage, virtues, and ideals, she will do everything in her power to block the transmission of terror, shame, and guilt. Yet when it comes to the transmission of massive trauma, the parent's conscious desires to protect her child seem to count for very little. The child suckles "the black milk" (Celan's phrase) of trauma, relishes and absorbs it, cultivates its bitter taste as if it were vital sustenance—as if it were existence itself. The transposition of trauma which, as we shall see, originates in the parent's unconscious needs and wishes must rely on and exploit the child's happier susceptibilities—to be at one with the parent, to be close to the parent, to partake in the parent's power, to be like the parent, to be loved and admired by the parent, to maintain a dialogue with the parent. The psychological process that comes from the child is normal. What the child is absorbing is abnormal.

The parent unwittingly and against her conscious will positions her trauma within the child; the child sets out to cure the parent and undo her trauma by placing himself in the parent's position.

Transposition is a feature in every child's life. Every child cultivates a morsel of suffering absorbed from an unconscious awareness of the parent's traumas. Every child gives up some portion, however large or small, of his own life to cure a parent's trauma. However, in the child of a Holocaust survivor, where the parent suffered a *massive* trauma, transposition is omnipresent.

How do the dreams, wishes, and nightmares of a parent enter a child's mind? How does a parent transmit his or her past to the child if he never says a word or if, in fact, he may not even consciously recall this past? Transposition is already present when the child's life begins. The parent projects her traumas through her caregiving gestures. The infant receives the traumas and makes them part of herself. The infant's ordinary susceptibility to receiving and taking in the parent via reciprocal dialogue prepares the soil for transposition.

An infant's survival depends on the ministrations of a mother whose capacity for empathy shields the child from internal and external stimuli that would otherwise overwhelm his still incipient and unformed ego. Occasionally, even the most empathic mother will unwittingly expose her child to experiences that are still beyond his emotional capacities. If this happens every once in a while, the child recovers, his ego continues to form and develop, and life goes on. However, when a mother fails to be empathic over an extended period of time, this constitutes a disruption and derailment of dialogue. The child begins to sense that he must protect himself. He senses that something more drastic and imperiling than his own immediate survival is at stake and that in addition to protecting himself, he must also protect his parent. In order to survive, the child must attempt to empathize with the mother and care for her. The child learns that he must become his parent's bridge to life.

A mother who lost her children in an extermination camp was prevented from mourning. To show any sign of sorrow or grief would have brought certain death. The bodies of her dead children were shoveled into mass graves. There were no burials, no tombstones, no time allotted for saying farewell to the dead. If she chose to not-die, the mother had to resume her robotic existence immediately. Because she was and still is unable to mourn, the mother is locked in a frozen dialogue with her dead loved ones, which unconsciously infiltrates her dialogues with her living child. Much as the survivor mother wants to live in the present, she clings to the dead, never letting them go. Not having been put to rest by a process of mourning, her dead ones remain alive, frozen in a state of potential animation.

The survivor mother is unable to make room in her heart for a fully animated dialogue with her living child. But the living child, who hungers for the emotional reciprocities of human dialogue, will do everything he can to bring life and animation to the mother.

Precocious attunement, where an infant absorbs the parent's trauma through a derailment in dialogue, is the key to a child's awareness of what he is not supposed to know. Inevitably, the other susceptibilities of childhood also collaborate in the unconscious transposition of a parent's trauma. Compare the natural, everyday experiences that assume importance in a child's life—eating, retaining and eliminating bodily wastes, asserting one's autonomy, displaying courage and initiative, exhibiting one's body with pride, showing off one's mind with joy, competing with one's siblings or parents—with the parent's Holocaust experiences—starvation, uncontrollable attacks of diarrhea that soiled one's garments and bedding, living conditions that made him feel like filthy vermin, fantasies and acts of escaping and hiding, being captured and recaptured, acting like a robot, trying to remain unnoticed.

Each phase of the child's early development invites a transposition of the parent's Holocaust experience. The survivor parents unconsciously focus on the issues that were and still are crucial to their salvation. Though the mother still cannot remember her starvation, she transmits the emotional experience of starvation through her preoccupation with buying, preparing, serving, and eating food. The father transmits the physical degradations he endured by being preoccupied with cleanliness and the elimination of feces. When the little child experiments with running away from the parent, the parent may be oblivious to the child's wish to be found and caught. Because of his own terrors of being found and caught, the parent looks away from the child's playful drama and lets him get lost. Or the moment before the child is about to run away, the parent grabs her and holds her so tightly that the child senses some inexplicable terror in the idea of escaping and being caught. When a girl is innocently competing with her mother for her father's attentions, the mother may suddenly decide to snip off her daughter's ponytail and send her to school with a crew cut. Of course, when the mother arrived at the camp at the same age her daughter is now, that is what her captors did to her. To survive the psychological trauma of her mother's hostile gesture, the daughter develops an unconscious fantasy that she has been selected by her mother to perform a special mission. She, and she alone, can repair her mother's trauma by sacrificing her own desires and longings. She becomes obese, thus effectively concealing her beauty under layers of fat. Or she starves herself until her body is transformed into the body of a concentration camp prisoner.

Thus, sometimes, it is the age of the living child that triggers the parent's unconscious need to undo and repair the past. If, for example, the mother was separated from her parents at the age of two and never saw them again, she may find some reason to tear her own child away from her when the child arrives at the age of two. Perhaps the child is placed in a hospital for an undiagnosable illness. Perhaps the child is sent off to day care so that she can begin to read and write. Perhaps the mother leaves the child in the care of a stranger while she takes a month's vacation. Similarly, if the father was rounded up by the Gestapo and placed in a ghetto when he was six, he might put his child in a ghettolike situation shortly before or after her sixth birthday. Maybe he places his daughter in a shelter for homeless children so that he can work at night, or he dispatches her to a convent so she can learn proper manners, or he enrolls her in a kibbutz so she can learn how to share with others. Because of these abrupt and unexpected derailments in dialogue, the child becomes a witness to what happened to the parent.

After a certain point in her development, the child begins to know about the parent's past because she wants to know. She becomes a witness through her own efforts and initiative. A parent's silence and secrecy actually stimulate the child's need and desire to uncover his past. Children are curious about everything, particularly about the "secrets" of the unseen. Of the myriad situations that come up in the course of an ordinary day, there are three enigmas that invite a child's most intense curiosity: what goes on in the unseen parts of her body, where babies come from, and what her parents do and say when she is not around. Sooner or later, the child figures out that her parents' secret life holds the key to unlocking the other two mysteries. For a child, the parents are god, the parents are how the world began and how the child began. She wants to know what goes on inside their bodies, who made them, what they were like when they were children, how they got to have grown-up bodies, how they make babies. From her earlier baby fantasies of digging into the hidden passageways, spaces, and crevices of her own body, a new fantasy about her parents begins to take shape. She gets the idea of building a tunnel back to the parents' past. Of course there are no *actual* time tunnels, but everyone has imagined such a possibility at one time or another. Tunnels to the past or future are among the familiar structures in science fiction novels and films. Children believe in these imaginary time tunnels, and while they are always partially successful, they are never nearly as successful as they imagine. In their tireless quest to expose their parents' secrets, children eventually get enough of a glimpse into the past to piece together a version of the historical truth. Since this history has been constructed by a child's immature mind with its tangle of untamed passions, the child's version of the past is a distortion of what actually happened to the parent. Nevertheless, like any mythology of how the world began, what a child digs up as she tunnels back to the parent's past always contains a few grains of truth.

In the best of circumstances, a child's tunneling results in a benign generational transmission. The child happens upon a secret wish or desire that the parent has as yet been unable to fulfill, and the child takes up the parent's position, fulfills his secret dream, and then returns to the present to live out her own life. In this case, the mission to rescue the parent is possible without a profound incursion into the life of the child. The child returns from her mission with a sense of having enlarged her own self and given a portion of the parent's unfulfilled life back to him. However, the best of circumstances does not apply to the transposition of massive trauma. The child of a survivor does not feel entitled to live her own life until she goes back to the psychotic world of the concentration camps and rescues the parent.

To return to the camp means to return to the naked truth, to the alternative of life *or* death. In the camp, if one person lived, another would be selected to die. The child of a survivor does not wish to die in order to save the parent. Like her survivor parent, she wants desperately to live. So that they both may live, the child employs her own body and mind as a bridge to transport the parent out of his psychotic universe. The enormity of the parent's trauma requires a messianic rescue mission. Until a survivor's child is helped to understand that she is *allowed* to live an ordinary life, that she is entitled to enjoy eating and breathing, dressing up, taking care of her body, looking pretty, learning and knowing, creating living works, and bearing living children, this mission impossible to cure the parent preoccupies and eats away at the present life of the child.

As Kestenberg said,

> In all cases, the need to discover, to reenact, or to live the parents' past was a major issue in the lives of survivors' children. This need is different from the usual curiosity of children about their parents. These children feel they have a mission to live in the past and to change it so that their parents' humiliation, disgrace and guilt can be converted into victory over the oppressors, and the threat of genocide undone with a restitution of life and worth.

The cases of transposition recorded in the psychoanalytic literature seem dramatic and extreme, but they correspond to my own clinical experiences with children of survivors. And while some analysts dispute the term *transposition,* preferring the more familiar *hysteria,* most would agree on the psychological phenomena which occur to some degree in all children of survivors.

In several of her published papers, Kestenberg described her treatment of Rachel, the twenty-six-year-old daughter of an extermination camp survivor. Rachel, a gifted painter who had given up her talents to devote herself to another mission, was born in the United States. Rachel's mission was to not only live out the experiences of her father and his relatives, but also to assume the roles of all the Jews who suffered the Holocaust atrocities.

Rachel's father had been transported to Auschwitz when he was a young adolescent. When Rachel arrived at pubescence and her childlike body began to assume the form of a woman, she brought her own body to the edge of starvation and death. To Rachel, the Holocaust was the emotional equivalent of starvation. She had imagined that she could feed starving babies with her own body. In her fantasies she put the starving babies into her body, held on to them until they were well fed, and then released them. Sometimes she would go a step further and keep them imprisoned inside her until they died. Then, when she finally released them, she imagined she was resurrecting dead babies and liberating them from their prisons. Through her self-tormenting ways of consumption and defecation, Rachel was, in her own way, giving order to the chaos of the Holocaust. She was doing and undoing the suffering. Rachel was equating the unknown processes that went on inside her body with the unknown secrets of the Holocaust.

The Israeli psychoanalyst Yolanda Gampel told of a seven-year-old Israeli child, Michal, who was suddenly afflicted with a severe disturbance in memory. This heretofore perceptive, bright, imaginative child could no longer recall recent events or lessons she had learned in school or words she had spoken the night before. Sometimes she would fall into an "absence" and awaken from it in a lost confusion, unsure of where she had been and what she had been doing. The analyst, after hearing about the child's symptoms, requested that Michal's mother give a detailed history of the family. During this interview, the mother related her own childhood in great detail and mentioned only in passing that Michal's father had come to live in Israel as a child. Michal's mother left her homeland as a teenager and emigrated to Israel, where she met and married him. No mention was made of the father's history before he went to Israel or before he married Michal's mother. The mother's story about the father, brief as it was, turned out to be untrue.

Michal had listened seriously and intently to her mother's animated narrative. When Michal's mother left the room, the analyst invited the child to draw pictures and play games. After a few minutes, Michal spoke up, saying she would not want "to be [sic] an electric fence in the Warsaw Ghetto, because they put the soldier's children there and if they touch the fence, they will electrocute themselves and die." Michal's terrible words suggested events from a past she could not have known. Gampel, who had treated other children of survivors, realized that Michal must be speaking of another child, perhaps one of her parents. This other child from the distant past had discovered that it was much wiser to be absent than aware. And now, it seemed, Michal was enacting the experience of this other child. Gampel decided to recheck the family history.

At the next interview, Gampel told the mother what Michal had said and asked if Michal might have heard a family story about the Holocaust. The mother confessed, "My husband was in the Warsaw Ghetto as a young child and later in a concentration camp, but we have never spoken about this with the children. How could she know? My husband always says he arrived in Israel as a child and there are never any further questions about his background."

When the father learned what Michal had told the therapist, he was touched and deeply disturbed by his little girl's uncanny attunement to his childhood feelings. He recalled that when he was six or seven years old, the same age that Michal was, he was rounded up and brought to the ghetto. Then a few months later he was transported to the concentration camp. He was willing to do anything to cure Michal of her absences. He gave his permission for the truth to be told to his daughter, even though he could not bear to be present at the retelling of his nightmare.

As Michal began to understand the connection between her memory absences and her father's absences, she realized she no longer *had* to be absent from her own life. Now that her father's truth had been told, Michal was no longer compelled to enact and concretize his past emotional experience. Michal's memory was restored, and young as she was, she came to understand the reasons for her father's strange emotional absences. The family continued to respect the father's need to be detached from his past, but now there was an intimacy, a connection between the father and his children that had never existed before. Michal, in enacting a truth her father could not speak, did manage to resurrect him. He was no longer frozen in a dialogue of absence, shut off from all feelings and thoughts in an icy cocoon of silence.

Absences designed to protect the self from memory, to spare the child any exposure to unspeakable atrocities, become empty spaces which invite fantasies of mutilation and torment. The silences create an emotional climate that compels the survivor's child to live a double life where what happens in the present assumes the meanings of what happened in the past. Ordinary events take on a double registration of present and past. The simplest detail of everyday life assumes a life-or-death dimension. A loop of cord hanging from a lamp becomes a hangman's noose to the survivor. The child hears the parent gasp and sees the parent frantically rearranging the cord. A policeman approaches on the street; the mother has a panic attack. She clutches the child's hand tightly and stands as still as a statue. Nothing is said, but the child registers the mother's reactions and knows "something" is wrong. The child comes to know that existence is precarious. You must always be alert. And, to be safe, you must be invisible.

In many cases the child of a survivor would overhear bits and fragments of the past as the parents whispered to each other in Yiddish. The child would catch a word here and there, just enough to get a sense of what had happened. In other cases, nothing is overheard, or at least the child does not recall having heard anything. Perhaps Michal only heard the words "Warsaw Ghetto" in passing. Perhaps she never heard anything else about her father's childhood. But she did grow up in the atmosphere of a father who was absent. She sensed her father's unbearable sadness; she witnessed his absences, and in her childlike longing to be closer to her father, she took his sadness and absence into herself. A child's desire to be loved and admired by the parent is so powerful that she will readily assimilate whatever she senses is vital to the parent. Michal identified with her father's absences and in doing so recreated in herself a history she had no conscious knowledge of.

Transposition compels the child to make the parents' traumas visible and concrete in their own lives. Concretization is a special form of transposition. The parents have undoubtedly hinted at some horror, and the child has pieced parts of the story together by tunneling. But essentially the trauma remains obscure. The trauma is not only about what actually happened, that is, the events in themselves, which are atrocious enough; the trauma also concerns the parents' buried and unspeakable responses to the devastation they saw and heard and could not stop from happening. The child senses the parents' terror, shame, and guilt about the "something" they feel they should have prevented but could not. These unspoken affects inspire the child to enact a scenario of terror, shame, and guilt. The child creates scenes and dramas that re-evoke these silenced affects and in doing so concretizes the presence of the lost ones.

The German psychoanalyst Ilse Grubrich-Simitis relates the story of a patient who was born to Polish parents who had lost two children in Auschwitz. After the liberation the parents found each other in a displaced persons camp and one year later settled in West Germany. They spoke only German with Mark, Grubrich-Simitis's patient, their later-born child. But when there were quarrels and the emotional atmosphere heated up, Mark would hear his mother cursing at him or his father in her mother tongue. Once he thought he heard the words "I wish you would burn like pinewood."

Mark's mother stayed at home with him from the time he was an infant until he was six years years old. She protected him zealously, never leaving him with a baby-sitter, never letting him out of her sight, always holding him on her lap to feed him, keeping him in the house all day, and forbidding him to play in the courtyard with the neglected, dirty, vulgar children of Nazis. When Mark started school, his mother immediately got a job working as a bookkeeper in his father's factory.

During his school years, Mark had few friends. With both parents at work, he spent most of his afternoons alone at home, longing for company and not having the slightest idea of how to comfort or entertain himself. His mother had always told him exactly what to do. But now that Mark was a "schoolboy," his mother all at once expected him to manage on his own.

Without knowing why, Mark began to experiment with inflammable materials—matches, candles, spirits, gas—during his lonely afternoons. It was as though the experiments kept him company; the flames were his friends. This went on for four years, without creating any more damage than a few ashes here, a few singed towels there. Ashes can be wiped up and damaged towels hidden until they can be thrown away. His parents never suspected what Mark was doing.

Then, one early evening, when he was ten years old, Mark "accidently" set fire to a curtain in the living room. The conflagration began just around the dinner hour, when most of the working-class parents who lived in Mark's apartment house were returning from their jobs. Within minutes, the living room was enveloped in smoke and flames. Mark was terrified. He was immobilized. If a neighbor had not come home just then, smelled the smoke, and crashed his fists through the door to the apartment, Mark might have been burned to death.

In his analysis, Mark, now a thirty-five-year-old adult, was able to grasp the extended unconscious meanings of his schoolboy experiments. By standing still as the flames drew closer and closer, he was repeating the helplessness of his parents' lost children. By arranging to be saved in the nick of time, he was resuscitating the lost children and reversing his parents' trauma. The lonely boy was also showing his mother that when a mother deserts her child, he might get into dangerous trouble.

As a result of these insights into his own behavior, Mark was finally, after three decades of silence, able to speak with his parents about their experiences in Auschwitz. From these painful conversations, Mark learned that his parents had assumed and imagined that their children had been burned alive. The moment they arrived on the selection ramp, the two children had been torn away from his mother, and she never saw them again. Yet she blamed herself for having left her children. And, like so many mothers who lost children in the extermination camps, she unconsciously encouraged her new son to enact and concretize the terror of her loss *and* her shame and guilt. After having protected Mark from every contingency, from starvation, from separations, from contaminating friendships, she suddenly left him alone to his own devices—with nothing to keep him company but the sight of flames and the smells of gas and "burning wood."

Mark's parents might easily have sniffed the ashes and scorch smells and become aware of what their son was up to while they were at work. The survivor parent's conscious wish is that her new family will erase the memory of the family that perished in the flames of Auschwitz. Unconsciously, however, the new living child is expected to be the return, the *revenant* of the dead ones. My patients who were children of survivors were often given the name of a mother, a father, a sister, or the "other child" who had been selected for extermination. Naming a child after a dead relative is a custom among many peoples. The intent is to honor the dead and to bless the infant with the physical, spiritual, and intellectual qualities of the departed one. However, in the case of the child of a survivor, the memorialization of the dead entails his resurrection.

A mother who has witnessed the murder of her child in an extermination camp no longer believes she can protect any child. The revenant tries to restore the mother's shattered belief in her mothering ability by resurrecting the lost child. The revenant knows she is expected to make a space inside herself to house the soul of the lost one. The revenant knows she must prepare to slip into the skin of the dead one when she reaches the age when he was murdered. The revenant knows she must fall into the interrupted biography of the dead one and complete it before she can carry on with her own life.

The revenant often feels that one resurrection is not enough to undo the damage done to her parents. In order to ensure that her parents can become whole again and emerge victorious over their captors, she believes she must undo the murder of all the dead; not only parents, siblings, children, relatives, and friends, but all those who perished in the Holocaust.

The child of a survivor has been empowered to embody several irreconcilable and contradictory missions. On the one hand, she is fighting to reinstate visions of love and goodness. On the other hand she represents the concretizations of hatred. She is expected to carry out and perform for her parent the unfinished work of mourning. Yet she is also expected to avenge the parents for the crimes committed against them by enacting their silenced hatred and rage. Should she weep for the dead so that their souls may be released from their icy purgatories? Should she dismember the persecutors and react with rage against the Almighty One for not protecting the Jews? Which trauma of the parent should the child make visible in her own life? Should it be the loss of her loved ones and her inability to mourn? Should it be her mortification at having to suppress all signs of rage? Is the survivor child honoring the dead by giving up her own life? Or is her refusal to live an enactment of the rage and hatred that the parent could not express when she was in the camp?

Transposition, where the child positions herself in the parent's past in order to cure and rescue him, also gives unconscious permission for narcissistic rage, narcissistic triumph, envy, spite, jealousy, and forbidden oedipal strivings. Up to a point, cross-generational transposition can be understood in a generous light, as an act of virtue on the part of a child who sacrifices her life to rescue her parent. But in this unconscious collaboration between a parent's unmet needs, wishes, and desires and a child's susceptibilities to receiving and curing the parent's traumas, there is another life that demands to be seen and to be heard. In the course of treating the child of a survivor, questions arise concerning the child's *ordinary* personal motives for pursuing her holy mission.

Rachel, for example, made a number of unconscious bargains with her conscience. Under the guise of a noble self-starvation that resurrected her father's dead family and, in Rachel's mind, all the Jews, Rachel obtained a license to compete with her parents and to defeat them. As Kestenberg indicated, "To compete with the mother, she had to sacrifice her life for her father; to compete with the father, she had to be a victim whom her mother could rescue and a hero whom she worshipped." Rachel identified with her father as hero and as victim. She also identified with her mother's self-sacrificing devotion to her husband. These identifications served three motives, each of them unconscious, and each of them designed to secure a fantasy victory where otherwise there could only have been helplessness and ultimate defeat. Rachel's most compelling motive, which could be traced to her father's massive trauma, was to triumph over the Nazis by resurrecting the Jews they had exterminated. Another, which could be traced to her childhood relationship to her parents, was to sneak in a forbidden oedipal triumph. Rachel would be more heroic than her father, and thereby win her mother's love and adoration. But she would also be more self-sacrificing than her mother and thereby win her father's love and adoration. The child was the victor; the parents, those defeated. Rachel's third motive, which had to do with her adolescent conflict over separating from her parents, was to protect her father from the grief of losing a child. However, this too was an unconscious bargain. Dominated by her preoccupation with bodily functions, Rachel was a helpless victim who would never be able to leave the shelter of her family home.

Rachel's sacrifice of body and life served yet another motive: that of rescuing her wounded narcissism. No matter how self-sacrificing or heroic Rachel was, she had to recognize that her mother and father shared a past and present existence that excluded her. This profound humiliation, this unavoidable evidence of the parents' superior power, inflamed Rachel's envy. By mutilating the precious gifts that had been given to her by her parents—her beautiful body, her artistic talents—and if necessary, sabotaging and destroying her very life, Rachel would demonstrate that she was more powerful than either of them. At the same time, this vengeful victory would succeed in making her dependent on them forever.

By posing as a child whose desires were confined to the innocent lusts of taking in and eliminating food, Rachel's genital and procreative desires could remain hidden. Rachel could be an oedipal victor and simultaneously avoid the responsibilities of genital desire. Instead of producing paintings or flesh-and-blood children, she continued to nourish and eliminate feces babies.

If Kestenberg had ignored the personal motives underlying Rachel's Holocaust enactments, the Nazis would have accomplished their mission of silencing the past, and there would have been no future. Rachel's children would have been lost forever. She might never have painted again. And she would never be able to weep for the dead or the unborn.

• • •

When finally, after three decades, psychologists were able to listen to the voices of the dead speaking through the children of survivors, our sympathies with the sufferings we witnessed prevented us from hearing the full range of voices in our living patients. In any sustained exploration of the human plight, there comes a point where the explorers begin to suspect and worry that they may have arrived at the boundaries of their expertise. The Holocaust provoked such a crisis in psychoanalysis. Psychoanalysis had to "pass through its own answerlessness, pass through a frightful falling mute," before analysts could bear witness to the full complexities of the transgenerational effects of massive psychic trauma.

Transposition is never the full psychological story of the child of a survivor. In order that he might begin to be able to go on living and perhaps even celebrate life, the child of the survivor *first* needs permission to leave the world of the dead. At that point, there is a crisis of truth in the therapy. The painful work of mourning the past has not been accomplished, and as the patient begins to believe he has a right to live a life that is his own, he will collaborate with the therapist's own cowardly wishes to stop at this good-enough, halfway truth. But the patient suspects and the therapist knows that permission without responsibility is a ticket back to the prison house. The child of a survivor, who has spent his life ferreting out truth, does not want to be abandoned with only half of a life restored. For somewhere he knows that he, just like everyone else, has sought self-glorification in the name of virtue; he knows that his missionary zeal has been a cover-up for personal vengeances, and he counts on his therapist to recognize this truth.

Until this fuller truth is spoken and worked through, some small or large portion of the patient's life will be devoted to a concretization of the hatred and vengeance the parents could not express. This preoccupation with vengeance stands in the way of his ability to mourn the dead as well as to mourn the loss of a childhood, adolescence, or adulthood that was consumed by vengeance.

Apocalyptic vengeances avoid the pain of mourning. Apocalyptic fantasies of rebirth and resurrection also deny and cancel out the work of mourning. The failure to mourn, to weep for the dead and for the unborn, guarantees a return of the repressed, until—one day—there is nothing but absence and silence, and no one to testify.

❦

NO VOICE IS EVER WHOLLY LOST

In writing about experiences of separation and loss, I have stressed the tenacity of the human dialogue. Beginning as infants, once we have engaged in this dialogue, we cannot live without it. Any dialogue, even one that entails fear, threat, suffering, and self-punishment, feels better to us than none at all. Thus the trauma of loss often leads to a repetition of trauma in dialogues with those who are still alive. A bereaved person enters into new relationships with a conscious desire to love and be loved, only to behave in ways that ensure a repetition of the devastating abandonment. Through the new relationship, the bereaved retains the hope of refinding his lost beloved, and the trauma of loss is transformed into a fixated and ritualized perverse scenario in which the bereaved engages in repetitive cycles of losing love and finding love, of castration and restitution, of abandonment and reunion, of death and resurrection.

Dialogue is the heartbeat of human existence. What we dread even more than actual extinction is loss of dialogue. We cripple our own selves and even destroy the world around us in our desperate quest to refind, recover, restore, reconstitute a lost dialogue. Yet because the reciprocal dialogue between infant and parent establishes certain everlasting connections between each individual life and some larger human community, self-mortification and destruction are not our only responses to loss of dialogue. Our cultural attainments, the sentences we utter or sign, our poems, dances, monuments, paintings, symphonies, songs, are all a way of refinding and restoring lost dialogues.

The transition from family dialogue to cultural dialogue is not a simple step. We are lured into human existence by a mother who gratifies our innate urges to be suckled, held, rocked, and caressed. That same mother also rations gratifications and places conditions on the fulfillment of desire. Because the infant senses the extent of her limitations, dependency, helplessness, and vulnerability, she begins to recognize that lawfulness—the where, when, and how of gratification—is an essential aspect of her humanity.

To fulfill their primary function of protecting the child, the mother and father offer a leniency and charity that temper the demands of social existence. They shield the child from the crippling indoctrinations that society often imposes on us. However, if the family is to maintain its viability as a social unit, it must also convey to the child the lawfulness of the larger social order. A prolonged and intense attachment between parent and child is essential to the preservation of the social ideals and values that enable us to participate in human culture. Insofar as the passions of family life serve to insulate and isolate the individual from the larger social order, these passions are also a threat to communal life and culture. To be human is to be vulnerable to the tensions between family passion and society at large.

The child's game of peekaboo is a dialogue that speaks of a never-ending human existence. The interchangeability of suspenseful anxiety and pleasurable excitement gives the child the courage to flirt with the uncertainties of loss. Each time the mother's face disappears, the infant feels as though he is being exposed to threats of extinction. But when her face reappears, the infant reestablishes his connections with the human community. The dialogue resumes. Even if the infant is ruthless and greedy in his appropriation of the breast, he need not fear that his lust will destroy his mother. He knows her face will always brighten with recognition. The regularity of the reappearing face is the infant's first sense of what it means to be part of a trustworthy universe. The recurrent rhythms of disappearance and reappearance become an intrinsic aspect of his humanness.

Without this marvelous fantasy of a never-ending cycle in which absence and disappearance alternate with resurrection and rebirth, a child would not survive the plight of being human. The illusion of the eternally reappearing face that inevitably brightens is crucial to the growth and development of a little child who derives his strength of hope from the confident expectation that his mother's face will reappear. But in an adult the fantasy of eternal return is a manic denial of separation and loss. It allows us to be ruthless in pursuing our ideals, even to brutalize others in the name of justice or virtue and all with the mistaken expectation that the familiar world, the human community, nature itself, will never disappear.

I have enlisted the phrase "no voice is ever wholly lost" in support of my belief that the human dialogue resists its own obliteration. However, in wanting so much to offer hope, I have created an incomplete sentence—one of those unwitting duplicities of language that could encourage the Pollyannaish denial I have been challenging. Indeed, to deny the darker inevitabilities of separation, loss, decay, and death is tantamount to inviting the forces of destruction to enter by a side door. So now, in order to acknowledge the dark side of all these matters, I must also record the full sentence: "No voice is ever wholly lost *that is the voice of humanity.*"

NOTES AND BIBLIOGRAPHY

Works traditionally cited with short titles will be identified by the following abbreviations:

Amer. J. Orthopsychiat.	*American Journal of Orthopsychiatry*
Amer. J. Psychiat.	*American Journal of Psychiatry*
Amer. Psychol.	*American Psychologist*
Int. J. Psycho-Anal.	*International Journal of Psycho-Analysis*
Int. Rev. Psycho-Anal.	*International Review of Psychoanalysis*
J. Amer. Acad. Child Psych.	*Journal of the American Academy of Child Psychiatry*
J. Amer. Psychoanal. Assn.	*Journal of the American Psychoanalytic Association*
J. Psychohist.	*Journal of Psychohistory*
J. Soc. Work and Policy in Isr.	*Journal of Social Work and Policy in Israel*
Psychoanal. Q.	*Psychoanalytic Quarterly*
Psychoanal. Study Child	*Psychoanalytic Study of the Child.* 1946–1970, New York: International Universities; 1971–1973, New York: Quadrangle; 1973–1993, New Haven: Yale University.
Psychosomat. Med.	*Psychosomatic Medicine*
S. E.	*Collected Papers of Sigmund Freud.* Standard Edition. London: Hogarth
Soc. Res.	*Social Research*
Soc. Sci. Med.	*Social Science and Medicine*

Author's note: The research and writings of John Bowlby, the British psychoanalyst, have not been mentioned in the text because his theories of attachment, separation, and loss are not congruent with the *internal* psychic processes that are the focus of this book. See Kaplan review of Bowlby's work (notes to chapter 1) and Spitz critique (notes to chapter 3).

Chapter 1: The Human Dialogue

Cole, Susan Letzler. 1985. *The absent one: mourning ritual, tragedy and the performance of ambivalence.* University Park and London: Pennsylvania State University Press.

Devlin, Judith. 1987. *The superstitious mind.* New Haven: Yale University Press.

Engel, George. 1961. Is grief a disease? *Psychosomat. Med.* 23:18–22.

Euler, Robert C., and Henry F. Dolyns. 1971. *The Hopi people.* Phoenix: Indian Tribal Series.

Freud, Sigmund. 1917. *Mourning and melancholia. S.E.* 14:237–58.

Geertz, Clifford. 1968. *Islam observed.* New Haven: Yale University Press.

———. 1973. *The interpretation of cultures.* New York: Basic Books.

Goodall, Jane. 1986. *The chimpanzees of Gombe.* Cambridge and London: Belknap/Harvard.

———. 1988. *In the shadow of man.* Revised edition. Boston: Houghton Mifflin.

Harlow, Harry F. 1958. The nature of love. *Amer. Psychol.* 13:673–85.

———. 1959. Love in infant monkeys. *Scientific American* 200:68–74.

———. 1960a. Affectional behavior in the infant monkey. *Central nervous system and behavior.* Edited by M. A. B. Brazier. New York: Josiah Macy, Jr., Foundation.

———. 1960b. Primary affectional patterns in primates. *Amer. J. Orthopsychiat.* 30:676–84.

———. 1962. The heterosexual affectional system in monkeys. *Amer. Psychol.* 17:1–9.

———. 1974. *Learning to love.* New York: Aronson.

Kaplan, Louise J. 1978. *Oneness and separateness.* New York: Simon and Schuster.

———. 1980. A theory of mourning. Review of *Loss,* by John Bowlby. *The New York Times Book Review,* Sunday, August 24.

Lewis, Michael, and Leonard A. Rosenblum. 1974. *The effect of the infant on its caregiver.* New York: Wiley.

Loewald, Hans W. 1962. Internalization, separation, mourning, and the superego. *Psychoanal. Q.* 31:483–504.

Platt, Larry A., and Richard V. Persico, Jr. 1992. *Grief in cross-cultural perspective.* New York and London: Garland Press.

Pollack, George H. 1961. Mourning and adaptation. *Int. J. Psycho-Anal.* 42:341–61.

Rosenblatt, Paul C., Patricia R. Walsh, and Douglas A. Jackson. 1976. *Grief and mourning in cross cultural perspective.* New Haven: HRAF Press.

Schaller, George B. 1963. *The mountain gorilla*. Chicago: University of Chicago Press.

Spitz, René A. 1945. Hospitalism. *Psychoanal. Study Child* 1:53–74.

———. 1946. Anaclitic depression. *Psychoanal. Study Child* 2:313–42.

———, 1962. Autoeroticism re-examined. *Psychoanal. Study Child* 17:283–315.

———. 1963. Life and the dialogue. *Counterpoint*. Edited by Herbert S. Gaskill. New York: International Universities Press.

———. 1964. The derailment of dialogue. *J. Amer. Psychoanal. Assn.* 12:752–75.

———. 1965. The evolution of dialogue. *Drives, affects, behavior*. Vol. 2. Edited by Max Schur. New York: International Universities Press.

Stone, Joseph L., Henrietta T. Smith, and Lois B. Murphy. 1973. *The competent infant*. New York: Basic Books.

Stroebe, Margaret S., Wolfgang Stroebe, and Robert O. Hansson. 1994. *Handbook of bereavement*. New York: Cambridge University Press.

Thompson, Laura, and Alice Joseph. 1965. *The Hopi way*. New York: Russell and Russell.

Wikan, Unni. 1988. Bereavement and loss in two Muslim communities. *Soc. Sci. Med.* 27:451–60.

———. 1990. *Managing turbulent hearts*. Chicago: University of Chicago Press.

Yamamoto, Joe et al. 1969. Mourning in Japan. *Amer. J. Psychiat.* 125:1660–65.

Zuckerman, S. 1932. *The social life of monkeys and apes*. London: Kegan, Paul, French and Trubner.

---

14 Mourning and burial rituals: Cole, 13–39. Devlin, 92. Platt and Persico, passim. Rosenblatt et al., 86–98.

15 Contrasting bereavement behaviors of Egyptian and Balinese: Wikan 1988.

15 Sadness in Bali: Wikan 1990, 142–71.

15 "We are very sensitive": paraphrase of Wikan 1988, 456.

16 animals are bereft: Goodall 1988, 220–24.

16 A chimpanzee infant: Goodall 1986, 101–3; 1988, 229–30.

16 A gorilla mother: Schaller, 269.

17 In the Shinto and Buddhist religions: Yamamoto et al.

17 Hopi mortuary and burial customs: Thompson and Joseph, 64.

18 The Spirit's journey to the Underworld: Thompson and Joseph, 64; Euler and Dolyns, 81–85.

18   Hopi religious beliefs: Euler and Dolyns, 80–81.
18–19   Classification and description of the two stages of bereavement: Pollack, 358–60. (Pollack also divides the acute phase into three stages.)
18   Grief as an illness: Engel.
19   "the *work* of mourning": Freud 1917, 14:244–45.
20–21   Harlow's studies: Harlow 1958–1962; Summary 1974.
22   "terry cloth adults": Spitz 1962, 287–78.
22   "together-together": Harlow 1960a, 1960b.
22   Spitz critique of Harlow: 1962, 1963, 1964, 1965.
22   two groups of infants: Spitz 1945, 1946.
23   desperate hunger for dialogue: Spitz 1965, 183.
23   Violence of dialogue-deprived infants: Spitz 1965, 184.
23   "affect exchange" in development of libidinal and aggressive drives: Spitz 1965, 178–82.
24   Infant research: Stone et al.; Lewis and Rosenblum. There have been numerous later studies on infant contributions to the infant-parent interaction, but these works are the foundations.
24   a living rhesus mother: Spitz 1962, 285.
24   "Therefore she offers her baby": Spitz 1962, 285–86.
25   "derailment of dialogue": Spitz 1964.
26   The basic dialogue: Spitz 1963, 1965; Kaplan 1978.

Chapter 2: Losing and Being Lost

Binger, C. M. 1973. Childhood leukemia—emotional impact on siblings. *The child in his family.* Vol. 2. Edited by E. J. Anthony and C. Koupernik. New York: Wiley.

Cain, A. C., and B. S. Cain. 1964. On replacing a child. *J. Amer. Acad. Child Psych.* 3:443–56.

Freud, Anna. 1967 [1953]. About losing and being lost. *Psychoanal. Study Child* 22:9–19. Based on a paper read at the 18th Congress of the International Psycho-Analytical Association in 1953.

Freud, Sigmund. 1899. *The interpretation of dreams. S.E. 5.*

———. 1915–16. *Introductory lectures on psychoanalysis. S.E.* 15.

———. 1920. Beyond the pleasure principle. *S.E.* 18:3–66.

———. 1960. *Letters of Sigmund Freud.* Selected and edited by Ernst L. Freud. Translated by Tania and James Stern. New York: Basic Books.

Freud, W. Ernest. 1987. Die Freuds und die Burlinghams in der Berggasse: Persönliche Erinnerungen. Sigmund Freud Lecture, University of Vienna, May 6. *Sigmund Freud house bulletin* 11:2–18.

———. 1988. Persönliche Erinnerungen an den "Anschluss," 1938. *Sigmund Freud house bulletin* 12:13–18.

Gay, Peter. 1988. *Freud: A life for our time.* New York: Norton.

Kaplan, Louise J. 1978. *Oneness and separateness.* New York: Simon and Schuster.

Kennedy, Hansi. 1984. Growing up with a handicapped sibling. *Psychoanal. Study Child* 40:255–74.

Schur, Max. 1972. *Freud: living and dying.* New York: International Universities Press.

Young-Bruehl, Elisabeth. 1988. *Anna Freud.* New York: Summit Books.

28–29   Ernst's *fort-da: S.E.* 18:14–15.

29   gone [o-o-o-o] as a first word: *S.E.* 5:note 461 [added 1919].

29   Ernst as an obedient child: *S.E.* 18:14; 5:note 461 [added 1919].

29   "the only use": *S.E.* 18:16.

29   Ernst's preoccupation with distressing aspects of his games: *S.E.* 18:15–16.

29–30   Ernst's disappearance game: *S.E.* 18:note 15.

30   "Go away, mother": paraphrase, *S.E.* 18:16.

32   Repetition compulsion: *S.E.* 18:32–38, 56–59.

33   Ernst's catastrophes: W. E. Freud 1987; 1988.

33   "called up to the front": *S.E.* 18:16.

33   Ernst's dream and interpretation. *S.E.* 5:note 461 [added 1919].

33   "Go to the fwont": *S.E.* 18:16.

33   Ernst and Sophie on the breadline: W. E. Freud 1988, 14.

33   Sophie's death: Young-Bruehl, 91–94; Gay, 391–93.

33   Heinz Rudolphe's death: Schur, 359–61; *Letters* 343–45.

34   life itself had lost all value: Gay, 422, citing Freud's August 18, 1923 letter to Oscar Ric.

34   no consolation: Gay, 422.

34   "Now that his mother": *S.E.* 18:note 15.

34   "violent jealousy": *S.E.* 18:note 15.

34   The family of Amy, Sally and George Gordon: composite of children and parents at the New York University Mother-Infant Nursery during 1973–77.

35–36   The dialogues between Sally and Amy: observations at the Mother-Infant Nursery; *Oneness and separateness.*

38–40   Amy's "gone and back" and "talk" games: observations of numerous children, including the children at the Mother-Infant Nursery, my own children and my grandaughter, Ariel.

41   parents do not lose children: A. Freud, 15.

41–42   A child gets lost: A. Freud, 16.

42–46   Cynthia Coles and her family: composite based on my clinical experiences with replacement children; Binger; Cain and Cain; Kennedy.

44   Double identification: A. Freud, 17.

46   The mislaying and losing of things: *S.E.* 15: "Parapraxes" 54, 77.

Chapter 3: The Death of a Virtuous Father

Barnes, Marion J. 1964. Reactions to the death of a mother. *Psychoanal. Study Child* 19:334–57.

Bowlby, John. 1960. Grief and mourning in infancy and early childhood. *Psychoanal. Study Child* 15:9–52.

———. 1963. Pathological mourning and childhood mourning. *J. Amer. Psychoanal. Assn.* 11:500–41.

Frankiel, Rita. 1994 *Essential papers on object loss.* New York: New York University Press.

Freud, Sigmund. 1917. Mourning and melancholia. *S.E.* 14:237–58.

Furman, Edna. 1964. Death and the young child. *Psychoanal. Study Child* 19:377–97.

———. 1974. *A child's parent dies.* New Haven: Yale University Press.

———. 1986. On trauma: When is the death of a parent traumatic? *Psychoanal. Study Child* 41:191–208.

Hummer, K. M., and A. Samuels. 1988. The influence of the recent death of a spouse on the parenting function of the surviving parent. *Childhood bereavement and its aftermath.* Madison, Conn.: International Universities.

Miller, J. B. M. 1971. Children's reactions to the death of a parent: a review of the psychoanalytic literature. *J. Amer. Psychoanal. Assoc.* 19:679–719.

Rochlin, Gregory. 1953. Loss and restitution. *Psychoanal. Study Child* 8:288–309.

———. 1959. The loss complex. *J. Amer. Psychoanal. Assn.* 7:299–316.

———. 1961. The dread of abandonment. *Psychoanal. Study Child* 16:451–70.

Scharl, Adele E. 1961. Regression and restitution in object loss. *Psychoanal. Study Child* 16:471–80.

Shambaugh, B. 1961. Loss reactions in a seven-year-old. *Psychoanal. Study Child* 16:510–22.

Silverman, P. R., S. Nickman, and J. Worden. 1992. Detachment revisited: The child's reconstruction of a dead parent. *Amer. J. Orthopsychiat.* 42:4; 494–503.

Spitz, René A. 1960. Discussion of Dr. Bowlby's paper. *Psychoanal. Study Child* 15:85–94.

Wolfenstein, Martha. 1966. How is mourning possible?" *Psychoanal. Study Child* 21;93–122.

———. 1969. Loss, rage and repetition. *Psychoanal. Study Child* 24:432–60.

———. 1973. The image of the lost parent. *Psychoanal. Study Child* 28:433–56.

---

51 Controversies: For an excellent summary of the disagreements about a child's capacity to mourn, see Frankiel, 327–33; also Bowlby, Furman, Miller, Silverman, Spitz, and Wolfenstein.
52 Abandonment fantasies: Rochlin
55–65 The family of Charles Evans, his two children, Wendy and Winnie, and his wife Marilyn: a composite based on clinical papers by Marion Barnes (a social worker who worked with Edna Furman at the Hanna Perkins Child Development Center in Cleveland) and Adele Scharl (a child psychiatrist at the Massachusetts Mental Health Center). My clinical experiences with young children's reactions to parental loss correspond to the therapy and therapy outcomes described by Barnes and Scharl. Both papers are particularly important because they focus on the differing reactions to parental loss of two siblings.

Chapter Four: The Red Thread

Burlingham, Michael John. 1989. *The last Tiffany.* New York: Atheneum.

Erikson, Erik. 1954. *Insight and responsibility.* New York: Norton.

Freud, W. Ernest. 1980. Notes on some psychological aspects of neonatal intensive care. *The course of life.* Vol. 1. Edited by Stanley I. Greenspan and George H. Pollack. Adelphi, Maryland: U.S. Government Printing Office, NIMH: 257–69. (Vol. 1 reprinted New York: International Universities Press, 1989, 485–501).

———. 1981. To be in touch. *J. Child Psychother.* 7:141–43.

———. 1983. Funeral tribute to Anna Freud. *Bulletin of the Hampstead Clinic* 6:5–8.

———. 1985. A conversation (with Jay Martin). *Psychoanal. Ed.* 4:29–56.

———. 1987a. Prenatal attachment and bonding. *Perinatal Psychology.* Edited by T. R. Verny. New York: Human Sciences Press (reprinted *The course of life.* 1989. Vol. 1, 1989, 467–83).

———. 1987b. Die Freuds und die Burlinghams in der Berggasse: Persönliche Erinnerungen. Sigmund Freud lecture, University of Vienna, May 6. *Sigmund Freud house bulletin* 11:2–18.

———. 1988. Persönliche Erinnerungen an den "Anschluss," 1938. *Sigmund Freud house bulletin* 12:13–18.

———. 1991. Das "Whose Baby? Syndrom": Ein Beitrag zum Psychodyanmischen Verständnis der Perinatologie. *Psychosomatische Gynäkologie und Geburtshilfe.* Edited by Stauber et al. Berlin: Springer-Verlag.

———. 1992. Wie ich Psychoanalytischer Frühchen-Forscher Wurde. Festansprache anlässlick der Verleihung des "Dr. phil.h.c." von der Philosophischen Fakultat der Universitat zu Koln am 10.02.92. *Zwischenschritte*, 11. Jahrg., 1/1992: 86–89.

———. (9/23/92–11/3/93) Correspondence with the author.

Freud, Sigmund. 1920. Beyond the pleasure principle. *S.E.* 18:3–66.

Gay, Peter. 1988. *Freud: A life for our time*. New York: Norton.

Heller, Peter. 1992. *Anna Freud's letters to Eva Rosenfeld*. Edited by Peter Heller. Translated by Mary Weigand. With contributions by Gunther Bittner and Victor Ross. Madison Conn: International Universities Press.

Schur, Max. 1972. *Freud: living and dying*. New York: International Universities Press.

Young-Bruehl, Elisabeth. 1988. *Anna Freud*. New York: Summit Books.

Translations of W. E. Freud's previously untranslated German papers by Felix Enslin, Henry Krish, and Lottie Krisch Sapadin.

---

66 Epigraph: W. E. Freud, correspondence, September 23, 1992.

67 "Cordial regards": Gay, 310; Freud Collection: Library of Congress.

67 "Last night . . . wonders of sexuality": Gay, 310; Freud Collection: Library of Congress.

67 Max Halberstadt's character and relationship with Ernst: W. E. Freud 1985, 37. (It is uncertain whether Max Halberstadt's father died before his birth or when he was an infant.)

67 Adoption of Heinz Rudolphe: Young-Bruehl, 118.

68 small private school: W. E. Freud 1985, 35.

68 Ernst did not miss Sophie: *S.E.* 18:14.

68 pretend it was *his* baby: W. E. Freud, 1987a, 468–69. (I am assuming that Ernst responded to his mother's pregnancies as W. Ernest Freud describes in his own writings.)

68–69 "For the first time in my life": Young-Bruehl, 93. Anna Freud to Lou Andreas Salome, March 26, 1922.

69 When Anna proposed . . . death of Sophie: Young-Bruehl, 93.

69 Death of Heinz: Schur, 358–60; Gay, 421–22.

69 "very weak . . . physical strength": Schur, 360, citing Freud's October 15, 1926 letter of condolence to his colleague, Binswanger.

69 betrayal of nursery school teacher/stepmother: W. E. Freud 1985, 35.

69 "it was like having found": W. E. Freud 1985, 35.

70 "I felt very excluded": W. E. Freud 1987b, 3.

70 spent a great deal of time daydreaming . . . "out of this world" and unrealistic: W. E. Freud 1985, 35.

70 Account of the fishing rod: W. E. Freud 1985, 35.

70 "I did not have much": W. E. Freud 1987b, 9.

71 "In reality, he is such a nice": Young-Bruehl, 119; Anna Freud to Sigmund Freud, August 4, 1921.
71 History of "About Losing and Being Lost" essay: Young-Bruehl, 276–314.
71 "the idealized family": Burlingham, 191.
71 Ernst idolized Bob Burlingham: W. E. Freud 1987b, 10. Burlingham, 191.
71 The Burlingham kids: W. E. Freud 1987b, 9–13.
72 circular flight: W. E. Freud 1987b, 9.
72 "dark cloud hanging," "it would all have to end": W. E. Freud 1987b. 13.
72 "the plasticene miracle": W. E. Freud 1983, 7; 1987b, 9.
72 Sigmund Freud permits his grandson to stay in Vienna: W. E. Freud 1987b, 13.
72 Max was surprised to learn: Heller, 110; Letter 7, March 18, 1929.
72 enjoyed the time they spent together: Heller, 141; Letter 27, June 25, 1930.
73 Freud-Burlingham "family": W. E. Freud 1987b, 9–15; Burlingham, 183–217; Heller, 74–78.
73 The Burlingham-Rosenfeld School (in German, Hietzing School because located in Hietzing suburb): W. E. Freud 1987b, 15.
73 Rosenfeld's role at the school: W. E. Freud 1987b, 15; Heller, 77–83; Ross in Heller, 31–33.
73 "I wanted to find comfort": Bittner in Heller, 16, citing Rosenfeld's unpublished memoirs.
73 "In no other place was I taught . . . learning buffet' ": W. E. Freud 1987b, 15–16.
74 "Education, it seems to me": Heller, 85.
74 Closing of the school: Ross in Heller, 33; Bittner in Heller, 3.
74 Eva Rosenfeld at Tegler; "for her future career": Bittner in Heller, 19.
74 "an ideal of what kind of person": Heller, 168, Letter 47, August 26, 1931.
74 Scharfenberg boarding school, "cheap, democratic, and very Spartan": W. E. Freud. 1985, 38.
74 Stories of arrest and torture: W. E. Freud 1988, 14.
74 Anna Freud asks Eva Rosenthal to escort Ernst across the border: Ross in Heller, 43–44. W. E. Freud 1988, 14.
74 On the streets of Berlin: W. E. Freud 1988, 14.
74 On the eve of April 30, 1933: Ross in Heller, 44.
74 a train for Vienna: W. E. Freud 1988, 14.
75 Once back in Vienna: W. E. Freud 1988, 14.
75 time out for . . . headaches, stomachaches: W. E. Freud 1985, 39.
75 no hobbies . . . photographer like his father: W. E. Freud 1985, 39–40.
75 Listening to *Kristallset:* W. E. Freud 1988, 13.
75 Rescue of Leopold Bellak: W. E. Freud 1988, 14.
76 "I could disappear without a trace" "You are neurotic": W. E. Freud 1988, 15.

76 Anna Freud and the Gestapo: W. E. Freud 1988, 16.

76 The emigration of Max Halberstadt: W. E. Freud 1985, 39.

76–77 Ernst remains in England; his struggles to find himself: W. E. Freud 1985, 40–41.

77 Psychoanalytic training "albeit late in life . . . the latter part of life.": W. E. Freud 1985, 41. His analyst was Willie Hoffer, who is well known for his writings on infancy.

77 Ernst Wolfgang Halberstadt/ W. Ernest Freud change of name: Correspondence, October 10, 1992.

77 "At last I found": W. E. Freud 1985, 42.

77 Birth of Colin: Young-Bruehl, 351.

77 Reading to Colin from Spirit of Saint Louis: W. E. Freud, 1988, 13.

77 Freud's remote relationship with Colin: Interview with a close friend of Colin's during Colin's adolescent years.

77–78 Freud's marriage and divorce: Since W. E. Freud has chosen to remain silent about his relationship with his wife, I have respected his reticence and only alluded briefly to the bare "facts" that there was a marriage, and finally a divorce. The information I have about his separation from his wife comes from his colleagues and students at Hampstead and his colleagues at the Yale University Child Study Center, where he visited during the years preceding the divorce. Naturally, as with all such personal matters where only the parties intimately concerned can have some idea of what "really" happened, it is difficult to distinguish facts from rumors.

78 Awarded a Doctor of Philosophy: W. E. Freud, 1992.

78 "Naturally, the loss of my mother": Correspondence, September 23, 1992.

79 "I got to know": W. E. Freud 1985, 33.

79 "It was basically": W. E. Freud 1985, 32–33.

79 "I owe it to my little brother": W. E. Freud 1985, 34.

79 Bonding begins earlier—playing at making babies: W. E. Freud 1987a, 468.

79 The sibling bonding to the fetus: W. E. Freud. 1987a, 469.

79–80 Fetal awareness: W. E. Freud 1987a, 472–73.

80 "Deprivation made me inventive": W. E. Freud 1992, 88.

80 "interaction, continuity, regularity, movement, rhythm, and stimulation": W. E. Freud 1987a, 474.

81 "bound between the breasts": W. E. Freud 1980, 486.

81 Whose Baby Syndrome: W. E. Freud 1981; 1991.

81 "Trustworthy motherliness": Erikson, 152.

82 "When my mother died . . . throughout her life." W. E. Freud 1983, 5.

82 Colin's death: personal communication from Young-Bruehl.

82 Circumstances of Colin's death: Interview with a close friend of Colin's during Colin's adolescence.

82 Responses to the loss of Colin: Correspondence, May 14, 1993.
82 Keynote address in Vienna: 1986, published by W. E. Freud 1988.
83 "To me coming to Vienna": W. E. Freud 1988, 2.
83 Although Bob Burlingham is not mentioned specifically in the address, I included his name along with Mabbie's because of the crucial role he played in Dr. Freud's life. Freud's unpublished funeral tribute (1970) to Bob is cited by his grandson, Michael, in Burlingham, 191–92.
83 I have reconstructed the family backgrounds of Freud's audience from the listings of the Vienna Psychoanalytic Conference and from information given to me by Dr. Otto Kernberg and other colleagues. The historical events referred to in W. E. Freud's address strongly suggest that, except for some personal friends of Freud's, there would be few, if any, children of Holocaust survivors attending that meeting.

Chapter 5: Broken Promises

Kaplan, Louise J. 1984. *Adolescence*. New York: Simon and Schuster.
Rochlin, Gregory. 1953. Loss and restitution. *Psychoanal. Study Child* 8:288–309.
———. 1959. The loss complex. *J. Amer. Psychoanal. Assn.* 7:299–316.
Silverman, Carol. 1993. Correspondence with the author.
Wolfenstein, Martha. 1966. How is mourning possible? *Psychoanal. Study Child* 21:93–122.
———. 1969. Loss, rage and repetition. *Psychoanal. Study Child* 24:432–60.
———. 1973. The image of the lost parent. *Psychoanal. Study Child* 28:433–56.

---

85 The farewell to childhood: Kaplan.
86 Nostalgia: Kaplan, 150–53; Wolfenstein 1966, 109–15.
86 "heaven lay about us": Wolfenstein 1966, 115, citing Wordsworth's 1807 ode, "Intimations of immortality from recollections of early childhood."
86 "the happy highways": Wolfenstein 1966, 115, and 1973, 438, citing A. E. Housman (1896) poem, "A Shropshire Lad."
88 Milly Wolfenstein: composite based on several of my own patients and Wolfenstein's 1969 clinical account of her patient "Ruth."
88 Descriptions of the racial tensions and upper-middle-income Jewish housing and educational priorities in Chicago during the 1950s and 1960s: Correspondence, Silverman.

Chapter Six: A Woman Succumbing

Feigelson, Caroline. 1993. Personality death, object loss, and the uncanny. *Internat. J. Psychoanal.* 74:331–46.

Freud, Sigmund. 1919. The uncanny. *S.E.* 17.

———. 1911. Psychoanalytic notes on an autobiographical account of a case of paranoia. *S.E.* 12.

Israels, Hans. 1988. Introduction to the new Schreber texts. *Psychosis and sexual identity: toward a post-analytic view of the Schreber case.* Edited by David B. Allison, Prado de Oliveira, Mark S. Roberts, and Alan S. Weiss. Albany: State University of New York Press.

Jentsch, Ernst. 1906. Zur Psychologie des Unheimlichen. *Psychiat. neurol. Wschr.* 8; 219–21; 226–27, as cited by Freud, 1919.

Kaplan, Louise J. 1991. *Female perversions.* New York: Nan A. Talese, Doubleday.

Lothane, Zvi. 1989. Vindicating Schreber's father:neither sadist nor child abuser. *J. Psychohist.* 16:3–18.

———. 1993. *In defense of Schreber: soul murder and psychiatry.* New Jersey: Analytic Press.

Niederland, William. 1974. *The Schreber case.* New York: Quadrangle/New York Times.

Schreber, Daniel P. 1903. *Memoirs of my nervous illness.* Translated by I. Macalpine and S. M. Hunter. Introduction by Samuel M. Weber. Cambridge:Harvard University Press, 1988.

———. Appendix D. 1903 [1909]. In what circumstances can a person considered insane be detained in an asylum against his declared will?

103–04 Dr. Schreber's biography and his relations with his wife and children: Niederland, chapters 7, 8, 9.

104 Gustave's suicide: Niederland, 66–67.

105–06 Descriptions and illustrations of Dr. Schreber's body straightening devices: Niederland, 52–55.

106 "Always bear in mind": *Memoirs,* Weber, Introduction, ix.

106 personality death: Feigelson. In *Female perversions,* I allude to the effects of Dr. Schreber's brain injury on his family. However, until reading Dr. Feigelson's paper, I was not sufficiently attentive to the crucial ways the earlier personality death of Dr. Schreber would have made his children more vulnerable to the traumatic effects of his actual death. My explanations of *the effects of the personality death of a parent on a child* are from my own clinical cases. In contrast to Feigelson, I stress the internal conflicts that are aroused in the observer.

107 "It feels uncanny": Feigelson, 337. The wife I refer to here is Dr. Feigelson, whose husband, the gifted psychoanalyst Dr. Charles Feigelson, suffered a massive brain injury several years earlier. Very likely, these words from her paper derive from her own personal experience.

107   References to Jentsch's paper: Freud 1919, 219, 226, 230, 233.
108   *umheimlich* and *heimlich:* Freud 1919, 219–26, 244–45.
110–15   Daniel Paul Schreber's life: *Memoirs,* Israels, 209–11; Niederland, chapters 7, 8, 9.
111   "WHO, AFTER ALL, HAS EVER HEARD OF [Dr] SCHREBER": *Memoirs,* Weber, Introduction, vii. To avoid confusion I omitted "Dr.," which refers to Judge Schreber, a doctor of jurisprudence.
111   "and marred only": *Memoirs,* 63.
111   "it really must be so lovely": *Memoirs,* 63, translation Kaplan.
111–12   Transformations into a woman: *Memoirs,* 147–49.
112   compression-of-the-chest device: *Memoirs,* 133.
112   head-compressing machine: *Memoirs,* 138.
112   "coccyx miracle", *Memoirs,* 139.
113   "It was *common sense*": *Memoirs,* 148.
113   "By a divine miracle": *Memoirs,* 43.
114   Permission to substitute perversion for psychosis: Kaplan, 482–83.
114   god's need for constant sexual enjoyment: *Memoirs,* 209.
114–15   Schreber's trial: Schreber [published 1909,] including appendices D and E of *Memoirs,* 255–356: Dr. Weber's "Expert Report" of April 5, 1902, "Judgment of the Royal Superior Country Court Dresden," July 14, 1902, and Final Judgment of December 20, 1902.
115   "God Himself was on my side": *Memoirs,* 79.

Chapter Seven: A Parent's Grief

Freud, Sigmund. *Letters of Sigmund Freud.* Selected and edited by Ernst L. Freud. Translated by Tania and James Stern. New York: Basic Books, 1960.

Gay, Peter. 1988. *Freud: A life for our time.* New York: Norton.

Greenleaf, Barbara Kaye. 1978. *Childhood through the ages.* New York: Mc-Graw-Hill.

Kaplan, Donald M. 1990. Review of *Tragic drama and the family. Int. Rev. Psycho-Anal.* 17:127–30.

Rothholz, Amy. 1987. *Iced Tigers.* Amagansett, New York: Amagansett Press.

Schur, Max. 1972. *Freud: Living and dying.* New York: International Universities Press.

Simon, Bennett. 1988. *Tragic drama and the family.* New Haven: Yale University Press.

Trachtman, Paula. 1993a, ed. *Out of season: An anthology of work by and about young people who died.* Amagansett, New York: Amagansett Press.

———— 1993b. Interviews with the author.

122 "He was indeed an enchanting": Freud 1960, June 11, 1923 letter to Kata and Lajos Levy.

122 Heinz was frail: Gay, 421, citing Freud's April 1923 postcard to Sandor Ferenczi. Freud-Ferenczi Collection, Library of Congress.

122 "I find this loss": Freud 1960, June 11, 1923.

123 "That was in 1920 . . . resigned to fate in advance" "To me this child": Schur, 360, citing Freud's October 15, 1926 letter.

123 "I am obsessed by": Gay, 422, citing Freud's August 13, 1923 letter.

123 "He meant the future to me": Gay, 422, citing Freud's August 18, 1923 letter. Freud Museum, London.

123 Child as symbol of fertility: Greenleaf, 24.

123–24 Sacrifice of children: Greenleaf, 17–18.

124 Democritus quote: Greenleaf, 21.

124 Western European tragic drama, themes of generation and regeneration: Simon.

124 convey a sense of threat and hopelessness: Kaplan, 127.

127 George Gordon's grief: based on interviews with Paula Trachtman, whose twenty-five-year-old daughter, Amy Elisabeth Rothholz, died on February 20, 1983, and the father, who wrote the prefaces to Amy's book *Iced tigers* and the anthology in her memory *Out of season.*

133 "the clouds pass:" Confucius, *I Ching,* epigraph, *Iced tigers.*

Chapter Eight: Weeping Mothers

Argentine National Committee of the Disappeared. 1986. *Nunca más.* New York: Farrar, Straus.

Anderson, Martin Edwin. 1993. *Dossier secreto.* Boulder, Colorado: Westview Press.

Amnesty International. 1992. *Report.*

Elshtain, Jean Bethke. 1994. The mothers of the disappeared: passion and protest in maternal action.

Representations of motherhood. Edited by Donna Bassin, Margaret Honey, and Meryle Kaplan. New Haven: Yale University Press.

Hollander, Nancy Caro. 1990. Buenos Aires: Latin mecca of psychoanalysis. *Soc. Res.* 57:889–919.

Lewis, Paul. Libya to give decision on Pan-Am 103 suspects. *The New York Times,* September 12, 1993, sec. A, p. 15.

———. UN tightens sanctions against Libya. *The New York Times,* November 10, 1993, sec. A, p. 10.

Lowenstein, Suse. 1993. Conversations with author: June 2, September 10, November 11.

Rock, David. 1987. *Argentina: 1516–1987*. Berkeley: University of California Press.
Sarlo, Beatriz. 1985. Hebe de Bonafini. In *Historias de vida*. Edited by Matilda Sanchez. Buenos Aires:Fraterna/Del Nuevo Extremo, 1985. Excerpted and translated by Marcy Schwartz Walsh in *Women's writings in Latin America*. Edited by Sara Castro-Klaren, Beatriz Sarlo, and S. Molloy. Boulder, Colorado: Westview Press, 1991.
Simpson, John, and Jana Bennett. 1985. *The disappeared and the mothers of the plaza*. New York: St. Martins Press.
Sullivan, Ronald. 1994. Court upholds Pan-Am 103 award. *The New York Times*, February 1, 1994, sec. D, p. 2.

135–38 Pan Am 103 and the construction of *Dark Elegy*: Suse Lowenstein.
136 History of legal proceedings against Pan Am: Suse Lowenstein; Lewis, September 1993; November 1993; Sullivan, 1994.
142 Recent history of Argentina: Rock, Argentine National Committee of the Disappeared, Anderson.
142 "First we will kill": Rock, 444.
143 Symptoms of parents and friends of the disappeared: Hollander, 913–14.
143 Uses of word "disappeared": Argentine National Committee on the Disappeared, *passim*.
144 History of *Las Madres*: Simpson and Bennett, 152–70.
144 March to Lujon: Sarlo, 287–88.
145 "After so many years": Sarlo, 281.
146 "It was like being born": Sarlo, 281.
146 Hebe's rebirth: Sarlo, 280–83.
146–47 "We must have left them" "In our own way": Sarlo, 281.
147 Jorge's disappearance: Simpson and Bennett, 154–55.
147 Hebe searches for Jorge: Sarlo, 281–83.
147 "Oh, poor thing": Sarlo, 282.
148 "There are more of us": paraphrase Sarlo, 283.
148 Hebe joins *Las Madres*: Simpson and Bennett, 155–59; Sarlo, 282–283.
148 Hebe signs her name: Sarlo, 285.
148 Description of Hebe's journey from Digue: Sarlo, 285.
148 "being more of a mother": Sarlo, 285.
148–49 Description of Calle Florida: Elshtain, 77.
149 "nobody who tells the truth": Simpson and Bennett, 159.
149 Petition and arrests: Simpson and Bennett, 160.
149–50 Meetings of *Las Madres*: Simpson and Bennett, 155–70.

149 Betrayal by Gustavo Niño/Captain Alfredo Astiz: Simpson and Bennett, 160–63.
150 Disappearances of Elena and Raúl: Simpson and Bennett, 155.
150–51 Return to the Plaza, Videla's order of the white cloths: Simpson and Bennett, 168; Sarlo, 287.
151–52 Alfonsín democracy: Rock, 385–403.
151 Radicalization of *Las Madres:* Simpson and Bennett, 169.
152 Hebe's strongly worded attack on Menem: Amnesty International *Report,* 56.
153 Menem's retaliations, traitors to the motherland: Amnesty International *Report,* 58.
153 *"Las Locas de la Plaza"*: Elshtain, 82.
153 they must have done *something*: Elshtain, 77.
153 demeaning female stereotype: Elshtain, 77.
153–54 Pathology in those who complied: Hollander 915–17.
154 "This experience [of speaking out for truth] is healing": Hollander, 917. Analysts interviewed: Diana R. Kordon and Lucila I. Edelman, authors of *Efectos psicológicos de la repression politica.*
154 "I have had to recapture": Sarlo, 281.

Chapter Nine: Necropolis

Barnes, Julian. 1985. *Flaubert's parrot.* New York: Alfred A. Knopf.

Bart, Benjamin F. 1967. *Flaubert.* Syracuse: Syracuse University Press.

Commanville, Caroline. 1886. *Souvenirs intimes,* v–xli, in *Correspondance.* Première 1830–1850. Paris: Louis Conard, Libraire-Editeur, 1910.

———. *Heures d'autrefois.* Unpublished, cited by Chevalley-Sabatier.

Ducourneau, Jean A., and Jean Bruneau. 1972. *Album Flaubert.* Paris: Editions Gallimard.

Flaubert, Gustave. 1830–1842. *Memoires d'un fou, novembre, et autres textes de jeunesse.* Edition critique par Yvan Leclerc. Paris, Flammarion, 1991.

———. 1857. *Madame Bovary.* Paris: A. Quantin, 1885.

———. *Correspondance.* Première Serie 1830–1850. Paris: Louis Conard, Libraire-Editeur, 1910.

———. *Correspondence.* Troisième Serie 1852–1854. Paris: Louis Conard, Libraire-Editeur, 1927.

———. *Letters.* Selected with an introduction by Richard Rumbold. Translated by J. M. Cohen. London: Weidenfeld and Nicolson, 1950.

———. *Les lettres d'Egypte de Gustave Flaubert.* Edited by Antoine Youssef Naaman. Paris: A. G. Nizet, 1965.

———. *Correspondence.* Vol. 1 (janvier 1830 à juin 1851). Edited by Jean Bruneau. Paris: Editions Gallimard-Pleiade, 1973.

———, and George Sand. 1993. *Flaubert-Sand: The correspondence.* Edited and translated by Francis Steegmuller and Barbara Bray. New York: Alfred A. Knopf.

Greenleaf, Barbara Kaye. 1978. *Childhood through the ages.* New York: McGraw-Hill.

Lottman, Herbert. *Gustave Flaubert.* Boston: Little, Brown and Co., 1989.

Oliver, Hermia. 1980. *Flaubert and an English governess: The quest for Juliet Herbert.* New York: Oxford University Press.

Sabatier, Lucie Chevalley. 1971. *Gustave Flaubert et sa nièce Caroline.* Preface by Jean Bruneau, Paris: La Pensée Universelle.

Steegmuller, Francis. 1939. *Flaubert and Madame Bovary.* New York: Farrar, Straus and Giroux.

———. 1980. Editor and translator of *The letters of Gustave Flaubert (1830–1857).* Cambridge, Mass., and London, England: Belknap/ Harvard University Press.

Société des Amis de Flaubert. 1980. *Les Rouennais et la famille Flaubert* (in honor of 100th anniversary of Flaubert's death).

Troyat, Henri. 1988. *Flaubert.* Translated by Joan Pinkham. New York: Viking Press, 1992.

Zaretsky, Eli. 1973. *Capitalism, the family and personal life.* New York: Harper/ Colophon Books.

---

155 "What a necropolis": Flaubert letter to Mlle. Leroyer de Chantpie, November 4, 1857. Steegmuller (1980), 96.

156 Like the artist, the hero . . . the child: Zaretsky, 58–59; Romantic and Victorian images of child; Peter Pan as hero: Greenleaf, 80–81.

157 Infant and child mortality rate: Greenleaf, 69–72.

157 Basis for my imaginings: Madame Flaubert's letters to Flaubert: Bruneau, 66–191. Flaubert's mother did not keep a diary, and though she wrote to her children when they were away from home, most of that correspondence—except for her son's letters to her—is still unpublished (Bruneau, 512–18). A few letters that Anne-Justine wrote to Gustave while he was attending Rouen College between 1831 and 1832 have been published. Her daughter, Caroline, wrote frequent letters to Gustave describing the activities and state of mind of their mother. A series of letters from Flaubert to his mother, from August to November 1849, suggest he is responding to a letter from her. The lengthy letters that Gustave wrote to his mother during his two years in Egypt reveal the profound nature of their attachment. (Of the twenty-two letters from Flaubert to his mother from December 1849 to July 1850, many indicate he is responding to one of her letters [Naaman, 44–46].) When Anne-Justine's granddaughter, also named Caroline, was growing up, Anne-

Justine would entertain her with stories about her own childhood. When Caroline was forty, she recorded her recollections of her grandmother's memories in *Souvenirs intimes*. Many years after that, Caroline confided her childhood memories of her grandmother to her own stepniece, Lucy Sabatier, who wrote *Gustave Flaubert et sa nièce Caroline*. Anne-Justine's life story is encapsulated in the many biographies of her famous son, and she also speaks to us through her son's letters and novels.

157   Prussian occupation: Flaubert's letters to Sand from September 10, 1870–April 30, 1871 in Steegmuller and Bray. Flaubert's letters to niece Caroline, December 18, 1870 and February 1, 1871 in Steegmuller 1980; Bart, 554–59; *Souvenirs intimes,* xxx–xxxi.

157–58   Burying of Flaubert's manuscripts: Flaubert to Sand, April 29, 1871 in Steegmuller and Bray.

158   Impending visit of granddaughter Caroline: Bart, 562.

158   Julie part of the household: Barnes, 23; Bart, 14.

158   Granddaughter Caroline's marriage to Commanville: Sabatier, 43–80.

158   Caroline's infatuation with drawing teacher, Johanny Maisiat: Sabatier, 50–52.

158   Dr. Franklin Grout's interest in Caroline: Sabatier, 60–62.

158   boring but rich lumber merchant: Sabatier, 55.

158–59   Granddaughter's love of Baron Leroy: Sabatier, 64–66.

159   Achille operates on his father's leg, gangrene sets in, father dies: Steegmuller 1939, 42; Steegmuller 1980, 36.

159   Gustave Flaubert's "flashes" and "absences": Steegmuller 1939, 5, 11–14; Barnes, 25. The attacks resembled epilepsy but there were no convulsions, only flashing lights and a trancelike state of consciousness. The doctors, including Flaubert's father, were perplexed. Steegmuller 1939, 13.

159–60   "the most poisonous invention of all creation": letter to Ernest Chevalier, June 7, 1844, Bruneau, 208; Conard I, 144.

160   Achille as chief of Rouen hospital: Steegmuller 1980, 38 and 40. Flaubert letter to Ernest Chevalier, June 4, 1846, Steegmuller 1980, 40.

160   Mother never visits Achille without an invitation: Flaubert letter to Louise Colet, January 13, 1854 in Steegmuller 1980, 208.

160   Juliette Roquigy, daughter of Achille and Julie Flaubert; the suicide of her husband in 1865 and the loss of her three-year-old daughter in 1868: Bart, 443.

160   "his good little rat": More than five hundred letters were exchanged between Flaubert and his sister, Caroline. Among his salutations were "Joli rat," "Mon bon rat," "Vieux rat." A typical signature of Caroline would be "Ta soeur et rat."

160   "She has married mediocrity": Steegmuller 1939, 7. Steegmuller cites Flaubert's private diary.

161 Birth and death anniversaries of Madame Flaubert's children: Barnes, 27; Lottman, 8. Most biographers either ignore the births and deaths of the first Caroline, Emile, and Jules, or when they do mention them, the names of the children and their birthdays and death days are incorrect. Sartre's impressionistic five-volume biography *The Family Idiot*, which was more about Sartre than Flaubert, created some of this confusion. Caroline Commanville's memory, 1886, v., of her grandmother's recollections of her three infants' deaths is misleading. She reports that after the birth of Gustave another child was born who died in a few months. She is probably referring to Jules Alfred's death, or conflating the deaths of Emile and Jules. Barnes, whose sources I trust absolutely, seems to have made an error on the age of Jules, who could only have been three years and five months, if his mother became pregnant with him the month that Emile was born.

161–62 The deaths of Caroline, Emile, and Jules: the precise details are unknown. My construction is based on the few details in Barnes, Bart, Troyat, Lottman, Commanville, what I have learned of Madame Flaubert's character, my knowledge of infant development, and what is known about the symptoms of infant illness and causes of infant death in mid-nineteenth-century France.

163 Description of Madame Flaubert's childhood: Commanville, x–xi; Bart, 1–7.

163 House on the rue du Petit Salut: Commanville, xii; Sabatier, 30; Ducourneau, photo, 14.

163 Flaubert apartment at Hôtel Dieu: Steegmuller 1939, 15; Ducourneau, photo, 15.

163 the sick and the dying: Steegmuller 1939, 15.

163 Achille Cleophas buys a family plot: Barnes, 27.

164 Birth of Madame Flaubert's second Caroline: Commanville, v.

164 Julie comes to live with Flaubert family: Steegmuller 1939, Barnes, 23; Bart, 14.

164 Caroline Flaubert's childhood illnesses: Lottman, 58.

164 Gustave and Caroline climb the trellis: letter to Louise Colet, July 7, 1853 in Conard 1927, 269.

164 Billiard room theatricals: Commanville, ix.

164 Relationship between Gustave and Caroline: Commanville, ix; Bart, 9–10.

165 The Flaubert family joins Caroline and Emile Hamard on their honeymoon trip: Steegmuller 1939, 3–11.

165 Upstairs, in Gustave's studio: Floor plan of Flaubert House at Croisset: Commanville, xxi; Oliver, 15; Ducourneau, drawings 46, 49.

165 Marble bust of Caroline: Oliver, 16; Ducourneau, photo, 48.
Caroline Hamard's death, birth of granddaughter and move from Hôtel Dieu to Croisset with infant: Steegmuller 1980, 36–37. Flaubert let-

ter to Maxime DuCamp, March 15, 1846; Steegmuller 1980, 37; Letter to Maxime DuCamp, March 22, 1846; Steegmuller 1980, 38.

166   Caroline Hamard's burial: Flaubert letter to Maxime Camp, March 25, 1846: Steegmuller 1980, 38.

166   Emile Hamard lives in small cottage nearby in Croisset: Société des Amis de Flaubert, 39.

166   Madame Flaubert as a weeping statue: Flaubert letter to Maxime DuCamp, March 15, 1846 in Steegmuller, 37.

167   "Since my father and sister died": Flaubert letter to Louise Colet, October 14, 1846 in Steegmuller, 85.

167   a man, at least, is free: thoughts of Emma Bovary, in Flaubert 1857, 102.

167   "My mother needs me": Flaubert letter to Louise Colet, September 30, 1846 in Steegmuller, 83.

167   Madame Flaubert follows her son on tour of Brittany: Sabatier, 33–34.

167   Caroline takes first steps in Brest; Sabatier 34.

168   Hamard is declared incompetent: July 4, 1848 letter to Ernest Chevalier; Steegmuller 1980, 92; Troyat, 63.

168   Death of Alfred LePoittevin: April 7, 1848 letter to Maxime du Camp, Steegmuller 1980, 94.

168   Madame Flaubert pays for trip to Egypt: Oliver, 22.

168   Gustave wrote at least once a month from Egypt: Naaman, 44–54.

168   "There is no desire . . . but none will ever enter in": Constantinople, December 15, 1850, Rumbold, 58.

168   Dismissal of Caroline's first governness: Flaubert letter to Louise Colet, July 2, 1853 in Steegmuller, 191.

169   Caroline's lessons with Flaubert: Commanville, xx, xxiv–xxv.

169   "the customary attribute of persons of her sex": Oliver, 24.

169   Madame Flaubert's discovery of Balzac's description of mother's visit to wet nurse: Flaubert letter to Louise Colet, December 27, 1852 in Steegmuller, 178.

170   Madame Flaubert's childhood: Commanville x–xi.

170   Gustave seemed retarded: Commanville, vi–vii; Bart, 15; Troyat, 5; Barnes, 27.

170   Once he learned to read, he read incessantly: Steegmuller 1939, 16–17.

170   Gustave wrote plays since he was nine: Commanville, ix; Troyat, 5.

170   Thirty-eighth birthday celebration, history of Louis XIII: Flaubert, 1831 in biographical sketch by Leclerc, 533.

170   The routine at Croisset: Commanville, xxii; Oliver, 21.

170–71   Madame Flaubert's money worries as she described them in a letter to the family lawyer: Oliver, 23. Citing Lettres inédités à. . . . Auriant, Sceaux: Palmugre, 1948.

171   "My poor dear old mother": letter to George Sand, April 16, 1872. Rumbold, 181.

170 Gustave died . . . ; Caroline's inheritance, Flaubert museum at Villa Tanit: Sabatier, 191–208; Steegmuller 1939, 324. Ducourneau, 206–7.

172 Courtship and marriage of Caroline and Franklin Grout: Sabatier, 194–96.

172 Madame Flaubert's glacial manner: Sabatier, 29, citing Caroline Commanville and Maxime du Camp.

172 "His mother transmitted": Commanville, xiii.

172 Gustave buried in tiny grave next to Madame Flaubert: Société des Amis, 80.

Chapter Ten: Berthe's Dead Mother

Centre International à Etudes Pedogogiques. 1973. La genèse du roman (et documents). *Madame Bovary*. Sèvres.

Chouard, Robert. 1991. *Promenades en Normandie: avec Madame Bovary and Gustave Flaubert*. Paris, Editions Charles Corbet.

Dunbar, A. H. 1899. *Scottish kings*. Edinburgh: Edinburgh.

Flaubert, Gustave. 1857. *Madame Bovary*. Translated by Louise J. Kaplan (1991). Paris: A. Quantin, Imprimeur-Editeur, 1885.

Green, André. 1983. Narcissisme de vie. Narcissisme de mort. Translated by Katherine Aubertin as "The dead mother," in André Green, *On private madness*. Madison, Conn: International Universities Press, 1986.

Heywood, Colin. 1988. *Childhood in nineteenth-century France*. Cambridge: Cambridge University Press.

Newman, Edgar Leon, and Robert Lawrence Simpson. 1987. *Historical dictionary of France from 1815 Restoration to Second Empire*. 2 volumes. New York/Westport, Conn.: Greenwood Press.

Société National Année. *Almanach de France*: 1833–1850.

Spitz, René. 1963. Life and the dialogue. *Counterpoint: libidinal object and subject*. Edited by Herbert S. Gaskill. New York: International Universities Press.

Steegmuller, Francis. 1939. *Flaubert and Madame Bovary*. Appendix, Gustave Flaubert, "Second Scenario." Chicago: University of Chicago Press, 1968.

Sussman, George D. 1982. *Selling mother's milk: The wet-nursing business in France*. Urbana, Ill.: University of Illinois Press.

Weissbach, Lee Shai. 1989. *Child labor reform in nineteenth century France*. Baton Rouge: Louisiana State University Press.

---

174 Date of Berthe's birth: *Almanach de France*. Flaubert stated that birth was a Sunday, when the sun rose at 6:00 A.M. Sunrise at 6:00 A.M. happened only once during the summer of 1841—on September 26. Schol-

ars at the Centre International have placed Berthe's birth in November of 1839. This year would not correspond to the family history set out by Flaubert, in Steegmuller, Appendix. Madame Bovary became pregnant a few months prior to the move to Yonville, in March 1841. The seasonal flowering of plants are another clue to the end-of-summer birth of Berthe. The events occuring after her birth, such as Emma's walk to the wet nurse six weeks later, also took place during the late summer.

All dates of significant events in Berthe's life have been constructed from known historical events, the seasons mentioned in the course of the novel, the flowering and decay of certain plants, and religious observances noted by Flaubert. The section on movable feasts and fasts from Dunbar, 349–50, 359–60 was another source. The chronology of major historical events from 1832–1851 in Newman and Simpson 1158–1172 allowed me to amplify certain events mentioned by Flaubert. The Agricultural Fair of 1842 is another standard date mark for Madame Bovary. Emma's abandonment by Rodolphe is generally set as the first Monday in September, 1843. Charles Bovary died the year before the 1848 French Revolution, which is set as the end of the novel.

174–86   Every scene depicted here is from my translation of *Madame Bovary,* but the scenes are written from the point of view of Berthe Bovary. Félicité serves as Berthe's observer.

176   Emma's mother dies of breast cancer: Steegmuller Appendix, 355.

177   The fate of children sent to wet nurses: Sussman, 101–20; 141–49; Newman and Simpson, 1125.

178   Madame Rollet's hovel: Flaubert's description and Chouard, 67, photo entitled "La maison de la nourrice" (la mère Rollet).

189   Conditions of child labor: Weissbach, 6–107. Diseases of laboring children: Weissbach, 11; Heywood, 212–19.

190   The "dead mother": Green, 142–73.

190   partially a creation of the child: Green, 142–43.

192   "Life as we know it": Spitz, 174.

192   Paper introduced with mechanical dolls: Spitz, 154–55.

193   "There is a strange fascination": Spitz, 155.

Chapter Eleven: Portraits of a Dead Mother

Artaud, Antonin. 1958. *The theater and its double.* New York: Grove Press.

Breton, André. 1925 [1953]. *Manifestoes of surrealism.* Ann Arbor: University of Michigan Press, 1969.

Fenichel, Otto. 1929. The economics of pseudologia fantastica. *Collected papers of Otto Fenichel,* second series. New York: W. W. Norton, 1954.

Freud, Sigmund. 1899. Screen memories. *S.E.,* 3:301–22.

———. 1901. Childhood memories and screen memories. *S.E.,* 6:43–52.

Gablik, Suzi. 1973. *Magritte.* Greenwich, Conn: New York Graphic Society.

Glover, Edward. 1929. The screening function of traumatic memories." *Int. J. Psycho-Anal.* 10:90–93.

Hammacher, A. M. 1985. *René Magritte*. Translated by James Brockway. New York: Harry Abrams.

Hubert, Renée Riese. 1978. The other-worldly landscapes of E. A. Poe and René Magritte. *Sub-Stance* No. 21.

Kaplan, Donald M. 1989. Surrealism and psychoanalysis: Notes on a cultural affair. *American Imago* 46: 319–28.

Kaplan, Louise J. 1987. *The family romance of the impostor-poet, Thomas Chatterton*. New York: Atheneum.

———. 1991. *Female perversions: The temptations of Emma Bovary*, New York: Nan A. Talese/Doubleday.

———. 1992. The perverse strategy in 'The Fall of the House of Usher.' *New Essays on Poe's Major Tales.* Edited by Kenneth Silverman. Cambridge: Cambridge University Press.

Magritte, René. 1938 [1979]. *La ligne de vie*. Lecture, Musée des Beaux-Arts d'Anvers, November 20, 1938. (A brief extract of this famous autobiographical lecture was published in the Belgian magazine *Combat,* December 10, 1938. The full lecture and the version traditionally cited by most Magritte scholars was published in the Belgian magazine *L'Invention collective,* No. 2, April 1940. Felix Giovanelli's English translation of the *L'Invention collective* version appears in *View* series 7, no. 2, 1946.) All citations below will be to René Magritte, *Ecrits Complets*. Edited by André Blavier. Paris: Flammarion, 1979. No. 46, *La ligne de vie I,* 142–48 is the version in *L'Invention collective.* No. 42, *La ligne de vie II,* 103–30, contains two versions; a longer version (undated, but evidently written toward the end of or after World War II), with Magritte's historical and political commentary, and an abbreviated version.

Melly, George. 1992. Robbing Banks. Review of *Magritte: Silence of the world. London Review of Books,* June 25, 1992, 7–8.

Scutenaire, Louis. 1977. *Avec Magritte*. Brussels: Lebeer Hossman. Includes text of *René Magritte,* 1947, Brussels: Selection, which was an extended version of Scutenaire's 1942 monograph, *René Magritte: La terre n'est pas une vallée de larmes.*

Silverman, Kenneth. 1991. *Edgar A. Poe: mournful and never-ending remembrance*. New York: Harper/Collins.

Spector, Jack. 1989. André Breton and the politics of dream: Surrealism in Paris ca. 1918–1924. *American Imago* 46:287–318.

Spitz, Ellen Handler. 1985. Pathography in practice. *Art and psyche*. New Haven: Yale University Press.

————. 1994. *Museums of the mind*. New Haven: Yale University Press.

Sylvester, David. 1992a. *Magritte: silence of the world*. London: Thames and Hudson, in association with the Menil Foundation.

————. 1992b. *René Magritte: catalogue raisonné*. The Menil Foundation/ Antwerp: Fonds Mercator.

Torczyner, Harry. 1977. *Magritte: ideas and images*. New York: Harry N. Abrams.

Viederman, Milton. 1987. René Magritte: coping with loss—reality and illusion. *J. Amer. Psychoanal. Assn.* 35:967–98.

Waldberg, Patrick. 1965a. *René Magritte*. Translated by Austryn Wainhouse. Brussels: Andre de Roche.

————. 1965b. *Surrealism*. Translated from the German. London: Thames and Hudson.

Wolfenstein, Martha. 1973. The image of the lost parent. *Psychoanal. Study Child* 28:433–56.

————. 1974. The past recaptured in the work of Magritte. Unpublished manuscript prepared for the Margaret S. Mahler Symposium. Philadelphia: May 1974.

————. The man in the bowler hat. Unpublished manuscript, cited by Spitz 1985.

---

195   Magritte family biographical references: Sylvester 1992a, 1992b.

195–96   The events from 1898 through 1912 are described in detail in Sylvester 1992b; Régina's depressions and her husband's responses are my constructions based on Sylvester's descriptions, a photograph of Régina and infant René, Sylvester 1992a, 11, the ensuing suicidal history and newspaper accounts of Régina's suicide.

196–97   Story of Régina's suicide as told to Scutenaire: Sylvester 1992a, 69–70.

197   Sylvester's search of the newspaper accounts of Régina's disappearance and the discovery of her body: Sylvester 1992b, 8–9.

        Among those who have been fooled by the Scutenaire version of Régina's suicide were Sylvester in his 1969 Magritte biography, Hammacher, Torczyner, Gablik, Wolfenstein, and Spitz.

197   Magritte's encounters with psychoanalysts who interpreted his paintings as symbols of castration: Torczyner 80–83, Hammacher, 18.

198   Tricking the psychoanalysts: Torczyner, 80. Letter of March 12, 1937 to Louis Scutenaire and Irène Hamois.

198   "Apropos the Freudian": Sylvester 1992a, 318; citing Magritte's letter of January, 1946 to his friend Achille Chavée.

198   "obsession with hidden faces": Sylvester 1992a, 24.

199   Hearing the story of his mother's death from Jeanne Verdeyan;

Sylvester 1992a, 14. Verdeyan may not have told the children directly, but they surely heard her repeating the story to visitors.

199 If it is possible to make someone believe something untrue: Fenichel, 133; Kaplan, L. 1987, 213–35.

200 Modern interpretations of castration: Kaplan, L. 1991, 43–77; 106–22.

200 Madonna mother, sexual mother: Kaplan, L. 1991, 43–77.

202 Magritte's father enjoyed children; Viederman, 975, interview with Georgette Magritte, October 1984.

202–03 Surrealist credos: Breton, Kaplan, D., Spector, Waldberg. The word "surrealist" was first used by Apollinaire to describe his play, *Les Mamelles de Tiresias,* but it was Breton who gave the term its official definition.

203 state of mind: Waldberg, 13, citing Blanchot.

203 Freud was flattered but: Kaplan, D. M., 320.

203 "a phenomenology of aggression": Gablik, 45.

203 "inflicts gratuitous suffering": Gablik, 46.

203 "something bleak": Gablik, 46.

203 "It is cruelty": Artaud, 104.

203 "the simplest surrealist act": Breton, 125.

203 "to make the most familiar objects howl": Magritte 109, 119; phrase not in *L'Invention Collective* version.

203–04 Memory of the cemetery, "We used to lift" "a painter who had come from the capital": Magritte 105, 116, 143.

204 screen memories: Freud 1899, 1901; Glover.

205 Magritte's reversals of darkness into light: Wolfenstein, man in bowler hat, 204–6, as cited by Spitz 1985, 84–85.

205 "great pride": Sylvester 1992b, 10, citing Scutenaire 1977, 69.

205 Losing and finding of Georgette: Wolfenstein, 1974. Sylvester 1992b, 20, presents two versions of the first refinding of Georgette. The meeting in the art supply shop, which came from Magritte, is the traditional reference. However, Madame Magritte remembered bumping into her future husband as he was strolling along with a friend in the Botanical Gardens.

205 "as if it were only a curtain": Magritte 106, 118, 142.

206 Discovery of *Song of Love:* Magritte, 105. There is some debate about who the friend was, or if possibly Magritte made the discovery on his own. Magritte recalls the event as 1924, however, after considering the various stories, Sylvester, 1992a, 61, concludes that it is "indisputable" that the *Song of Love* revelation came during the summer or end of 1923.

206 "that pictorial experience which puts the real world on trial": Magritte 145. Phrase is omitted in *La ligne de vie I.* The phrase, which was in the original lecture, is probably derived from Breton, who recommended a "prosecution of the real world." Waldberg, 17.

206–07 Grelots as "the Magritte trademark": Sylvester 1992a, 92.
207 Description of various grelots: Sylvester 1992a, 84.
207 "showing objects": Magritte 109, 119, 143.
207 "I caused the iron bells": Magritte 109, 120, 143.
208 Images of birds: Viederman, 988–89.
208 "One night in 1936": Magritte 110, 121, 143
209 Misdating of paintings: Sylvester, 1992a, 222–23.
209 Sheila Legg/Paul Colinet story: Sylvester 1992a, 240–42.
210 "Against the general pessimisms": Le Surrealisme en plein soliel, dossier la querelle du soleil. Ecrits complets, 195; Sylvester 1992a, 208.
210 "a backward child": Sylvester 1992a, 210 (a paraphrase of Breton).
210 The Belgian potato joke: Sylvester 1992a, 269.
211 "Up Yours": Sylvester 1992a, 268–75.
211 "to fling it in their faces": Sylvester 1992a, 269.
211 "It's my natural propensity": Sylvester 1992a, 272.
211 "well-made paintings" "In the future": Sylvester, 272; Gablik, 153.
211 Bourgeois parlor: Melly, 7.
211 Pilgrimage to Poe house . . . he wept: Torczyner, 15.
211–12 Life of Poe: Silverman, Kaplan, L. (1992), and Hubert.
214 Magritte's undermining of Poe's utopian vision: Hubert, 77.

Chapter Twelve: Images of Absence, Voices of Silence

Barocas, H. A., and C. B. Barocas. 1973. Manifestations of concentration camp effects on the second generation. *Amer. J. Psychiat.* 130:7.

Bergman, Martin, and Milton E. Jucovy. 1982. *Generations of the Holocaust.* New York: Columbia University Press.

Celan, P. (1958) *Bremen Speech.* Literature Prize of the Free Hanseatic City of Bremen, as quoted in Felstinger translation, translating Celan's last poem. *American Poetry Review* 1982 (July/August), 23.

Deak, I. 1989. The incomprehensible Holocaust. *The New York Review of Books,* September 28, 1989, 63–72.

Epstein, Helen. 1979. *Children of the Holocaust: conversations with sons and daughters of survivors.* New York: G. P. Putnam.

Felman, Shoshana, and Dori Laub. 1992. *Testimony: crisis of witnessing in literature, psychoanalysis and history.* New York and London: Routledge.

Felstiner, J. 1992. Translating Paul Celan's "Todesfuge." *Probing the limits of representation: Nazism and the "Final Solution".* Edited by S. Freidlander. Cambridge: Harvard University Press.

Fogelman, Eva. 1988. Therapeutic alternatives for Holocaust survivors and second generation. *The psychological perspectives of the Holocaust and of its aftermath*. Edited by R. L. Braham. New York: Columbia University Press, pp. 79–108.

Gampel, Yolanda. 1982. A daughter of silence. *Generations of the Holocaust*.

———. 1992. Thoughts about the transmission of conscious and unconscious knowledge to the generation born after the Shoah. *J. Soc. Work and Policy in Isr.* Special issue "Holocaust trauma: Transgenerational transmission to the second generation." 5–6:85–105.

Grubrich-Simitis, Ilse. 1984. From concretization to metaphor. Translated by Veronica Machtlinger. *Psychoanal. Study Child* 39:301–20.

———. 1981. Extreme traumatization as cumulative trauma. Translated by Veronica Machtlinger. *Psychoanal. Study Child* 36:415–50.

Jucovy, Milton E. 1992. Psychoanalytic contributions to Holocaust studies. *Int. J. Psycho-Anal.* 73:267–91.

Kestenberg, Judith S. 1972. Psychoanalytic contributions to the problem of children of survivors from Nazi persecution. *Israel Annals of Psychiatry and Related Disciplines* 10:249–65.

———. 1982a. Ways of children's involvement in their parents' Holocaust past, the choice of crucial themes in survivors and their children. *Generations of the Holocaust*.

———. 1982b. A metapsychological assessment based on an analysis of a survivor's child. *Generations of the Holocaust*.

———. 1989. Transposition revisited: clinical, therapeutic and developmental considerations. *Healing their wounds*. Edited by P. Marcus and A. Rosenberg. New York: Praeger.

Langer, Lawrence L. 1991. *Holocaust testimonies*. New Haven: Yale University Press.

Laub, Dori, and Nan Auerhahn. 1993. Knowing and not knowing massive psychic trauma. *Int. J. Psycho-Anal.* 74:2.

Levi, Primo. 1986. *The drowned and the saved*. Translation by Raymond Rosenthal. New York: Summit Books.

Pines, Dinora. 1992. The impact of the Holocaust on the second generation. *J. Soc. Work and Policy in Isr.* Special issue: Holocaust trauma: "Transgenerational transmission to the second generation." 5–6:85–105.

Weisel, Elie. 1975. For some measure of humility. *Sh'ma*, October 31, 1975, 314–15. Cited by Grubrich-Simitis, 1981, 416.

---

216 Epigraph: Celan, *Bremen Speech*.
217 Celan's Holocaust experiences, postwar writings and suicide: Felman and Laub (Felman), 26.

217 "acquiring an overall": "The prisoner felt overwhelmed . . . incomprehension," Levi, 17.

217–18 Impossibility of witnessing: Levi; Felman and Laub (Laub). An event without a witness, 75–92.

218 Jucovy, 271.

219 In an extermination camp: Grubrich-Simitis 1981, 415–25.

220 Dream of returning home: Levi, 14.

221 "death, total, absolute death": Wiesel, 314.

221 Holocaust statistics: Deak.

222 Symptoms of second generation: Fogelman, Barocas and Barocas, Kestenberg 1972, Epstein. Grubrich-Simitis 1984.

223 "*transposition*": Kestenberg, 1982a, 1982b, 1989.

224 "black milk": Black milk of daybreak we drink you at night, Celan, "Todesfuge."

224 The mechanisms of transposition: Kestenberg 1972, 1982a, 83–102, 148–49; Grubrich-Simitis, 1984.

226–27 Choice of crucial developmental themes; Kestenberg, 1982b, 97–102; 1989, 67–82.

227–28 Time tunneling: Kestenberg 1989, 76–77; Jucovy, 271.

229 "In all cases": Kestenberg 1982a, 101.

229–36 The cases of Rachel (Kestenberg), Michal (Gampal), and Mark (Grubrich-Simitis) have been put into a narrative form by the author; some of the details are author's elaborations—in keeping with spirit of the case reports.

229 Case of Rachel: Kestenberg 1982b, 137–58; 1989, 68–9.

230–32 Case of Michal: Gampal, 120–2.

231 Double registration: Bergmann and Jucovy: (M. Bergmann) 254–56; Jucovy, 271.

232 Concretization: Grubrich-Simitis 1984, 301–10.

232–34 Case of Mark: Grubrich-Simitis 1984, 311.

234 Revenant: Jucovy, 271.

235 "To compete with the mother": Kestenberg 1982b, 145–46.

237 Crisis of therapy: Acceptance of Holocaust reality; analysis of personal motives: Jucovy, 270–79; Kestenberg 1982b; Grubrich-Simitis 1984, 312–18.

237 Mourning and commemoration: Jucovy, 278–79.

Epilogue: No Voice Is Ever Wholly Lost

241 "No voice is ever wholly lost *that is the voice of humanity*": Hesiod, Aristotle; the epigraph to No Voice Is Wholly Lost: Harry A. Slochower, 1945.

ACKNOWLEDGMENTS

Naturally, my deepest gratitude goes to the many mothers, fathers, and children who entrusted me with their histories of loss and mourning. In the Notes I have also acknowledged the authors whose memoirs, case studies, biographies, theories of attachment and loss, and socio-cultural perspectives form the background of this work.

For their steadfast belief in me and in this work, and for their wisdom in solving the large and small dilemmas that arose in connection with its composition and production, I want to thank my literary agent, Elaine Markson, and my editor, Frederic W. Hills.

These formal acknowledgments cannot express the full extent of my gratitude to the two people who grappled on a day-to-day basis with the essential literary and theoretical issues. Laureen Connelly Rowland, Fred Hills's assistant editor, gave to each word and each turn of phrase a patient, thoughtful, and critical reading, and furthermore was able to make me give my full attention to each one of her queries and comments—which, I usually discovered, were amazingly insightful. As always, I could count on my husband, Donald M. Kaplan, for another kind of critical reading. He knew at once when I had not sufficiently worked through a theoretical dilemma and he knew exactly how to guide me toward a better solution. Beyond these scholarly and intellectual matters, when the going got rough Donald's humor and emotional sensitivity saved the day.

INDEX

  Croisset estate of, 157–58, 163, 169, 171
  death of, 157, 171
  Flaubert's relationship with, 160, 161, 162, 166, 167–71, 190–91, 192
  Flaubert's writings and, 11, 168, 169, 170–71, 172–73
  marriage of, 157, 159, 162, 163, 170, 190
  migraines of, 162, 165, 168
  parents of, 163, 170
  in Rouen, 157–58
  soliloquy of, 158–71
Flaubert, Caroline, 161–62, 163, 191
Flaubert, Emile-Cleophas, 162, 163, 164
Flaubert, Gustave, 155
  birth of, 162
  Brittany walking tour of, 167
  death as viewed by, 187–88
  in Egypt, 168
  epilepsy of, 159, 160, 173
  father's relationship with, 173
  finances of, 170–71
  gravesite of, 163–64, 172
  law studied by, 159–60
  manuscripts of, 157–58
  marriage as viewed by, 158
  mother's relationship with, 160, 161, 162, 166, 167–71, 190–91, 192
  niece's relationship with, 158, 160, 169, 170, 171–72
  reading by, 169, 170
  in Rouen, 157–58, 167
  sister's death and, 165–66, 167, 187, 188
  sister's relationship with, 164–65, 168
  studio of, 165, 169
  as writer, 11, 168, 169, 170–71, 172–73
Flaubert, Jules Alfred, 162, 163, 164
Flaubert, Julie, 160
Flaubert, Juliette, 160
fort-da game, 28–29, 33, 34, 37–39, 44, 53, 67, 70, 78, 99
foundlings, 23, 52
Franco-Prussian War (1870–71), 157–58
Freud, Anna, 67–74, 76, 77, 78, 82, 83
Freud, Colin, 77–78, 82–83
Freud, Ernst L., 76, 77
Freud, Martha, 69, 76, 83
Freud, Martin, 76, 83
Freud, Mathilde, 67, 69

Freud, Sigmund:
  children's games as viewed by, 29, 34, 38
  daughter's death and, 10–11, 34, 69, 123
  daughter's relationship with, 67
  grandson's death and, 34, 122–23
  in London, 76
  Magritte and, 198
  psychoanalytic school of, 10, 197–98
  surrealism and, 203
  "uncanny" investigated by, 108–9
Freud, Sophie, *see* Halberstadt, Sophie Freud
Freud, W. Ernest:
  Anna Freud's relationship with, 67–74, 76, 77, 78, 82, 83
  birth of, 67
  brother's death and, 69, 79
  Burlingham family and, 71–74
  as child analyst, 77–84
  childhood of, 67–75
  education of, 68, 73–77
  as father, 77–78, 82–83
  father's relationship with, 33, 67, 69–70, 72–73, 83
  Freud's relationship with, 69, 72, 73, 83
  games invented by, 28–31, 33, 34, 53, 67, 68, 70, 78
  happiness of, 72–74
  Jewishness of, 74–76
  in London, 76–78
  mother's death and, 11, 33–34, 66, 67–68, 69, 78, 79, 82, 83, 99
  mother's relationship with, 28–30, 33
  name changed by, 77
  neonatal studies by, 78–82
  stepmother of, 69–70
  "trawling" by, 70, 79
friendships:
  in adolescence, 96–97, 100
  mourning and, 57, 61
frustration, 53, 89
funerals, 14, 16, 17, 128, 129, 166

Gablik, Suzi, 203
Gadhafi, Mu'ammar al-, 135, 138
games, children's:
  catch-me, 184
  fantasies in, 39, 41, 44
  fort-da, 28–29, 33, 34, 37–39, 44, 53, 67, 70, 78, 99

mother-child relationship (*cont.*)
  separation in, 10, 28–30, 36–39, 53
  trauma and, 225–27
  see also infant-mother relationship
mothers:
  absences of, 28–30, 36–37, 53, 182
  as caretakers, 125, 156–57
  death of, 11, 13–14, 16, 33–34, 66–84, 99
  depression of, 10, 81, 186, 188, 191, 192, 195, 196, 200, 202, 205–6, 207
  familial role of, 157
  grief of, 127–28, 131, 135, 138, 140–54
  guilt felt by, 37, 81, 125–26
  ideals of, 55–56
  imprisoned delinquents as, 22–23
  love of, 20–23, 156–57
  needs of, 119
  overprotective, 45
  "perfect," 59
  psychological death of, 10, 190–94, 199–201, 203, 204, 207–8, 214–15
  sexuality of, 200–201
  social protest by, 143–54
  substitute, 21–22, 23, 53, 81, 193, 194
  "terry cloth," 21–22, 193, 194
  "wire," 21
  working, 34–37
mourners, professional, 14
mourning:
  of childhood, 85–87, 96, 97
  by children, 49–50, 59–65
  conventions and, 9, 16
  cultural differences in, 14–15
  as detachment, 51
  emotional process of, 52, 127–33
  friendships and, 57, 61
  inner presences and, 19–20
  personal vs. public, 16–17, 18
  psychological death and, 106–7, 116
  prevention of, 153–54, 225–26
  rituals of, 9, 14–18, 155
  work of, 19, 51, 106, 116, 235, 237
  see also grief
murders, child, 124
Museum of Modern Art, 211
Muslims, Balinese vs. Egyptian, 15–16, 18
mutilation, 200–201, 204, 222

nannies, 156
narcissism:
  in child-parent relationship, 41, 119, 120–21

  of children, 120–21, 126
  of parents, 55, 119, 120–21, 124, 126–27
  transformation of, 126–27, 154
  wounded, 236
Nazis, 74, 75–76, 82–84, 210, 218, 221, 233, 236
needs:
  of children, 117–18
  of fathers, 119
  of mothers, 119
  parental, 119
  unmet, 98, 99, 117–18
Neonatal Intensive Care Unit (NICU), 78–82
Nervenklinik hospital, 111, 112, 115
New York, N.Y., 117
nightmares, 32
nostalgia, 86, 156
nuclear war, 91
nurturance, 20, 81

obesity, 227
orality, 21
orphans, 23, 52

pain:
  avoidance of, 50
  pleasure vs., 41, 84, 99
Pan American Airways, 136, 137
Pan Am Flight 103 bombing, 134–42
panic, 97, 219, 231
paranoid psychosis, 111–16
parents:
  adolescent resentment of, 95–96
  adolescent's relationship with, 85, 87–88, 95–96
  alternatives to, 121
  anger of, 117–18, 125
  broken promises by, 88–90, 94–95, 100–101
  death of, 46, 51–54, 85, 101–2, 118, 128, 129
  dialogue between, 127–32
  fantasies of, 124–26
  generational transmission by, 10, 117–18, 119, 120, 122, 124, 224, 228, 235
  genetic inheritance of, 122
  grief of, 10, 14, 42–43, 117–33, 155
  guilt felt by, 37, 81, 125–26
  ideals of, 54, 55, 58, 64, 65, 66–67, 119, 121, 126

ABOUT THE AUTHOR

Louise J. Kaplan, Ph.D., is a distinguished psychologist, lecturer, and critically acclaimed author. She is coeditor of *American Imago* and a visiting faculty member of the Chicago Center for Psychoanalysis. Previously, she was an associate professor of the clinical psychology graduate programs at New York University and the City University of New York. While at NYU, Dr. Kaplan was Director of the Mother-Infant Research Nursery; at CUNY, she was the director of Child and Adolescent Clinical Services. She is the author of several books, including *Oneness and Separateness, Adolescence*, and most recently, *Female Perversions*, which was a finalist for the National Book Critics Circle Award. Dr. Kaplan lives in New York City.

CPSIA information can be obtained
at www.ICGtesting.com
Printed in the USA
FSHW011334230221
78873FS

9 780684 818207